Research Methods in Political Science

An Introduction Using *MicroCase*®

Seventh Edition

Michael K. Le Roy

WHITWORTH UNIVERSITY

THOMSON

WADSWORTH

Australia • Canada • Mexico • Singapore • Spain • United Kingdom • United States

Dedicated to the memory of Michael
Corbett (1943 – 2001) and his
wonderful wife, Julia

Michael Corbett, the original author of the first four editions of this text, received his Ph.D.
from the University of Iowa. He was a professor of political science at Ball State University,
where he taught courses covering an introduction to political science, research methods in
political science, and public opinion. A scholarship fund has been established in his name by
the Political Science Department at Ball State University.

THOMSON

™

WADSWORTH

Research Methods in Political Science
An Introduction Using MicroCase®
Seventh Edition
Michael K. Le Roy

Publisher: Michael Rosenberg

Managing Development Editor: Karen Judd

Senior Editorial Assistant: Megan Garvey

Consulting Editor: Julie Aguilar

Technology Project Manager: Yevgeny Ioffe

Marketing Manager: Trent Whatcott

Marketing Assistant: Aimee Lewis

Marketing Communications Manager: Heather Baxley

Senior Content Project Manager: Michael Lepera

Art Director: Linda Helcher

Print Buyer: Linda Hsu

Copyeditor/Proofreader: Margaret Moore

Cover Image: ©Charles Smith/Corbis

Text Designer/Compositor: Brent Veysey

Printed in the United States of America
1 2 3 4 5 6 7 12 11 10 09 07

Library of Congress Control Number: 2007942098

ISBN-13: 978-0-495-50283-8
ISBN-10: 0-495-50283-9

Thomson Higher Education
25 Thomson Place
Boston, MA 02210
USA

For more information about our products, contact us at:
Thomson Learning Academic Resource Center
1-800-423-0563

For permission to use material from this text or product,
submit a request online at http://www.thomsonrights.com.
Any additional questions about permissions can be
submitted by e-mail to thomsonrights@thomson.com.

ABOUT THE AUTHOR

Michael Le Roy is a professor of political science and Vice President of Academic Affairs at Whitworth University in Spokane, Washington. He received his Ph.D. in Political Science at Vanderbilt University. Between 1992 and 1994, Michael was a Fulbright scholar at Gothenburg University in Sweden. He teaches comparative politics, international political economy, and research methods in political science. While at Wheaton, Le Roy received two teaching awards, including the Faculty Achievement Award for Excellence in Teaching from Wheaton in 1999 and the Excellence in Teaching Award from the American Political Science Association in 2000. He is the author of *Comparative Politics: An Introduction Using ExplorIt*, 4th Edition (Belmont, CA: Wadsworth, 2007). His research on civil society, xenophobia, and the European Union has been published in *Comparative Politics*. Comments about this book from students and faculty are welcome and may be sent directly to the author at the following e-mail address: mleroy@whitworth.edu.

CONTENTS

ACKNOWLEDGMENTS

Never again will *Research Methods in Political Science* be published without first acknowledging the debt that we owe to Michael Corbett. Many of us who have used this book for years must acknowledge that our teaching evaluations in this challenging course have been improved (sometimes vastly!) by Michael's creative approach to bringing mainstream data analysis and research methodologies to life for political science undergraduates. His untimely death was a great loss to his colleagues at Ball State University and the profession as a whole.

Improvements to the 7th edition would not have been as strong without the careful attention and suggestions of numerous faculty who use this text. Their obvious care for student learning was apparent in each of their reviews. This book has benefited substantially from their efforts.

Previous editions of this book have also benefited from many faculty who have reviewed and improved the book over the years. Their assistance has been invaluable:

Thomas J. Baldino (Wilkes University)

Stephen Bennett (University of Cincinatti; Emeritus)

J. Barron Boyd (Le Moyne College)

Marcelle Chenard (previously College of St. Elizabeth)

Harold D. Clarke (University of Texas at Dallas)

Timothy Conlan (George Mason University)

Jay A. DeSart (Utah Valley State College)

Maurice Eisenstein (Purdue University)

Lev Gonick (Case Western Reserve University)

Kerstin Hamann (University of Central Florida)

Joseph Harry (previously Northern Illinois University)

Jan Hardt (University of Central Oklahoma)

Jan Hillard (University of Wisconsin)

Randolph Horn (Samford University)

Mark Hyde (Providence College)

Ming Ivory (James Madison University)

Laurence Jones (Angelo State University)

Patricia M. Keilbuch (University of Colorado, Colorado Springs)

Michael Krukones (Bellarmine College)

Edgar C. Leduc (University of Rhode Island)

Leslie Leip (Florida Atlantic University)

Myron Levine (Albion College)

Edward Mautz (University of La Verne)

Andy Merrifield (Sonoma State University)

Gregory Moore (Eckerd College)

Goktug Morcol (Penn State University)

Kelly Patterson (Brigham Young University)

James E. Prather (Georgia State University)

Paul D. Senese (University at Buffalo, SUNY)

Chuck Smith (West Virginia State University)

Arturo Vega (University of Texas, San Antonio)

Matt Wetstein (San Joaquin Delta College)

Nancy Zingale (University of St. Thomas)

I would like to thank David Tatom and Karen Judd for seeing the value in the MicroCase series and cheering this revision through to its publication. The books in the MicroCase series continue on as strongly as they ever have thanks to the support and editorial oversight of Julie Aguilar, MicroCase Technology Program Manager. I also want to thank Brent Veysey for designing such a student-friendly layout and format for these pages. I also wish to thank Rebecca Green, Assistant Editor at Wadsworth Publishing, for her assistance in the development of this revision.

Lastly, Michael Corbett was always right to acknowledge the central role that a spouse plays in the development and publication of an intellectual project. From my own experiences as an author, I know that my own wife is often denied my company morning, noon, and night when I am in the midst of writing. When one can pursue a scholarly career with a supportive spouse, it is a double blessing indeed! Michael Corbett was so blessed, as I am, to have a loving and supportive wife. Because of this blessing he dedicated each edition of his work to Julia Corbett (professor of religious studies at Ball State University) and gave her credit for her helpful feedback, advice, and inspiration. This book is dedicated to Michael's memory and to Julia who survives him.

I also need to acknowledge the sources of the data files used here. The GSS data files are based on selected variables from the National Opinion Research Center (University of Chicago) General Social Surveys for 2004 and 2006. The principal investigators are James A. Davis and Tom W. Smith. The NES data files are based on selected variables from the 2004 and 2006 American National Election Studies provided by the National Election Studies, Institute for Social Research, at the University of Michigan, and by the Inter-university Consortium for Political and Social Research. The principal investigators are Virginia Sapiro, Steven Rosenstone, and the National Election Studies.

The data in the HOUSE file (and the data for the creation of the U.S. Senators file) are from a variety of readily available sources such as a world almanac or an encyclopedia, the Thomas website (*http://thomas.loc.gov*), the census, or other government publications. The data in the GLOBAL file and the STATES file are from a variety of sources such as the *Statistical Abstract of the United States*, the census, *The Uniform Crime Reports*, *The World Almanac and Book of Facts*, and others. Much of the data in the GLOBAL file is based on the World Values Survey, for which we must thank Ronald Inglehart at the Institute for Social Research, University of Michigan. See Appendix C for further information about these data sources.

Finally, I wish to thank my colleagues and students at Whitworth University. Julia Stronks, Patricia Van Inwegen, and John Yoder provide an encouraging environment for the scholarship of teaching in my department at Whitworth and I am grateful for their support. I also wish to acknowledge my attentive students who have made this edition better thanks to their diligent efforts. I am grateful to all of my students but I extend a special thanks to Evan Case, Kirk Harris, Brittney Peterson, and Laura Thaut.

Michael K. Le Roy
Spokane, Washington

GETTING STARTED

INTRODUCTION

Welcome to the real world of political science research. There is nothing make-believe about what you will be doing here. All of the data are real. In fact, they are some of the best data available to professional researchers, and you will be using some of the same research techniques they use.

This book is designed to teach you the basics of political research through a "hands-on" approach. Each chapter begins by explaining the topic and then guides you through worksheets that help you better understand the topic. The worksheet exercises are based on the Student MicroCase software that comes with this book. Although this statistical software is very powerful, you will find that it is easy to use. Further, having learned the MicroCase software, you will understand the basic underlying procedures involved in other statistical analysis systems that you might learn later (such as SPSS* or SAS**).

This section gives you the information you need to begin using Student MicroCase. You will receive further instructions as necessary.

SYSTEM REQUIREMENTS

The software that accompanies this workbook is designed for the Windows 98 operating system or higher. The software can be installed to a personal computer or accessed from a computer located on a network.

- Windows 98, ME, 2000, XP, Vista

- Pentium II 233MHz

- 32MB RAM (64MB recommended)

- 800×600, 16-bit high-color display

- 8× CD-ROM drive

- 20MB of hard drive space (if you want to install it)

---

*Statistical Package for the Social Sciences
**Statistical Analysis System

Macintosh Note: To run the software on a Macintosh, you will need emulation software or hardware installed. For more information about emulation software or hardware, check with your local Macintosh retailer or try the website *http://macs.about.com.*

You can run Student MicroCase in two different ways:

- Install it to your computer's hard drive and run it from there (recommended).

- Run it from a network installation (see notes about this use below)

NETWORK VERSIONS OF STUDENT MICROCASE

A network version of Student MicroCase is available at no charge to instructors who adopt this book for their course. Students using the network version of Student MicroCase will be required to use their personal copy of the data files to complete their worksheet exercises. From the site they will access to download the software, students are given the option to download just the data files to a floppy disk or other portable memory device (e.g., memory stick). As the requirements of computers lab may vary, check with the lab to see which method is preferred. The network version is available from the Instructor Companion page for this book at *http://politicalscience.wadsworth.com.*

INSTALLING STUDENT MICROCASE

If you will be using a version of Student MicroCase that is installed on a network, skip to the section "Starting Student MicroCase."

NOTE: When installing Student MicroCase to a hard drive, this installation is designed for one student only. If multiple students will be using the same computer, install the network version of the software.

A card has been packaged with this book. This card contains a PIN code and a website address from which you can download the Student MicroCase software needed to complete the exercises in this book. You must have this card to obtain the software. Only one person may use this card.

To install Student MicroCase to a hard drive, you will need to follow the instructions on the card to register for access. Once you are on the download screen, follow these steps in order:

1. Select DOWNLOAD to begin downloading the software.

2. You will then be presented with a choice:
   a. Run this program from its current location. This is the recommended option, and this option will allow the installation to begin as soon as the file is downloaded to your computer.
   b. Save this program to disk. This option will allow you to save the downloaded file to your computer for later installation. This option also provides you a file that

will reinstall the software in the event this is needed. If you select this option, you will then need to specify where to save the file. Be sure to select a location where you can easily find the file. This file is named STU602355. Once the file has downloaded, locate the downloaded file and open or double-click the file name.

3. A security warning may appear next. Select [Yes].

4. The next screen will display the name of this book. Click [OK] to continue.

5. The next screen shows where the files needed for the installation will be placed. We strongly recommend you accept the default location, but if desired, you can specify a new location. Click [Unzip] to begin the install.

6. During the installation, you will be presented with several screens, as described below. In most cases you will be required to make a selection or an entry and then click [Next] to continue.

   If you have another version of the MicroCase software on your computer, you may first see a screen asking if you wish to remove earlier versions of the software. If you wish to retain these other installations, clear the box on each line by clicking once on it. Once all boxes are clear, click [Next].

The next screen that appears is the **License Name** screen. Review the licensing terms and then select the "I accept the terms of the licensing agreement" option to continue. Click [Next].

You are now asked to **Choose the Destination** for the program files. You are strongly advised to use the destination directory that is shown on the screen. Click [Next] to continue.

The final screen asks if you want a shortcut icon placed on your desktop. The default setting is yes. Make your selection and click [Finish] to complete the installation.

7. The Student MicroCase program will now be installed. When the installation is finished, you are now told the installation is complete. Click the [OK] button to close the window.

STARTING STUDENT MICROCASE

As indicated previously, there are two ways to run Student MicroCase: (1) from a hard drive installation or (2) from a network installation. Each method is described below.

Starting Student MicroCase from a Hard Drive Installation

If Student MicroCase is installed to the hard drive of your computer (see earlier section "Installing Student MicroCase"), locate the Student MicroCase "shortcut" icon on the Windows desktop, which looks something like this:

To start Student MicroCase, position your mouse pointer over the shortcut icon and double-click (that is, click it twice in rapid succession). If you did not permit the shortcut icon to be placed on the desktop during the install process (or if the icon was accidentally deleted), you can follow these directions to start the software:

- Click [Start] from the Windows desktop.
- Click [Programs].
- Click [MicroCase].
- Click [MicroCase - RMPS6].

After a few seconds, Student MicroCase will appear on your screen.

Starting Student MicroCase from a Network

If the network version of Student MicroCase has been installed to a computer network, you must provide the data files that accompany your book. You may have this data on a floppy diskette, or a memory stick, or by using another method. Check with your instructor or network advisor for more guidance. If a Student MicroCase icon appears on the Windows desktop, double-click it to start the program. (**Note:** Your instructor may provide additional information that is unique to your computer network.)

STUDENT MICROCASE MENUS

Student MicroCase is extremely easy to use. All you do is point and click your way through the program. That is, use your mouse arrow to point at the selection you want, and then click the left button on the mouse.

Two menus provide the beginning points for everything you will do in Student MicroCase. When you start Student MicroCase, the DATA MANAGEMENT menu appears first. To do statistical analysis, you must switch to the STATISTICS menu. You can toggle back and forth between those two menus by clicking the menu names shown on the left side of the screen.

Not all options on a menu are always available. You cannot, for example, do a statistical analysis until you have a data file open. You can tell which options are available at any given time by looking at the colors of the options. The unavailable options are dimmed. For example, when you first start Student MicroCase, only the OPEN FILE and NEW FILE options are immediately available. As you can see, the colors of those options are brighter than the colors of the other options shown on the screen. Furthermore, when you move your mouse pointer over the available options, they will become highlighted.

SOFTWARE GUIDES

Throughout this workbook, "Software Guides" provide the basic information needed to carry out each task. Here is an example:

> ➤ Data File: **STATES**
> ➤ Task: **Mapping**
> ➤ Variable 1:   **1625) %GWBUSH04**
> ➤ View: **Map**

Each line of the software guide is actually an instruction. Let's follow the simple steps to carry out this task.

Step 1: Select a Data File

Before you can do anything in Student MicroCase, you need to open a data file. To open a data file, click the OPEN FILE task. A list of data files will appear in a window (e.g., GSS, NES, STATES, etc.). If you click on a file name once, a description of the highlighted file is shown in the window next to this list. In the MicroCase Guide shown above, the ➤ symbol to the left of the Data File step indicates that you should open the STATES data file. To do so, click STATES and then click the [Open] button (or just double-click STATES). The next window that appears (labeled File Settings) provides additional information about the data file, including a file description, the number of cases in the file, and the number of variables, among other things. To continue, click the [OK] button. You are now returned to the main menu of Student MicroCase. (You won't need to repeat this step until you want to open a different data file.) Notice that by looking at the file name shown on the top line of the screen, you can always see which data file is currently open.

Step 2: Select a Task

Once you open a data file, the next step is to select a program task. Six analysis tasks are offered in this version of Student MicroCase. Not all tasks are available for each data file, because some tasks are appropriate only for certain kinds of data. Mapping, for example, is a task that applies only to ecological data and thus cannot be used with survey data files.

In the software guide we're following, the ➤ symbol on the second line indicates that the MAPPING task should be selected, so click the MAPPING option with your left mouse button.

Step 3: Select a Variable

After a task is selected, you will be shown a list of the variables in the open data file. Notice that the first variable is highlighted and a description of that variable is shown in the Variable Description window at the lower right. You can move this highlight through the list of variables by using the up and down cursor keys (as well as the <Page Up> and <Page Down> keys). You can also click once on a variable name to move the highlight and update the variable description. Go ahead—move the highlight to a few other variables and read their descriptions.

If the variable you want to select is not showing in the Variable Description window, click on the scroll bars located on the right side of the variable list window to move through the list. See the following figure:

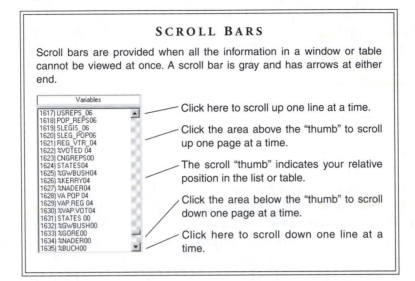

By the way, you will find an appendix at the back of this workbook that contains a list of the variable names for key data files provided in this package.

Each task requires the selection of one or more variables, and the software guides indicate which variables should be selected. The software guide example here indicates that you should select 1625) %GWBUSH04 as Variable 1. On the screen, there is a box labeled Variable 1. Inside this box, there is a vertical cursor that indicates that this box is currently an active option. When you select a variable, it will be placed in this box. Before selecting a variable, be sure that the cursor is in the appropriate box. If it is not, place the cursor inside the appropriate box by clicking the box with your mouse. This is important because in some tasks the software guide will require more than one variable to be selected, and you want to be sure that you put each selected variable in the right place.

To select a variable, use any one of the methods shown below. (**Note:** If the name of a previously selected variable is in the box, use the <Delete> key or <Backspace> key to remove it, or click the [Clear All] button.)

- Type in the **number** of the variable and press <Enter>.

- Type in the **name** of the variable and press <Enter>. Or you can type just enough of the name to distinguish it from other variables in the data—BUSH would be sufficient for this example.

- Double-click the desired variable in the variable list window. This selection will then appear in the variable selection box. (If the name of a previously selected variable is in the box, the newly selected variable will replace it.)

- Highlight the desired variable in the variable list, and then click the arrow that appears to the left of the variable selection box. The variable you selected will now appear in the box. (If the name of a previously selected variable is in the box, the newly selected variable will replace it.)

Once you have selected your variable (or variables), click the [OK] button to continue to the final results screen.

Step 4: Select a View

The next screen that appears shows the final results of your analysis. In most cases, the screen that first appears matches the "view" indicated in the software guide. In this example, you are instructed to look at the Map view—that's what is currently showing on the screen. In some instances, however, you may need to make an additional selection to produce the desired screen.

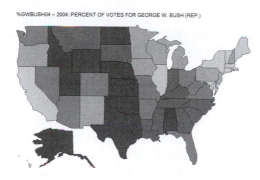

%GWBUSH04 -- 2004: PERCENT OF VOTES FOR GEORGE W. BUSH (REP.)

(OPTIONAL) Step 5: Select an Additional Display

Some software guides will indicate that an additional "Display" should be selected. In that case, simply click on the option indicated for that additional display. For example, this software guide may have included an additional line that required you to select the Legend display.

Step 6: Continuing to the Next Software Guide

Some instructions in the software guide may be the same for at least two examples in a row. For instance, after you display the map for murder in the example above, the following software guide may be given:

> Data File: **STATES**
> Task: **Mapping**
> ➤ Variable 1: **1253) KID ABUSE**
> ➤ View: **Map**

Notice that the first two lines in the software guide do not have the ➤ symbol in front of the items. That's because you already have the data file STATES open and you have already selected the MAPPING task. With the results of your first analysis showing on the screen, there is no need to return to the main menu to complete this next analysis. Instead, all you need to do is select KID ABUSE as your new variable. Click the [⟲] button located in the top left corner of your screen and the variable selection screen for the MAPPING task appears again. Replace the variable with 1253) KID ABUSE and click [OK].

To repeat: You need only do those items in the software guide that have the ➤ symbol in front of them. If you start from the top of the software guide, you're simply wasting your time.

If the software guide instructs you to select an entirely new task or data file, you will need to return to the main menu. To return to the main menu, simply click the [Menu] button located at the top left corner of the screen. At this point, select the new data file and/or task that is indicated in the software guide.

That's all there is to the basic operation of Student MicroCase. Just follow the instructions given in the software guide and point and click your way through the program.

ONLINE HELP

Student MicroCase offers extensive online help. You can obtain task-specific help by pressing <F1> at any point in the program. For example, if you are performing a scatterplot analysis, you can press <F1> to see the help for the SCATTERPLOT task.

If you prefer to browse through a list of the available help topics, select Help from the pull-down menu at the top of the screen and select the **Help Topics** option. At this point, you will be provided a list of topic areas. A closed-book icon represents each topic. To see what information is available in a given topic area, double-click on a book to "open" it. When you double-click on a book graphic, a list of help topics is shown. A help topic is represented by a graphic with a piece of paper with a question mark on it. Double-click on a help topic to view it.

If you have questions about Student MicroCase, try the online help described above. If you are not very familiar with software or computers, you may want to ask a classmate or your instructor for assistance.

EXITING FROM STUDENT MICROCASE

If you are continuing to the next section of this workbook, it is not necessary to exit from Student MicroCase quite yet. But when you are finished using the program, it is very important that you properly exit the software—do not just walk away from the computer or remove your memory device. To exit Student MicroCase, return to the main menu and select the [Exit Program] button that appears on the screen.

CHAPTER 1

A Brief Overview of Research Methods in Political Science

Tasks: Univariate, Mapping
Data Files: NES 04, GLOBAL, GSS, STATES, HOUSE

INTRODUCTION

To give you an overview of things to come, this chapter provides

- an explanation of the goals of the book

- a description of the organization of the book

- a brief overview of the overall research process in political science

- an introduction to the use of the MicroCase software with the data files

GOALS OF THE BOOK

This book will describe and explain the basic features of the research process in political science. These features will also be demonstrated through the Student Version of the MicroCase Analysis System, but the same ideas and basic procedures would also apply if you were using a different statistical analysis system such as SPSS or SAS. After completing this book, you will be able to

- define and explain the core concepts used in the discussion of research methods in political science

- explain the basic strategy and stages—from the beginning stage to the ending stage—of political science research

- create a data file and do the appropriate statistical analysis of variables in data files

ORGANIZATION OF THE BOOK

This first chapter gives an overview of the research process in political science. Each of the subsequent chapters covers certain aspects of the research process in political science: measurement, sampling, data preparation, variables, hypotheses, and so on. The final chapter puts the pieces back together into an integrated whole.

Each chapter has two major parts. The first part discusses and explains the topic of the chapter. The second part provides step-by-step computer exercises that demonstrate the topic of the chapter; for this part, you will go to a computer and follow the directions included in the exercise. As you go through the exercises, you will respond to the questions on the worksheets.

THE OVERALL POLITICAL RESEARCH PROCESS

As a political science student, you need to understand the basic processes of political research. You need to be able to evaluate the research done by others, and you need to be able to carry out your own research. Sometimes students say, "I'm not really interested in the research aspects of political science; I'm more interested in analyzing political issues." Even for these students, however, it is important to understand research methods and to be able to evaluate the research of other people. The discussion of political issues often involves assumptions or questions that could be investigated empirically—through systematic, "objective" sensory observations rather than just an expression of opinions.

For example, there are often discussions of the effects of providing economic assistance to the poor. Such discussions generate a great deal of heat, because different people bring different values and different assumptions about reality to the discussion. What kinds of people are most likely to receive assistance? How long do people usually rely on assistance? Does assistance produce a group of people who become dependent on it and cannot help themselves? Does assistance usually provide temporary help for people who then get back on their feet economically? What kinds of psychological effects does assistance have on the people who receive it? Many of those questions about reality could be assessed through research or through analysis of research findings that already exist.

We might further be interested in the kinds of people who hold different views concerning assistance to the poor. Some people, for example, take a negative view of those who receive economic assistance; others take a more positive view. What accounts for the difference between these views? How are these attitudes concerning public assistance to the poor related to other political and social attitudes that people hold?

Using comparative data (for different political units such as cities, states, or nations), we might further be interested in the effects of public assistance on the overall political system. In the United States, for example, what differences are there from one state to another in terms of public assistance policies? What effects do these policies have? Does spending on public assistance help or hurt the economy of a state? How is spending on public assistance related to such matters as the crime rate or the education level in the state? We could also ask those *types* of questions about nations, since there are great variations among the countries of the world in terms of assistance to the poor.

Many political controversies involve questions of how political reality operates; these questions can be investigated through political research. However, you need to be able to evaluate whether the research has been done properly and whether its conclusions are justified on the basis of the research.

As students of politics, we attempt to develop descriptions and explanations of aspects of political reality. Different political scientists have different views on the best way to define politics; they also have different views on which particular aspects of politics are the most important to study. Nevertheless, although we may do a great deal of exploratory research when moving toward our goals, our overall goal is to describe and explain political reality, no matter how we may define the term. This leads to research on many questions related to politics at various levels and in various types of situations. The following questions provide a very small sample of the types of questions that political scientists have investigated:

- What kinds of people are most likely to become fascists?

- Which city government structure is the most efficient in achieving its goals?

- In which economic situations within nations is rebellion most likely to occur?

- What effects does educational level have on people's political views?

- How do people's religious beliefs affect their political beliefs? How, for example, are their religious beliefs related to their attitudes toward war? Toward abortion? Toward welfare?

We can all come up with our own *opinions* on such matters, but the scientific approach in political science requires that we go beyond this. Our goal is to develop explanations of political reality that can be verified by other researchers who employ the scientific approach.

There are various approaches within political science, but the scientific process has a general overall strategy. We will briefly review the typical stages of doing research in political science. Note that in reality, however, the order in which these stages occur is not necessarily the order in which they are presented below. For example, in the stages below, the researcher develops the hypotheses first and then collects the necessary data to test those hypotheses. However, in reality a political scientist might already have access to important data and then develop hypotheses that could be tested using those data.

Stage 1: Formulating the Research Idea
The first stage in the research process is to develop the research idea. Research ideas can come from various sources. They might be based on the interests of the researcher—for example, a person might be interested in political tolerance and decide to investigate the sources of tolerance or intolerance. The research idea might originate in questions raised by others (e.g., students or professional colleagues). The researcher might be working on one idea and come across materials that lead to the development of another idea.

The researcher might start out with a specific hypothesis or set of hypotheses. Conversely, the researcher might start with a fairly broad research idea (e.g., the question of the extent to which people's political attitudes are linked to their personality traits) and then narrow this idea down to a set of specific hypotheses as the research process unfolds.

Stage 2: Conducting the Literature Review

The next stage is to find out what research has already been done in this area. Scientific research is cumulative; we build onto what has already been done rather than start from scratch each time we do research. It might be that someone else has already done the research you want to do, or that someone has done research that has important implications for the research you want to do. At any rate, the political researcher must find out what has already been done and what needs to be done in this particular area. In conducting the literature review, the political researcher will primarily examine the books and the professional journals in this area.

Stage 3: Formulating the Hypothesis

At some point, the researcher formulates a specific hypothesis or set of hypotheses. The hypothesis should grow out of a theoretical framework—an explanation of the aspects of political reality being investigated. A researcher starts, for example, with a theory to explain how and why certain personality traits affect political attitudes. The researcher then develops one or more hypotheses in order to test the theory. Since a hypothesis is a prediction based on the theory, the test of the hypothesis has implications for the validity of the theory.

Stage 4: Defining the Concepts

We need to measure the concepts we are dealing with. Before the measurement process begins, however, it is important that we have a clear idea of exactly what these concepts are. For example, if we are going to do research on political tolerance, we need to start with a clear notion of what we mean by political tolerance. Thus, we need to formulate clear definitions of our concepts early in the research process. A *conceptual* (or *nominal*) *definition* is a statement of the meaning of a concept.

Stage 5: Operationalizing the Concepts

If we want to use a concept in scientific research, we need a way to measure the concept. An *operational definition* is a specification of the steps by which a concept is measured. For example, how would you go about measuring the concept of political tolerance? You would probably develop a series of questions to ask people. In this case, the operational definition of political tolerance would consist of the specific set of questions and the procedures for developing an actual measurement of political tolerance.

An operational definition must be so specific and complete that someone else could use your operational definition and obtain the same results that you did. It is important in scientific research that the procedures we use be made explicit so that others can replicate our research. Thus, we need to be clear about how we define concepts, how we measure concepts, how we analyze data, and so on.

Stage 6: Measuring the Data

At this point, the actual measurement process is carried out. If we are collecting new data, this process begins with data collection. We might collect data through surveys, from public records (such as the voting records of public officials), from aggregate data sources (such as the United States Census), through experiments, or through other methods.

Sometimes the data already exist. We might, for example, use data that were collected by an organization (the Census Bureau, a survey organization, the *Congressional Record* staff, and so on) to be used for various purposes. However, even in this situation, we are still involved in measurement, because the measurement process also includes alterations in existing data. For example, in the General Social Survey (GSS) data file you will be using for the worksheets, there are several questions that might be used to measure racism. Instead of using those questions individually, a researcher might develop a composite measure of racism based on a combination of several questions.

Stage 7: Selecting the Statistical Technique

After the data have been collected, the researcher must select the appropriate statistical techniques to test the hypotheses. There are many different methods of statistical analysis; some are more useful in a particular situation than others. To a very great extent—as you will see—we select the statistical technique on the basis of the characteristics of the data we are using.

Stage 8: Drawing Conclusions

After the statistical analysis, the researcher draws conclusions about the theoretical meaning of the results. Do the results support the theory with which the researcher started? How has the research contributed to what was already known in this particular area? Do the results suggest that further research is needed? Have new questions been raised by the research?

Stage 9: Writing the Research Report

After the study is finished, the researcher writes a report on it. The nature of the report can vary, depending on the audience for which it is intended. Essentially, however, it includes information describing the stages of this particular research: the background of the research question, the literature review, the operational definitions, the data-collection procedures, the statistical results, and the conclusions.

EXPLORING THE DATA FILES

Important: For the worksheet portion of each chapter, go to the computer you will be using and start MicroCase by following the directions in the "Getting Started" section at the beginning of the book. If you have not yet carefully read the "Getting Started" section, please do that before continuing.

In this section, we will explore the data files that came with your Student MicroCase software. We will open data files, view variable lists and variable descriptions, select variables for analysis, obtain frequency distributions (with bar graphs and pie charts), and so on. In the course of doing this, you will see that it is easy to use Student MicroCase. After this exploration, the worksheets at the end of the chapter will guide you through a second tour and provide you with questions to answer.

The Data Files

There are seven data files included with Student MicroCase:

- **HOUSE**   Selected information on the voting behavior and backgrounds of U.S. representatives for the 109th Congress (2005–2006)

- **NES**   A selection of variables from the 2006 American National Election Study survey of a national sample of adults in the United States

- **NES 04**   A selection of variables from the 2004 American National Election Study survey of a national sample of adults in the United States

- **GSS**   Selected variables from the 2006 General Social Survey of a national sample of adults in the United States

- **GSS 04**   A selection of variables from the 2004 General Social Survey of a national sample of adults in the United States

- **STATES**   A selection of variables (e.g., rate of violent crime, percentages of the votes given to presidential candidates, and data from the 2000 U.S. Census) for the 50 U.S. states updated in 2006

- **GLOBAL**   A variety of variables for 172 nations each with a population of 200,000 or more, updated in 2006

These data files represent a variety of different kinds of data. Four files (NES, NES 04, GSS, and GSS 04) contain survey data. The STATES file and the GLOBAL file each contain aggregate data from a variety of sources including some data originally collected through survey methods. The HOUSE file contains data from public records (e.g., information on how representatives voted on a term-limits bill) and from other sources (e.g., census data on the population characteristics of representatives' districts).

In addition to the data files that are included with Student MicroCase, you will see in Chapter 7 that you can create a MicroCase data file yourself.

Exploring Data Files Based on Individuals

Three of the data files are based on data collected from or about individuals. The NES and GSS files are based on surveys of individuals, and the HOUSE file contains data characterizing individual U.S. representatives or qualities of their districts. By contrast, the STATES file and the GLOBAL file contain aggregate data—information for larger units. Let's first explore a data file based on individuals and then explore a data file based on larger units.

Exploring Univariate Statistics and Graphs

Follow the directions in the software guide below.

> ➤ Data File: **NES 04**
>   ➤ Task: **Univariate**

Below the software guide, you sometimes will be provided additional information or tips on how to follow the instructions in the guide—especially at the beginning of this book. This information will be in bold, as it is here. For this particular example, remember that these two instructions mean you should open the NES data file and then select the UNIVARIATE task. You will need to select the STATISTICS menu before selecting the UNIVARIATE task.

Before we select a variable, note the variable list on the left side of the window that opened when you selected the UNIVARIATE task. Click on several of the variables and read their descriptions in the Variable Description box in the lower right corner of this window. Now let's select a particular variable.

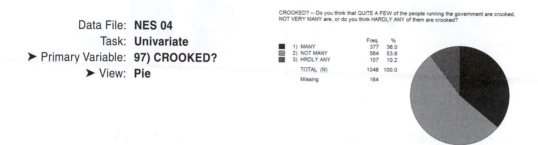

	Data File:	**NES 04**
	Task:	**Univariate**
➤	Primary Variable:	**97) CROOKED?**
	➤ View:	**Pie**

Remember that you must perform only those tasks that have the ➤ symbol in front of them. Here you have already performed the instructions in the first two lines, so there is no ➤ symbol in front of these two lines. So, you begin with the third line, which asks you to select 97) CROOKED? as the Primary Variable. Note also that in this particular situation you do not actually need to do anything else for the fourth line, because the default view was the pie chart, so it was automatically selected for you.

Also remember that you can select the variable—97) CROOKED?—in several different ways. You could have double-clicked the name of the variable in the box that lists the variable numbers and names, you could have typed in the number of the variable [97] in the Primary Variable box, or you could have typed in the name of the variable [CROOKED?] in the Primary Variable box. You also could have highlighted the variable name in the variable number or name box and clicked on the little arrow on the left side of the Primary Variable box.

At this point you see a pie chart representing the distribution of responses for a question asking people how many public officials they thought were crooked. This pie chart presents the results graphically so that you can quickly and easily grasp the basic distribution. These results show that 377 respondents (36.0%) believe that many public officials are crooked, 564 respondents (53.8%) believe that not many public officials are crooked, and 107 respondents (10.2%) believe that hardly any public officials are crooked. The *Total (N)* of 1,048 refers to the total number of respondents who answered this question. The *Missing* figure of 164 means that there were 164 respondents who did not answer this question. Next, let's view these same results in a different way.

Data File: **NES 04**

Task: **Univariate**

Primary Variable: **97) CROOKED?**

➤ View: **Bar - Freq.**

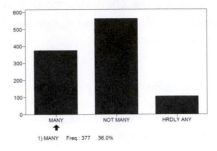

To obtain this graph, simply click the [Bar-Freq.] option.

Now you have a bar graph that gives you the same information you had in the pie graph. When you click on a particular bar, the results below the bar graph change to give details about the category represented by that particular bar. For example, when you click on the middle bar (the *Not Many* category), the results below the bar graph show that there are 564 respondents in this category (or 53.8% of all the respondents who answered this question). We can also see this information in a table format along with some additional statistics.

Data File: **NES 04**

Task: **Univariate**

Primary Variable: **97) CROOKED?**

➤ View: **Statistics (Summary)**

CROOKED? -- Do you think that QUITE A FEW of the people running the government are crooked, NOT VERY MANY are, or do you think HARDLY ANY of them are crooked?

Mean:	1.742	Std.Dev.:	0.629	N: 1048
Median:	2.000	Variance:	0.396	Missing: 164

99% confidence interval +/- mean: 1.692 to 1.792
95% confidence interval +/- mean: 1.704 to 1.780

Category	Freq.	%	Cum.%	Z-Score
1) MANY	377	36.0	36.0	-1.180
2) NOT MANY	564	53.8	89.8	0.409
3) HRDLY ANY	107	10.2	100.0	1.999

To obtain this table, simply click the [Summary] option.

We won't worry about what these results mean now. We'll learn more about this later. Be aware that you can print any of this information (if you have a printer available) by clicking the printer icon at the top of the screen.

Searching for Variables

There are many variables in the data files you will be using. Finding a particular variable in one of these files might be difficult if you were trying to find the variable by just scrolling through the variable names and descriptions. However, MicroCase makes the job of searching for a variable easy and convenient. Let's see how this works.

First, assuming that you still have the statistical results for 97) CROOKED? on the screen, return to the window that lists the variables by clicking on the [🔄] button. Note that while we will demonstrate the search procedure within the UNIVARIATE task, this applies to all other statistical tasks as well. That is, whenever you select any statistical task, a window containing a list of variables will appear on the screen. When that window appears, you can then search for a variable or set of variables.

Click on the [Search] button under the list of variables. A window will appear with a box in which you can type a search term. When you specify a particular search term, the program will search for any variable that has that term in its name or its variable description. For example, let's search for any variable that contains the word "trust" in either its name or variable description. So, type the word *trust* in the box and click [OK].

Note that this search produced a list of nine variables containing the word "trust." You can select variables for statistical analysis from this list using the same methods that you use to select variables from the full list. When you want to return to the full list of variables, simply click the [Full List] button.

Click on the [Full List] button, and let's do another search. If you wanted to search for any variable dealing with attitudes toward women, you could use the term "women," and then you could do another search using the term "woman." However, you can combine both of these searches into one search by simply typing the letters "wom." This will find any variable that contains "wom" in its name or variable description. Try this: Click on the [Search] button, type in *wom* as the search term, and click [OK].

Here's another tip. When you are searching for variables related to some particular topic, think about all relevant terms that might reasonably be used as search terms for that topic. In the preceding example, if you were interested in attitudes concerning sexual equality, you might search for all variables that contain any of the following terms (and perhaps others as well): sexual, equality, women, woman, female, gender, sexism, and affirmative.

By the way, in case you prefer to search through a paper copy of the list of variables, Appendix C contains a list of variables for the HOUSE and GLOBAL data files.

Exploring a Data File Based on Larger Units

The procedures for examining either the STATES file or the GLOBAL file will be similar to each other. The biggest difference between analysis of those two data files and analysis of the three data files based on individuals (NES, GSS, and HOUSE) is that we can use the MAPPING task with the STATES and the GLOBAL files. For present purposes, let's use the GLOBAL file. We will begin with a brief look at univariate statistics for some variables in this file and then go to the MAPPING task.

Univariate Statistics

The type of results for the UNIVARIATE task for GLOBAL will be partly similar to and partly different from those for the NES 04 data file we examined earlier. Let's first look at a situation when the type of results does not differ from the type of results we achieved when examining the NES 04.

➤ Data File: **GLOBAL**
➤ Task: **Univariate**
➤ Primary Variable: **314) CIV LIBS04**
➤ View: **Pie**

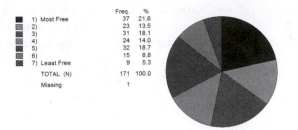

CIV LIBS04 -- Ratings of civil liberties on a scale of 1 to 7, 1 = most free, 7= least free, for the year 2004. (FITW 2005)

	Freq.	%
1) Most Free	37	21.6
2)	23	13.5
3)	31	18.1
4)	24	14.0
5)	32	18.7
6)	15	8.8
7) Least Free	9	5.3
TOTAL (N)	171	100.0
Missing	1	

Here we see a pie chart for the variable 314) CIV LIBS04. Note that this particular variable has only seven categories. Now let's look at a variable that has more categories.

Data File: **GLOBAL**
Task: **Univariate**
➤ Primary Variable: **99) HIV PREG**
➤ View: **Bar - Freq.**

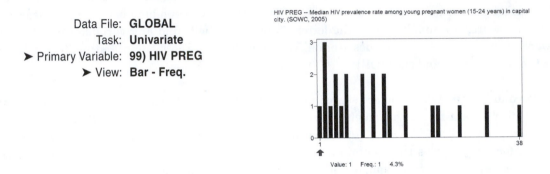

HIV PREG -- Median HIV prevalence rate among young pregnant women (15-24 years) in capital city. (SOWC, 2005)

Value: 1   Freq.: 1   4.3%

The category range for HIV PREG (which goes from 1 to 38) is much greater than the range for CIV LIBS04. Note that the pie chart option has been dimmed on the screen. Because pie charts with more than 10 slices are difficult to interpret, MicroCase does not allow you to create a pie chart with this many categories. Instead, a bar graph is shown by default, provided there are fewer than 100 potential categories.

In the previous two analyses, the categories were based on whole numbers (that is, the categories did not have any numbers to the right of the decimal point). Let's see what happens when we have a variable that uses decimal points.

Data File: **GLOBAL**

Task: **Univariate**

➤ Primary Variable: **28) BIRTHRATE**

➤ View: **Statistics (Summary)**

BIRTHRATE -- Crude birth rate indicates the number of live births occurring during the year per 1,000 people estimated at midyear. (WDI, 2005)

Categories generated by truncating last digit. Median is estimated.

Mean:	23.748	Std.Dev.:	11.587	N:	169
Median:	21.759	Variance:	134.260	Missing:	3

99% confidence interval +/- mean: 21.445 to 26.051
95% confidence interval +/- mean: 21.996 to 25.500

Range	Freq.	%	Cum.%	Z-Score
8.16 - 8.25	1	0.6	0.6	-1.345
8.36 - 8.45	1	0.6	1.2	-1.328
8.56 - 8.65	2	1.2	2.4	-1.311
8.66 - 8.75	1	0.6	3.0	-1.302
8.76 - 8.85	2	1.2	4.1	-1.294
8.86 - 8.95	1	0.6	4.7	-1.285
9.16 - 9.25	2	1.2	5.9	-1.259
9.26 - 9.35	1	0.6	6.5	-1.250
9.36 - 9.45	3	1.8	8.3	-1.242
9.46 - 9.55	2	1.2	9.5	-1.233
9.56 - 9.65	3	1.8	11.2	-1.225
9.66 - 9.75	1	0.6	11.8	-1.216
9.76 - 9.85	2	1.2	13.0	-1.207
9.96 - 10.05	1	0.6	13.6	-1.190

As shown in the left column, the categories for the birthrate variable have two decimal digits. Because two digits of precision are used for these categories, each nation tends to have a unique population growth rate. Because most categories represent a single nation, it doesn't make much sense to show the rate graphically. Notice the summary statistics located at the top of the screen. For this variable, we see that the mean (average) birthrate for these 172 nations is 23.748.

Mapping Variables

We will now map some of the variables in the GLOBAL file. Let's begin with the birthrate variable that we just used.

Data File: **GLOBAL**

➤ Task: **Mapping**

➤ Variable 1: **28) BIRTHRATE**

➤ View: **Map**

BIRTHRATE -- Crude birth rate indicates the number of live births occurring during the year per 1,000 people estimated at midyear. (WDI, 2005)

You have already opened the GLOBAL data file, so you need to first select the MAPPING task, and then select 28) BIRTHRATE for Variable 1. The first view is the Map view. (Remember, the ➤ symbol indicates which steps you need to perform if you are doing all examples as you follow along in the text. So, in the next example, you need only select the [Legend] option—that is, you don't need to repeat the first four steps, because they were already done in this example.)

The resulting map shows the 172 countries in terms of five different colors, and these colors correspond to the five levels of the birthrate. Look at the legend on your computer screen to see the birthrates that correspond to particular colors.

Data File: **GLOBAL**
Task: **Mapping**
Variable 1: **28) BIRTHRATE**
View: **Map**
➤ Display: **Legend**

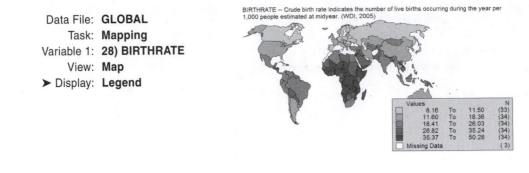

As indicated by the ➤ symbol, if you are continuing from the previous example, select the [Legend] option.

The nations are divided roughly equally into five groups. Here the 33 nations that have the highest birthrate are in the highest fifth. Next are the 34 nations in the second highest fifth. And so it goes down to the 34 nations in the lowest fifth.

We can easily see from this map that the highest birthrate countries are in Africa and that some of the lowest birthrate countries are in Europe. Another way to examine these results is to look at the spot map. First, deselect the legend by clicking on the [Legend] option again. Then select the [Spot] option.

Data File: **GLOBAL**
Task: **Mapping**
Variable 1: **28) BIRTHRATE**
View: **Map**
➤ Display: **Spot Fill**

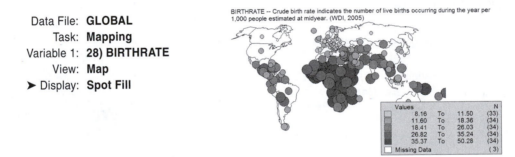

These spots are colored in the same way as the countries. Additionally, the size of the spot indicates how high the birthrate is—the larger the spot, the higher the birthrate. Deselect the spots by clicking [Spot] again.

For the variable being mapped, you can get specific information for a particular nation by simply clicking on it. Click on the United States and you will see that its birthrate is 13.88 and that it ranks 123 (out of 172 nations) in terms of birthrate. Click on Russia and you will see that it has a birthrate of 9.82 and that it ranks 149 out of 172. Click on Angola and you will see that it has a high birthrate (50.28) and that it is ranked number 1 out of 172 countries in terms of birth rate.

You say that you didn't find Angola on the map? Well, there's an easy way to do this. MicroCase has a [Find Case] option that makes it easy to locate a geographic area. You will first need to click the [Find Case] box to deselect it (the box will have been checked while you were clicking on countries). Now, continue with this example by selecting the [Find Case] option again as indicated by the following software guide.

Data File: **GLOBAL**
Task: **Mapping**
Variable 1: **28) BIRTHRATE**
View: **Map**
➤ Display: **Find Case: Angola**

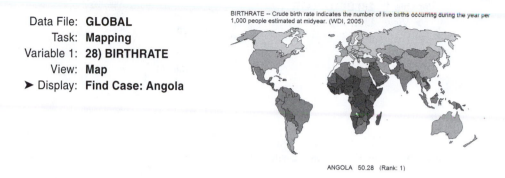

BIRTHRATE -- Crude birth rate indicates the number of live births occurring during the year per 1,000 people estimated at midyear. (WDI, 2005)

ANGOLA 50.28 (Rank: 1)

Once you have selected the [Find Case] option, locate Angola in the list of nations. Click on the box next to Angola to select it and then click [OK] to close the window. The selected case is highlighted on the map, and its value on the variable is shown.

Angola will now be highlighted, and an arrow will point to it. Go ahead and find some other countries this way.

While the methods for finding particular countries on the map are interesting ways to examine birthrates, you might want a listing of all the countries at once. This can be done quite easily.

Data File: **GLOBAL**
Task: **Mapping**
Variable 1: **28) BIRTHRATE**
➤ View: **List: Rank**

RANK	CASE NAME	VALUE
1	Angola	50.28
2	Somalia	49.99
3	Guinea-Bissau	48.56
4	Niger	48.23
5	Mali	47.53
6	Congo, Dem. Republic	44.97
7	Chad	44.77
8	Malawi	44.36
9	Congo, Republic	44.17
10	Uganda	43.98

As indicated by the ➤ symbol, select the [List: Rank] option. The number of rows shown on your screen may be different from that shown here. Use the cursor keys and scroll bar to move through the list if necessary.

The window that opens lists all 172 nations from highest to lowest in terms of birthrate. As we saw earlier, Angola has the highest birthrate (50.28), and (if you scroll down) Georgia has the lowest (8.16). You might, however, want an alphabetized list of countries. This is also easy.

Data File:	**GLOBAL**	
Task:	**Mapping**	
Variable 1:	**28) BIRTHRATE**	
➤ View:	**List: Alpha**	

RANK	CASE NAME	VALUE
--	Afghanistan	
109	Albania	17.05
86	Algeria	21.64
1	Angola	50.28
105	Argentina	18.24
158	Armenia	9.36
130	Australia	12.50
154	Austria	9.50
114	Azerbaijan	16.26
104	Bahamas	18.33

As indicated by the ➤ symbol, select the [List: Alpha] option.

This presents an alphabetized list of nations with the value and ranking for each nation.

You can also have two maps on the screen at the same time to compare the results. Return to the list of variables and follow the software guide below.

Data File:	**GLOBAL**
Task:	**Mapping**
Variable 1:	**28) BIRTHRATE**
➤ Variable 2:	**22) URBAN %02**
➤ Views:	**Map**

BIRTHRATE -- Crude birth rate indicates the number of live births occurring during the year per 1,000 people estimated at midyear. (WDI, 2005)

r = −0.621**

UBRAN %02 -- Percent urban, 2002 (HDR, 2004)

If you are continuing from the previous example, return to the variable selection screen for the MAPPING task by clicking on the [[↺]]. 28) BIRTHRATE should still be selected for Variable 1. Now select 22) URBAN %02 for Variable 2.

Compare the two maps on the screen and you will see that they look very different. Thus, nations that are more urban have lower birthrates. Let's change the second variable and view two more maps.

Data File: **GLOBAL**
Task: **Mapping**
Variable 1: **28) BIRTHRATE**
➤ Variable 2: **109) CONTRACEPT**
➤ Views: **Map**

BIRTHRATE -- Crude birth rate indicates the number of live births occurring during the year per 1,000 people estimated at midyear. (WDI, 2005)

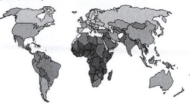

r = −0.793**

CONTRACEPT -- Percentage of women using contraception. (HDR, 2004)

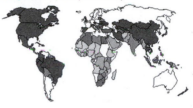

For the map showing 109) CONTRACEPT, note that some countries are not colored. These countries are missing cases for this variable—we do not have data for this particular variable for these countries. For all of the data files we're using with Student MicroCase, there will be some missing data for some of the variables.

For those countries that have data available for both variables (birthrate and percentage of women using contraception), note that the two maps are very different. That is, if a country is dark on one map (e.g., high in terms of birthrate), then it is light on the other map (a low percentage of women use contraception). This means that countries that have a high birthrate have a low percentage of women using contraception, and vice versa.

Your Turn
Now it's your turn. The worksheets that follow include instructions and questions to give you a better feel for Student MicroCase and the data files included with it. Enjoy!

worksheet

CHAPTER
1

NAME: _____

COURSE: _____

DATE: _____

Workbook exercises and software are copyrighted. Copying is prohibited by law.

You will need to use Student MicroCase to answer the following questions. Make sure you have already gone through the "Getting Started" section that appears before Chapter 1 and the preliminary part of this chapter.

1. Let's begin with a look at the HOUSE file.

> ➤ Data File: **HOUSE**
> ➤ Task: **Univariate**
> ➤ Primary Variable: **11) PARTY**
> ➤ View: **Pie**

How many of the U.S. representatives are Democrats? _____

What percentage of the U.S. representatives are Republicans? _____%

Sometimes a U.S. representative might be an Independent or belong to a minor political party. We treat these representatives as missing in statistical analysis because there are too few of them for meaningful analysis. How many U.S. representatives are in the missing category here? _____

Actually, the number of Independents in the 109th Congress depends on when you check. The file notes for this file contain important information that needs to be taken into account. Click on FILE SETTINGS on the menu bar at the top and then select FILE NOTES. Read through these notes.

Which representative started his career as a Democrat but later switched to Independent status and then became a Republican?

_____

While you're looking at the file notes for the HOUSE file, read the information in the second paragraph about continuous variables. When you see a variable name such as DIST $(U), what does the (U) mean?

_____

2. Return to the variable list and scroll down to the end of the list.

How many variables are there in this data file? _____

worksheet

Click on the [Search] button and search for any variables containing the word tax. List below the variables (numbers and names) found by this search.

_____

_____

_____

Click on [Full List] to return to the full list of variables, and then follow the software guide below.

    Data File: **HOUSE**
      Task: **Univariate**
➤ Primary Variable: **58) TAX CUTS**
    ➤ View: **Pie**

Write the variable description for 58) TAX CUTS below.

_____

_____

_____

_____

How many U.S. representatives voted in favor of this bill? _____

What percentage of U.S. representatives voted against this bill? _____%

All U.S. representatives who did not vote on this bill are listed as missing. How many representatives did not vote on this bill? _____

3. Let's look at the roll-call results for a bill concerning fuel efficiency standards.

    Data File: **HOUSE**
      Task: **Univariate**
➤ Primary Variable: **53) FUEL EFF**
    ➤ View: **Pie**

Write the variable description for 53) FUEL EFF below.

_____

_____

_____

_____

worksheet

CHAPTER **1**

How many U.S. representatives voted in favor of this bill? _____

What percentage of U.S. representatives voted in favor of this bill? _____%

How many U.S. representatives did not vote on this bill? That is, how many are listed as missing for this variable? _____

4. Open the GSS file and follow the software guide below.

> ➤ Data File: **GSS**
> ➤ Task: **Univariate**
> ➤ Primary Variable: **63) POL. VIEW**
> ➤ View: **Pie**

Write in the percentages of people who classified themselves as liberals, moderates, and conservatives.

Liberal _____%   Moderate _____%   Conservative _____%

How many respondents answered this question? That is, what is the total number of cases (N) for this question? _____

How many people were classified as missing for this particular variable? (In this situation, missing means that these people didn't answer this question.) _____

5. Return to the list of variables and click on [Search]. For the search term, type abortion and click [OK].

How many variables did this search produce? _____

This list of variables contains some questions about abortion in what might be termed emergency situations (e.g., the health of the mother is in danger) and some questions about abortion in what might be termed nonemergency situations (e.g., the woman isn't married and doesn't want to marry the man). Let's compare the results for two of these questions. First, obtain the results for one of the emergency-situation questions.

> Data File: **GSS**
> Task: **Univariate**
> ➤ Primary Variable: **187) ABORT HLTH**
> ➤ View: **Pie**

What percentage of the respondents in this survey would allow an abortion if the woman's health is endangered by the pregnancy? _____%

How many people answered this question? _____

How many missing cases were there for this question? _____

Chapter 1 Worksheet

19

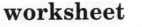   

You might think it is odd that so many people did not answer this question. In fact, not everyone in the GSS survey was asked this question. The National Opinion Research Center (NORC) used a large sample in its 2006 GSS survey and asked a little less than half of the sample some of the questions. This is an example of that situation. Even though less than half of the sample was asked this question, this proportion represents an adequate sample. We will return to sampling in a later chapter. Now let's look at the results for a nonemergency-abortion question.

> Data File: **GSS**
> Task: **Univariate**
> ➤ Primary Variable: **190) ABORT SING**
> ➤ View: **Pie**

What percentage of the respondents in this survey would allow
an abortion if the woman is single and does not want to marry the man?   _____%

Compare the percentage who would allow an abortion if the woman's
health is in danger with the percentage who would allow an abortion if the
woman is single and does not want to marry the man. Do the results for
these two questions support the idea that in the United States many people
favor or oppose abortion depending on the specific circumstances?   Yes   No

Print these results and attach them to your assignment. (**Note:** If you have been instructed not to submit the printout, just skip this task.)

6. Open the STATES file and follow the software guide below.

> ➤ Data File: **STATES**
> ➤ Task: **Univariate**

With the variable list on the screen, click on several of the variables and look at the variable descriptions. Note that the variable descriptions give the range for the variables. For example, scroll to the end of the variable description for 110) %HISP.00, and note that the range is 0.7 to 42.1—indicating that the percentage of a state's population of Hispanic origin ranged from 0.7% to 42.1%.

Look at the variable description for 1622) %VOTED 04. Write the variable
description below, and specify the range for this variable.

_____

_____

_____

Range = _____

> Data File: **STATES**
> Task: **Univariate**
> ➤ Primary Variable: **1622) %VOTED 04**
> ➤ View: **Statistics (Summary)**

What was the average (mean) percentage who voted in the states in 2004?

_____%

Were there any missing cases for this variable?

Yes   No

7. We will now use the MAPPING task with the STATES file.

> Data File: **STATES**
> ➤ Task: **Mapping**
> ➤ Variable 1: **1625) %GWBUSH04**
> ➤ View: **Map**
> ➤ Display: **Legend**

Look at the first line of the legend to see what the lightest color represents and how many states are represented by this color. This color represents those states whose percentage of votes for Bush ranged from 37.0% to 45.3%. The 10 in parentheses at the end of this line means that there were 10 states in this category.

Look at the darkest color category (the fifth and highest category). Specify the low value, the high value, and the number of cases in this category.

Low Value = _____

High Value = _____

Number of Cases = _____

Click on the [Legend] button to deselect the legend, and let's search for a particular state.

> Data File: **STATES**
> Task: **Mapping**
> Variable 1: **1625) %GWBUSH04**
> View: **Map**
> ➤ Display: **Find Case: Texas**

We might expect that Bush would do very well in his home state. What percentage of the vote did he receive in Texas?

_____%

Look at the rank for Texas on this variable. Is Texas the state in which Bush did best?

Yes   No

Click on [Find Case] twice to search for another case. We might expect that Bush would not do well in Kerry's home state, Massachusetts.

> Data File: **STATES**
> Task: **Mapping**
> Variable 1: **1625) %GWBUSH04**
> View: **Map**
> ➤ Display: **Find Case: Massachusetts**

What percentage of the vote did Bush receive in Massachusetts?

_____%

Look at the rank for Massachusetts on this variable. Is Massachusetts
the state in which Bush did his worst in terms of vote percentage?   Yes   No

8. Let's look at the alphabetized list of states for this variable.

> Data File: **STATES**
> Task: **Mapping**
> Variable 1: **1625) %GWBUSH04**
> ➤ View: **List: Alpha**

Write in the percentage of the vote received by Bush in each of the
following states.

New York = _____%

Idaho = _____%

Florida = _____%

Click on the printer icon to print the alphabetized list of states for this variable and attach the
printout to your assignment. (**Note:** If you have been instructed not to use the printer, skip these
printing instructions.)

9. Let's look at the ranked list of states for this variable.

> Data File: **STATES**
> Task: **Mapping**
> Variable 1: **1625) %GWBUSH04**
> ➤ View: **List: Rank**

Write below the names of the three states that are ranked highest on this
variable—the three states that gave the highest percentages of votes to
Bush. Also write in the percentage for each of these states.

Rank 1 State: _____   Percentage = _____%

Rank 2 State: _____   Percentage = _____%

Rank 3 State: _____   Percentage = _____%

10. Let's compare two maps. We might expect that the states where Bush did best would be the states
where Kerry did worst, and vice versa. If there were only two candidates, that would be correct. However, a third candidate, Nader, was also in the race, which could complicate the matter. So, let's find out.

> Data File: **STATES**
> Task: **Mapping**
> Variable 1: **1625) %GWBUSH04**
> ➤ Variable 2: **1626) %KERRY04**
> ➤ View: **Map**

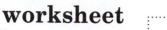

Note: Return to the list of variables. Since 1625) %GWBUSH04 is already selected in the Variable 1 box, you do not need to do anything about it. Put your mouse pointer in the Variable 2 box and click once to make this the active box. Then select 1626) %KERRY04 as the second variable.

Compare the two maps. Do they look similar to one another (states that are dark on one map are dark on the other; states that are light on one map are light on the other), look opposite of one another (states that are dark on one map are light on the other), or seem to be unrelated to one another? (Circle one.)

        Similar   Opposite   Unrelated

Now describe any patterns that you might observe.

_____

_____

_____

11. To demonstrate missing data, let's briefly look at another variable in the STATES file.

      Data File: **STATES**
           Task: **Mapping**
➤ Variable 1: **1253) KID ABUSE**
     ➤ View: **Map**

This map shows the distribution of reported child abuse cases per 1,000 children aged 18 or younger. One of the states is not colored, which means we do not have child abuse data for this state. Let's take a more detailed look at which state is missing data for this variable.

      Data File: **STATES**
           Task: **Mapping**
   Variable 1: **1253) KID ABUSE**
     ➤ View: **List: Rank**

In the MAPPING task, the cases that have missing values will be listed at the end of the ranked list. Scroll down the list to the end, and write below the name of the state that is missing for this child abuse variable.

_____

That's all for this lesson.

CHAPTER 2

Measurement I: The Basic Ideas

Tasks: Univariate, Mapping
Data Files: NES 04, GSS, GSS 04, HOUSE, GLOBAL

INTRODUCTION

In political research, we need to be able to measure the concepts with which we deal. Chapters 2 and 3 cover different aspects of the measurement process in political research. This chapter covers the following measurement topics:

- Concepts

- Variables

- Variation

- Conceptual (or nominal) definitions: the meaning of concepts

- Operational definitions: the measurement of concepts

- Reliability and validity

CONCEPTS

A **concept** is an abstraction based on characteristics of perceived reality.

In everyday life we use many different concepts, such as *work, test, book, love, school, success, motivation, food,* and *car.* When we perceive reality, we categorize and label it in terms of the concepts we possess—or we develop new concepts when our perceptions of reality are not covered well by the concepts we already have. That is, a concept is a term that we use to stand for a set of characteristics of a category of persons, objects, or events. For example, the concept *dog* stands for a set of characteristics of a category of objects—despite the many breeds and differences among dogs, we can easily apply this concept to the part of perceived reality that we have labeled *dog.*

In political science, we deal with many different political concepts. Here are some examples of concepts used in political science:

political party identification	political efficacy	public interest
freedom	political alienation	political trust
voting participation	political development	ideology
war	political tolerance	voter intent

VARIABLES

A *variable* is a measured concept.

When we use a concept in scientific research, we need to be able to measure it. Once we have measured the concept, we have what is known as a variable. Consider, for example, the concept of political participation. We might measure political participation among a set of people by asking each person a series of questions about his or her activities in the political system. For example, the investigators in the 2004 National Election Study asked respondents the following question that could measure one dimension of political participation:

> *We would like to find out about some of the things people do to help a party or a candidate win an election. During the campaign, did you talk to any people and try to show them why they should vote for or against one of the parties or candidates?*

The respondents answered this question in the following manner:

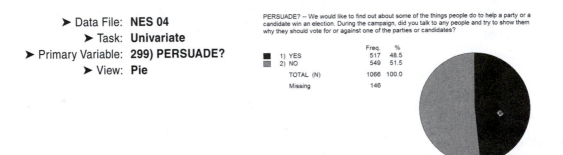

➤ Data File: **NES 04**
➤ Task: **Univariate**
➤ Primary Variable: **299) PERSUADE?**
➤ View: **Pie**

PERSUADE? -- We would like to find out about some of the things people do to help a party or a candidate win an election. During the campaign, did you talk to any people and try to show them why they should vote for or against one of the parties or candidates?

	Freq.	%
1) YES	517	48.5
2) NO	549	51.5
TOTAL (N)	1066	100.0
Missing	146	

We call this question, and the possible responses to the question, a *variable* because it measures one dimension of the concept of political participation. Researchers might also want to include other variables to measure additional dimensions of political participation. For example, one might also include questions about whether or not respondents volunteered for a campaign or made campaign contributions. Thus, we start with a concept, we develop a way of measuring this concept, we measure the concept, and we have a variable. This process is indicated as follows:

Concept → Measurement → Variable

Later, we will see that there are different *types* of variables (dependent, independent, and so on), depending on their roles in the particular research that uses them.

VARIATION

Variation means differences within a set of measurements of a variable.

There is variation within variables. When we measure political participation using the question that asks whether or not the respondent talked to others in an effort to persuade his or her vote choice, not everyone gave the same answer. While 48.5% of the respondents said that they had tried to persuade others to vote for or against a specific party or candidate, 51.5% said that they did not do this. Thus, there is *variation* in this dimension of political participation. However, if everyone in some group had the same level of political participation, there would be no variation in political participation within that group.

Let's take another example. For the variable *political party identification,* some people are Democrats, some are Republicans, some are Independents, and some identify with minor political parties. Thus, there is variation in the variable *political party identification.* On the other hand, if everyone had the same preference, there would be no variation in political party identification.

The concept of variation is extremely important in research. The basic goal of scientific research is to explain variation in one variable by relating it to variation in one or more other variables.

CONCEPTUAL (OR NOMINAL) DEFINITIONS

A *conceptual* (or *nominal*) *definition* is a statement of the meaning of a particular concept.

A conceptual definition (also called a nominal definition) specifies what we mean by a particular concept. How are conceptual definitions related to dictionary definitions? Dictionary definitions are a subset of conceptual definitions. There is nothing magic about dictionary definitions. The people who write dictionary definitions cannot be experts on everything. Thus, if you have a great deal of knowledge in some particular area, you will probably develop your own conceptual definitions of concepts relevant to that area. Further, the dictionary would not even provide definitions for specialized concepts within political research (e.g., political efficacy).

If we plan to use a concept in research, it is very important that we have a clear idea of what we mean by that concept. Otherwise, we can encounter great problems when we attempt to measure the concept. If you are vague about what a concept means, that vagueness will probably be reflected in your measurement of the concept. Thus, when you formulate a conceptual definition, keep the following cautions in mind:

1. Make sure the definition is clear enough that other people can understand what you mean.

2. Make sure you have defined the concept itself, rather than linking it to a related—but different—concept. Consider this definition: *Political interest is the extent to which people participate in politics.* This definition says that political interest is the same thing as political participation. Obviously, this is not correct. Some people are interested in politics but do not participate, and some who participate in politics do so for reasons (e.g., social interaction) that are really not related to any interest in politics.

3. Make sure the definition is not circular. A circular definition defines a concept in terms of itself so that no real information is given about the meaning of the concept. Example 1: *Political participation means participation in politics.* Example 2: *Political party identification means identification with a political party.* Neither of those definitions assigns any meaning to the concept involved—each says that the concept means itself.

OPERATIONAL DEFINITIONS

An ***operational definition*** is a specification of the process by which a concept is measured.

To use a concept in scientific research, we must have a way to measure it. The process used to measure a particular concept is referred to as the *operational definition*. Thus, a conceptual definition first specifies what we *mean* by a particular concept, whereas an operational definition specifies the way we will *measure* the concept.

For example, in our question that asks respondents whether or not they persuaded someone to vote for a particular candidate or party, we were trying to measure one dimension of political participation. However, we need to provide a "rule" that tells the observer when a respondent has "participated" in politics. That rule must refer to one or more *indicators*.

To measure a concept, a researcher must select one or more indicators.

Indicators are the specific observations that are made in order to measure a particular concept.

An operational definition must be clear and complete, and it must provide guidance so that the researcher can make consistent measurements. This is important for the measurement process itself and so that other researchers can use the same operational definitions in related research or in replicating the original research. Let's look at some examples.

Operational Definition of Support for Capital Punishment
For our first example, let's look at a concept that is often measured with a single indicator from survey data.

Conceptual Definition   Support for capital punishment means favoring the death penalty as a punishment for criminals convicted of certain crimes.

Operational Definition   Support for capital punishment is operationally defined in terms of a favorable response to the following question from the NORC GSS:

➤ Data File: **GSS**
➤ Task: **Univariate**
➤ Primary Variable: **107) EXECUTE?**
➤ View: **Pie**

EXECUTE? -- Do you favor or oppose the death penalty for persons convicted of murder?
(CAPPUN)

	Freq.	%
■ 0) OPPOSE	930	33.0
▓ 1) FAVOR	1885	67.0
TOTAL (N)	2815	100.0
Missing	1695	

Indicator The indicator of support for capital punishment is the response category "1) Favor" because it is the answer that *indicates* support for capital punishment.

Here we are measuring support for capital punishment in terms of survey data, and we are using only one variable (in this case, one question). Notice that the complete question is given along with the response categories (favor or oppose) and the codes (the numbers assigned to the response categories). In this case, a person who favors capital punishment will be coded 1 and a person who opposes capital punishment will be coded 2.

An operational definition does not necessarily fully capture the meaning of the concept defined. Sometimes we cannot develop an operational definition that does justice to the richness of the concept with which we are dealing. At other times we could develop an operational definition that would better capture the concept being defined, but the additional cost to implement it (e.g., adding 10 detailed questions about a concept to a survey) may not be worth it.

In the example above, the single question gives us a rough indication of the attitudes of most people concerning capital punishment. However, if we wanted to do an in-depth study of attitudes toward capital punishment, that single question would be inadequate. For example, that question concerns the death penalty for just one situation—for persons convicted of murder. Also, it does not indicate whether the death penalty should be allowed or required in this situation. To measure this concept more fully, we would need a series of questions for various circumstances.

Operational Definition of Political Trust

Now let's measure a concept that requires more than one variable.

Conceptual Definition Political trust means the belief that public officials are honest and competent.

Operational Definition Political trust is operationally defined in terms of responses to the following agree/disagree questionnaire items:

A. *Public officials in this country are basically honest.*
   1) Agree 2) Disagree

B. Our public officials have the knowledge to do their jobs well.
    1) Agree 2) Disagree

C. Most public officials in this country are crooks.
    1) Agree 2) Disagree

D. Our public officials are not really competent to do their jobs.
    1) Agree 2) Disagree

In this operational definition there are actually *four indicators of political trust*. These include agreement that public officials are basically honest and that they have the knowledge to do their jobs well, and disagreement with the statement that public officials are crooks and not competent to do their jobs.

An overall political trust score is computed for each person by adding the number of *trusting* responses given to the four questions. The trusting responses are *Agree* for questions A and B and *Disagree* for questions C and D. Thus, each person has a score between 0 and 4.

As you can see, this example is based on survey data and on multiple indicators: We ask respondents more than one question in order to get at their levels of political trust. A single question would not be adequate to operationally define a concept that had any degree of complexity.

Operational Definition of Electoral Party Competition at the State Level
Now we will look at an example that is based on voting results in the states rather than on survey data. Specifically, the party competition measure is based on the results of gubernatorial elections.

Conceptual Definition   Electoral party competition at the state level means how close the Democratic Party and the Republican Party have come to receiving equal proportions of the two-party vote in statewide elections.

Operational Definition   Electoral party competition at the state level is operationally defined for each state by the formula

$$\text{Degree of Party Competition} = 1 - (W - L)$$

- where **W** and **L** are the proportions of the vote received by the winning candidate and the losing candidate, respectively, in the gubernatorial elections between 1996 and 2006.

- **W** and **L** are computed on the basis of election results in Michael Barone and Grant Ujifusa, *The Almanac of American Politics 2000* (Washington, DC: National Journal, 2000).

- The degree of party competition will vary between 0 (one party received 100% of the votes) and 1.0 (each party received 50% of the votes).

We could modify this operational definition of electoral party competition to include different elections (e.g., U.S. Senate elections or presidential elections) or to include a composite of more than one type of election. Further, a researcher could develop more than one measure of party competition and determine whether it makes much difference in the research results.

Given just about any concept, there is more than one way to operationally define it. However, some ways are usually better than others. *The way in which a concept is operationally defined can affect the results of the research.* Therefore, it is very important to give a great deal of attention to this measurement problem.

RELIABILITY AND VALIDITY

Reliability means the extent to which a measurement procedure consistently measures whatever it measures.

Validity means the extent to which a measurement procedure measures what it is intended to measure.

When we measure a concept, we want this measurement procedure to produce consistent results; that is the problem of *reliability*. We also want to make sure that we are actually measuring the concept we are trying to measure; that is the problem of *validity*.

We can see the problem of validity more clearly when we try to measure citizen attitudes on the issue of abortion. Let's try to measure these attitudes using the following question from the General Social Survey: "Do you believe that abortion should be legal if a woman wants an abortion for any reason?"

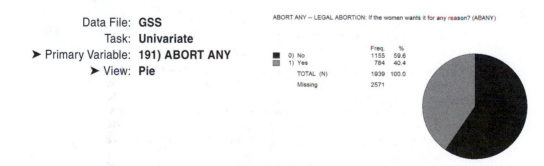

Data File:	**GSS**
Task:	**Univariate**
➤ Primary Variable:	**191) ABORT ANY**
➤ View:	**Pie**

ABORT ANY -- LEGAL ABORTION: If the women wants it for any reason? (ABANY)

	Freq.	%
0) No	1155	59.6
1) Yes	784	40.4
TOTAL (N)	1939	100.0
Missing	2571	

According to this question, only 40.4% of the U.S. population surveyed believes that abortion should be legal if the woman wants it for any reason. If this is a reliable measure of abortion attitudes, then other questions related to abortion ought to yield similar results. Let's see what people think about abortion in cases where a woman has been raped.

Data File: **GSS**
Task: **Univariate**
➤ Primary Variable: **189) ABORT RAPE**
➤ View: **Pie**

ABORT RAPE -- LEGAL ABORTION: If she became pregnant as a result of rape? (ABRAPE)

		Freq.	%
■	0) No	429	22.4
▨	1) Yes	1483	77.6
	TOTAL (N)	1912	100.0
	Missing	2598	

You should immediately notice that this result is very different from the preceding question that asks about abortion "for any reason." In this instance, 77.6% of the population surveyed believe that abortion should be legal for a woman who has been raped. The fact that these two results are so different tells us that *neither* one of these variables taken on its own is a ***reliable*** measure of public attitudes toward abortion. Part of the problem here is that one of the questions is very general (abortion for any reason) and the other is very specific (abortion in cases of rape). A reliable result should provide similar measurements across the two questions. Because each of these results taken on its own is not reliable, they are also not valid measures of abortion attitudes.

Now most political science majors are intuitively aware of the fact that abortion is a very complex issue. For this reason, political scientists try to achieve more reliable measures by asking many questions about abortion. Variables 185–191 in the GSS file represent seven different questions that have been asked in the 2006 survey. After asking these seven questions, political scientists combine the responses to get a more reliable measurement of attitudes toward abortion.

Data File: **GSS**
Task: **Univariate**
➤ Primary Variable: **192) ABORT TOT**
➤ View: **Pie**

ABORT TOT -- SUPPORT FOR LEGAL ABORTION. THE NUMBER OF SITUATIONS IN WHIHC THE RESPONDENT SAID ALLOW THE ABORTION [ABORT.DEF, ABORT.WAN, ABORT.HLT, ABORT NO$, ABORT RAP, ABORT SIN, ABORT ANY]

		Freq.	%
■	0) ILLEGAL	173	9.8
■	1)	158	9.0
■	2)	172	9.8
■	3)	372	21.1
■	4)	96	5.4
■	5)	82	4.6
■	6)	86	4.9
■	7) LEGAL	625	35.4
	TOTAL (N)	1764	100.0
	Missing	2746	

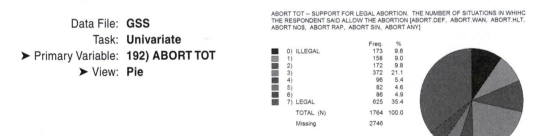

Now let's compare the reliability of this abortion measure in the 2006 GSS to the reliability in the 2004 GSS.

➤ Data File: **GSS 04**
➤ Task: **Univariate**
➤ Primary Variable: **189) ABORT TOT**
➤ View: **Pie**

ABORT TOT -- SUPPORT FOR LEGAL ABORTION> THE NUMBER OF SEVEN SITUATIONS IN WHICH THE RESPONDENT SAID ALLOW THE ABORTION [NOTE: ABORT.DEF, ABORT.WANT, ABORT.HLTH, ABORT NO$, ABORT RAPE, ABORT SING, ABORT ANY]

		Freq.	%
■	0) ILLEGAL	89	11.4
▨	1)	66	8.5
■	2)	80	10.2
■	3)	146	18.7
■	4)	52	6.7
■	5)	39	5.0
■	6)	38	4.9
■	7) LEGAL	271	34.7
	TOTAL (N)	781	100.0
	Missing	2031	

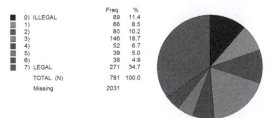

Research Methods in Political Science

If you carefully compare the two results taken in 2004 and 2006, you will see that the *Illegal* category from the 2006 survey contains 9.8% of the population compared to 11.4% of the population in the 2004 survey. 35.4% of the population in the 2006 survey seems to believe that abortion should be *Legal* compared to 34.7% of the population in the 2004 survey. If you compare all of the other categories, you will notice that not one of them differs more than three percentage points from the other. It appears that this approach provides a pretty reliable measure of abortion attitudes over time.

A measurement procedure might be reliable without being valid. The process by which we try to measure a concept might be consistent without actually measuring the concept it is intended to measure. On the other hand, a measurement procedure cannot be valid without being reliable. Thus, reliability is a necessary, but not a sufficient, condition for validity.

Reliability is concerned with consistency of the measurement approach, but **validity** is concerned with the accuracy of a measurement approach. For example, let's say a researcher wanted to measure ideology—that is, the extent to which a person is liberal, moderate, or conservative. The researcher must then select a variable to measure this concept. In this case the researcher selects the variable 5) PARTY from the NES 04 file as the measure of ideology.

➤ Data File: **NES 04**
➤ Task: **Univariate**
➤ Primary Variable: **5) PARTY**
➤ View: **Pie**

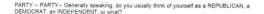

PARTY -- PARTY-- Generally speaking, do you usually think of yourself as a REPUBLICAN, a DEMOCRAT, an INDEPENDENT, or what?

		Freq.	%
■	1) DEMOCRAT	382	33.9
▨	2) INDEPENDEN	399	35.4
▤	3) REPUBLICAN	347	30.8
	TOTAL (N)	1128	100.0
	Missing	84	

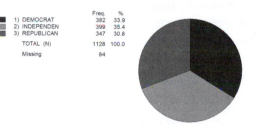

In some ways this approach may seem sound, but it assumes that all Republicans are ideologically conservative, that all Democrats are ideologically liberal, and that all moderates are Independents. While this may be accurate in many cases, we can also guess that it is not accurate in all cases. Let's check our assumptions about the validity of 5) PARTY as a measure of ideology using the Subset function of the UNIVARIATE task.

Data File: **NES 04**

Task: **Univariate**

➤ Primary Variable: **25) IDEOLOGY**

➤ Subset Variable: **5) PARTY**

➤ Subset Category: **1) Democrat**

➤ View: **Pie**

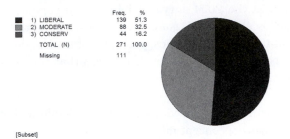

IDEOLOGY -- We hear a lot of talk these days about liberals and conservatives. Where would you place YOURSELF on this scale, or haven't you thought much about this?

	Freq.	%
1) LIBERAL	139	51.3
2) MODERATE	88	32.5
3) CONSERV	44	16.2
TOTAL (N)	271	100.0
Missing	111	

[Subset]

To find out the percentage of Democrats that identify with each ideological category, select 25) IDEOLOGY as the primary variable, then select 5) PARTY as the subset variable. When you click OK, you will see another window that asks which category you would like to analyze. Select "Democrat" here.

This particular analysis gives you a pie chart that tells you the percentage of people in each ideological category that are Democrats. According to this analysis, 51.3% of Democrats identify themselves as liberal, 32.5% identify themselves as moderate, and 16.2% identify themselves as conservative. Clearly, not all Democrats are liberal. Some are moderate and some are conservative. This raises questions about our ability to use 5) PARTY as a *valid* measure of ideology.

It is not easy to assess reliability and validity. We have given you a very basic understanding of this problem here, but you will need to learn more before you can confidently assess this for yourself. What is important here is to recognize that we must be very careful about the way that we operationalize concepts. If our measurement procedures are not solid, our research conclusions will rest on shaky ground.

TERMS INTRODUCED IN THIS CHAPTER

Concept

Variable

Variation

Conceptual (nominal) definition

Operational definition

Indicator

Reliability

Validity

FOR FURTHER READING

As indicated in this chapter, the way in which a concept is operationally defined can affect the results of a study. In the following article, the authors measure media exposure to campaign ads in a different way (outside the lab) than it previously had been measured, and their study produces different results. Paul Freedman and Ken Goldstein, "Measuring Media Exposure and the Effects of Negative Campaign Ads," *American Journal of Political Science* 43 (October 1999): 1189–1208.

It can be difficult for scholars to reach agreement on the most useful meaning of a concept or on the best way to measure that concept. For example, scholars differ on the best ways to conceptually define and operationally define racism. See, for example, the various articles in the special issue on race of the *Public Opinion Quarterly* 61 (Spring 1997)—such as the article by David O. Sears et al., "Is It Really Racism? The Origins of White Americans' Opposition to Race-Targeted Policies." Along those same lines, see Simo V. Virtanen and Leonie Huddy, "Old-Fashioned Racism and New Forms of Racial Prejudice," *Journal of Politics* 60 (May 1998): 311–332.

For an example of operationally defining the concept of political information among Americans, see Stephen Earl Bennett, "Comparing Americans' Political Information in 1988 and 1992," *Journal of Politics* 57 (May 1995): 521–532.

There has been a great deal of discussion among political scientists about how to conceptualize and measure political tolerance. For a good example—and references to other major works in this area—see James H. Kuklinski et al., "The Cognitive and Affective Bases of Political Tolerance Judgments," *American Journal of Political Science* 35 (February 1991): 1–27.

For examples of the measurement of several state-level concepts (e.g., welfare effort), see Robert D. Brown, "Party Cleavages and Welfare Effort in the American States," *American Political Science Review* 89 (March 1995): 23–33.

worksheet

NAME: _____

COURSE: _____

DATE: _____

These exercises will give you a better understanding of the topics discussed in the preceding pages. In one sense, however, you will be working backward. We ordinarily develop a concept and then formulate the operational definition. But because you will be working with the data files supplied with Student Micro-Case, the foundations for the operational definitions will already exist and you will be determining what concepts are being measured.

While this may be working backward, it is not unrealistic—a substantial amount of political research is carried out with data files that have already been developed by someone else. For example, there is a tremendous amount of research in political science that uses data from the American National Election Studies (NES) or the General Social Surveys (GSS), and the data files with Student MicroCase include a good selection of variables from each of those major sources.

1. Look at the univariate statistics for variable 25) IDEOLOGY in the NES 04 data file.

   ➤ Data File: **NES 04**
   ➤ Task: **Univariate**
   ➤ Primary Variable: **25) IDEOLOGY**
   ➤ View: **Pie**

   Write in the percentages of people in each ideological category.

   Liberal _____% Moderate _____% Conservative _____%

   What was the total number of people who answered this question? _____

   How many missing cases were there for this variable? _____

Most people are willing to classify themselves along a liberal-conservative continuum. However, is that ideological identification strongly related to the views that people hold on specific political issues? Not necessarily. We can legitimately conceptualize this variable as self-identification on the liberal-conservative dimension, but we would have a validity problem if we treated it as an actual measure of liberalism or conservatism.

There are several reasons why a person's ideological identification might not be strongly related to the views that the person holds on specific political issues. One reason is that people might be liberal on some types of issues and conservative on other types of issues. For example, some people who are liberal on economic issues (e.g., spending programs to provide services) are conservative on the social issues (e.g., abortion, prayer in school, pornography, euthanasia).

If you wanted to use one of the questions from the NES 04 to measure liberalism (or conservatism) on economic issues, which question might you use to measure this concept? (Use the search procedure.)

Write in the variable number and name. _____

If you wanted to use one of the questions from the NES 04 to measure liberalism (or conservatism) on the social issues, which question might you use to measure this concept?

Write in the variable number and name. _____

2. When we examine the political attitudes that people hold, background variables such as gender might be important. For example, males and females might have different attitudes on certain political issues. Other personal, social, or economic background characteristics (such as education level) can also affect the political opinions that people hold. Different background characteristics can lead to different experiences in society, and those differences in experiences can lead to different political views. Let's find some other background characteristics of people in the NES data file.

Look through the list of variables in this data file, and list below the variable numbers and names of three background variables other than the two already mentioned (sex and education) that might influence people's attitudes:

_____   _____   _____

We can operationalize many background variables sufficiently well for most purposes with a single indicator. For example, we can use a single indicator—here a single question—to operationally define the variable sex. We do not need a series of questions to measure the concept of sex. Later in these worksheets, we will use some concepts that require multiple indicators.

3. When we operationally define a concept, we do not necessarily fully capture the meaning of that concept. Look at the description for variable 4) EDUCATION. What do we mean by the concept of education? We might give a broad conceptual definition of education as the acquired learning of an individual, especially as developed through formal processes such as schooling. In doing research, however, we often need to settle for rough indicators of the concept we are trying to measure. As a result, we might use a specific indicator such as years of schooling to operationally define a broader concept such as education.

Obtain the univariate statistics for 4) EDUCATION.

> Data File: **NES 04**
> Task: **Univariate**
> ➤ Primary Variable: **4) EDUCATION**
> ➤ View: **Statistics (Summary)**

How many people (frequency) completed high school (but no more than high school)? _____

Those who have a high school degree all spent the same number of years in school. However, did they all have the same amount of education, in the broader sense? Briefly explain why two people who have the same number of years of school might not have the same amount of education.

_____

_____

4. Scroll through the variable descriptions in the NES 04 file or use the search procedure to find a variable that corresponds to each of the concepts listed below. Write the MicroCase variable number and name next to the concept. (The first one has been done as an example.)

CONCEPT	VARIABLE NUMBER & NAME
Presidential approval rating	16) BUSH APP
View of social security reform	_____
Presidential voting preference	_____
View on the war in Afghanistan	_____
View on the war in Iraq	_____

5. Now let's go to the GSS data file.

> ➤ Data File: **GSS**
> > ➤ Task: **Univariate**

Following is a list of conceptual definitions for several concepts. From the list of variables in the GSS file, find one question that could be used to operationally define each of the concepts. List the numbers and names of the variables in the spaces provided.

Environmentalism is the belief that the environment should be improved and protected. _____

Support for the Supreme Court prayer decision is the belief that the Supreme Court was right in ruling that state and local governments cannot require prayers in public schools. _____

Support for freedom of speech is a willingness to allow freedom of expression to others regardless of their political or religious views. _____

6. When a concept is complex, we usually need more than one indicator to operationally define the concept. Look at the variable descriptions for the following variables: 92) ATHEIST SP, 95) RACIST SP, 98) COMMUN.SP, 101) MILIT SP, 104) HOMO. SP

Those five variables can be used as indicators to operationally define a particular concept. Specify the overall concept indicated by those five variables, and give a conceptual definition for this concept.

Concept:

_____

_____

_____

Conceptual Definition:

_____

_____

_____

7. Look at the variable descriptions for the following variables: 146) FED.GOV'T?, 153) CONGRESS?, and 151) SUP.COURT?

Those three variables might be used individually to measure three separate concepts. However, they also might be combined to measure a broader concept. Specify the broader concept indicated by those three variables, and give a conceptual definition for this concept.

Concept:

_____

_____

_____

Conceptual Definition:

_____

_____

_____

8. As we learned in this chapter, the way we operationally define a concept can affect the results of our study. Let's examine this issue in greater depth. Say that we wanted to use a question from the GSS data file to operationally define the concept of support for abortion. We'll use variable 185) ABORT DEF (if there is a strong chance of serious defect in the baby) to operationally define support for abortion and obtain univariate statistics for it.

worksheet

Data File: **GSS**
Task: **Univariate**
➤ Primary Variable: **185) ABORT DEF**
➤ View: **Pie**

What percentage of people would allow an abortion in this situation? _____%

If you were using this question as an indicator to operationally define the
concept of support for abortion, what would you conclude about the extent to
which people in the United States favor or oppose abortion?

_____

_____

Instead of using 185) ABORT DEF to operationally define support for abortion, we might have used
a different question such as 188) ABORT NO$ (if the family has a very low income and cannot afford
any more children). Let's analyze this variable.

Data File: **GSS**
Task: **Univariate**
➤ Primary Variable: **188) ABORT NO$**
➤ View: **Pie**

What percentage of people would allow an abortion in this situation? _____%

If you were using this question as an indicator to operationally define the
concept support for abortion, what would you conclude about the extent to
which people in the United States favor or oppose abortion?

_____

_____

_____

How much difference in the results would it make whether you used
185) ABORT DEF or 188) ABORT NO$ to operationally define the
concept support for abortion? (Circle one.)

No difference   A small difference   A substantial difference

If you look at the variable list and descriptions, you will see that the GSS data file contains a series of
questions about abortion in different situations.

On the basis of the differences in results for the two questions previously
examined, does it seem necessary to have many different questions on this
topic to operationally define attitudes toward abortion?   Yes   No

Note that there is also a variable that is a composite measure (an index) of responses to seven
individual abortion questions. This variable (ABORT TOT) is the number of situations out of the seven

options presented in which a respondent would allow an abortion. Look at the univariate results for this variable.

> Data File: **GSS**
> Task: **Univariate**
> ➤ Primary Variable: **192) ABORT TOT**
> ➤ View: **Pie**

What percentage of people would not allow an abortion in any of the seven situations?   _____%

What percentage of people would allow an abortion in all seven situations?   _____%

If attitudes toward abortion were not dependent on the situation, then we might expect that just about all the respondents in this survey would have a score of either 0 (oppose abortion in all situations) or 7 (allow abortion in all situations). Is this the case? Are just about all the respondents either totally opposed to abortion or totally in favor of allowing abortion?   Yes   No

9. Look at the univariate statistics for variable 74) WELFARE $.

> Data File: **GSS**
> Task: **Univariate**
> ➤ Primary Variable: **74) WELFARE $**
> ➤ View: **Pie**

Write the description for this variable.

_____

_____

_____

What percentage of people think too little is being spent on welfare?   _____%

Now look at the results for variable 89) WELFARE $2.

> Data File: **GSS**
> Task: **Univariate**
> ➤ Primary Variable: **89) WELFARE $2**
> ➤ View: **Pie**

Write the variable description.

_____

_____

_____

What percentage think too little is being spent on assistance to the poor? _____%

It might be argued that the terms "welfare" and "assistance to the poor" mean basically the same thing. However, many people react differently depending on the terminology used. If you were going to operationally define a concept such as support for spending on welfare, this kind of problem would have to be considered. Again, the way in which we operationally define our concepts can affect the kinds of results we get in our research.

10. Whenever you use a data file with a number of variables in it, it is important to be able to find variables that deal with particular concepts. The search feature in MicroCase makes this easy to do. Let's say that we were doing research concerning the ways in which the political attitudes of people are related to various religious identifications and beliefs they possess. We would want to search for any variables having concepts related to religious orientations. Let's start by searching for any variable that contains the sequence of characters "relig"—which will include any variable that contains either the word *religion* or the word *religious*.

So, with the variable list for the GSS file on the screen, click on [Search], type **relig,** and click [OK]. How many variables did that search produce? _____

Look at the variable descriptions of those variables.

If you had to use one of those variables to operationally define the concept of support for religious freedom, which variable would you use? _____

If you had to use one of those variables to operationally define the concept of religious preference, which variable would you use? _____

If you had to use one of those variables to operationally define the concept of frequency of attendance at religious services, which variable would you use? _____

Although the preceding search picked up any variables that included the sequence "relig," it did not necessarily pick up a complete list of variables in this file that relate to religious identifications or beliefs. What other words or phrases might be used in searching for variables that concern religion or religious-political issues in the United States?

Find two other variables that relate to religion or religious-political issues, and write the variable numbers and names below.

_____   _____

11. Let's examine some variables in the HOUSE data file.

➤ Data File: **HOUSE**
➤ Task: **Univariate**

Search for two variables that indicate the seniority of representatives—the number of terms they have served in Congress.

Write in the variable numbers and names. _____ _____

> **Note that the only difference between those two variables is that one is grouped into categories and the other is not.**

Now search for a variable that measures support for the war in Iraq.

Write in the variable number and name. _____

Search for variables that measure each of the concepts listed below, and write in the variable numbers and names.

Support for a bill to build a fence on the U.S.-Mexican border _____

Support for a bill to expand oil production in Alaska _____

Support for a bill to allow federal research on embryonic
stem cells _____

12. Now let's look at variation within variables, which is an extremely important idea that we will consider throughout this book. First, let's look at a variable that has fairly low variation.

> Data File: **HOUSE**
> Task: **Univariate**
> ➤ Primary Variable: **14) INCUMBENT**
> ➤ View: **Pie**

What percentage of the representatives were re-elected to the 109th
Congress? _____%

The overwhelming majority of representatives were re-elected in 2004. Thus, there is low variation in that variable. Even when almost all the observations for a variable are the same, there is little variation in the variable.

Now let's look at a variable that has high variation.

> Data File: **HOUSE**
> Task: **Univariate**
> ➤ Primary Variable: **59) ANWR**
> ➤ View: **Pie**

What percentage of the representatives voted in favor of this bill to
expand oil production in Alaska? _____%

High variation occurs when the observations are evenly divided among the possible categories or values of a variable. In this situation, maximum variation would be a 50-50 split in the vote. As you can see, the actual results here are not far from a 50-50 split.

worksheet

CHAPTER 2

While you have the pie chart on the screen, print it. (**Note:** If you have been instructed by your professor not to use the printer, just skip this printing task.) Note that your name and the date are printed along with the pie chart. Attach this printout to your assignment.

Look at the univariate statistics for 58) TAX CUTS and 60) LEAVE IRAQ
Which of those two variables has greater variation in it? (Circle one.)

        58) TAX CUTS   60) LEAVE IRAQ

13. Let's briefly examine some concepts from the GLOBAL file.

> ➤ Data File: **GLOBAL**
> ➤ Task: **Mapping**

Search for variables that could be used to operationally define the concepts below, and write the variable numbers and names in the spaces indicated. (The first one has been done for you as an example.)

CONCEPT	VARIABLE NUMBER & NAME
Level of economic development	133) ECON DEVEL
Average life expectancy	_____
Extent of civil liberties enjoyed by citizens	_____
Possession of nuclear weapons	_____
Involvement in armed conflict	_____
Income inequality	_____

Chapter 2   Worksheet

Measurement II: Types of Data

Tasks: List Data, Univariate, Mapping, Cross-tabulation
Data Files: NES 04, NES, STATES, GSS, HOUSE, GLOBAL

INTRODUCTION

Political scientists use different types of data for different types of research. In this chapter, we will look at types of political science data in terms of three classifications:

• Cases (units of analysis)

• Approaches to data collection

• Levels of measurement

CASES — UNITS OF ANALYSIS

A *case* (or *unit of analysis*) is the item (person, city, nation, and so on) for which we have data.

Different kinds of research require different kinds of units of analysis. For example, if you wanted to investigate attitudes concerning abortion, individual people would be the units of analysis. However, if you wanted to investigate the relationship between welfare expenditures and per capita income in the 50 states, then states would be the units of analysis. The unit of analysis is important because different research questions require different units of analysis. Further, when interpreting the results of a study, we need to limit the conclusions to the type of unit of analysis used in the research.

Individual Data

The basic distinction here is between individual data and aggregate data. *Individual data are based on single entities rather than on collections of entities.* The most prominent example of individual data is survey research, in which the unit of analysis is the individual person.

We can see the way that individual data are put together for use in MicroCase or any other analysis program. Let's take a look at the GSS file.

➤ Data File: **GSS**
➤ Task: **Univariate**
➤ Primary Variable: **1) SEX**
➤ View: **Pie**

This analysis tells us the number of men and women that were surveyed for the General Social Survey. The MicroCase program actually tabulates the sex of every individual in the GSS data file and gives these results in this summary form. The graphic tells you that there are 2,003 men in the survey and 2,507 women. We can look at the data for each individual using the LIST DATA task.

➤ Data File: **GSS**
➤ Task: **List Data**
➤ Cases to be listed: **All Cases**
➤ Variables to be listed: **All Variables**

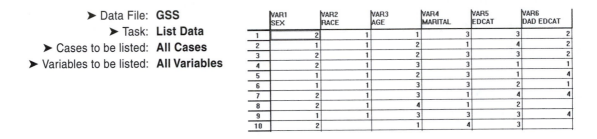

To find the LIST DATA task, return to DATA MANAGEMENT menu.

What you can see from the use of this task is very similar to a spreadsheet. Each row represents a specific person who was surveyed for the 2006 General Social Survey. Each column includes the question that the respondent was asked. By using the LIST DATA function, you can see that the first person in the survey is a woman (coded as a "2"), the second person in the survey is a man (coded as a "1"), and the third person is a woman, and so on. Now, if you scroll down to the bottom of the survey, you will see that the 4,510th person is a man. You will also be able to note that there are 4,510 people (or cases) surveyed in the 2006 General Social Survey.

Another example of research in which the individual person is the unit of analysis is the analysis of roll-call votes of public officials, in which the individual public official is the unit of analysis. However, individual data are not necessarily based on persons. For example, if we were studying the content of newspaper editorials, the individual editorial would be the unit of analysis.

Aggregate Data

The verb *to aggregate* means to put together. Thus, ***aggregate data*** *are data that are based on groups of units put together.* For example, census data are collected through surveys in which the individual is the unit of analysis. However, after these data have been aggregated, the individual is no longer the unit. Instead, we can obtain census data for cases such as cities, counties, states, congressional districts, and census tracts. For each of these units, we can get information (in the form of averages, rates, percentages, or sums) on population size, education, income, racial distribution, sizes of farms, number of manufacturing establishments, and so on.

➤ Data File: **STATES**
    ➤ Task: **Mapping**
  ➤ Variable: **2) TOTPOP03**
    ➤ View: **Map**
  ➤ Display: **Legend**

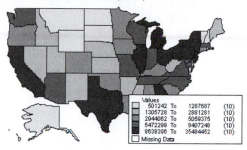

This map displays the population of each state in the STATES data file. Instead of individual people, the unit of this analysis is the state. If you look at the legend or click on one of the states, you can see that each state has a different population.

Now let's compare what you know about individual data to aggregate data. Let's list the data for the STATES file to see what it looks like.

Data File: **STATES**
    ➤ Task: **List Data**
➤ Cases to be listed: **All Cases**
➤ Variables to be listed: **All Variables**

	VAR1	VAR2	VAR3	VAR4	VAR5	VAR6
	STATE NAME	TOTPOP03	LND AREA	WATER AR	SOUTHNESS	WESTNESS
ALABAMA	ALABAMA	4500752	50750.2	1675	57.70	88.5
ALASKA	ALASKA	648818	570373.6	91316		
ARIZONA	ARIZONA	5580811	113642.2	364	49.23	115.5
ARKANSAS	ARKANSAS	2725714	52075.3	1110	55.23	94.5
CALIFORNIA	CALIFORNIA	35484452	155973.2	7736	51.58	124.5
COLORADO	COLORADO	4550688	103728.8	376	50.25	109.0
CONNECTICUT	CONNECTICUT	3483372	4845.4	699	48.20	73.5
DELAWARE	DELAWARE	817491	1954.6	536	50.33	77.0
FLORIDA	FLORIDA	17019068	53937.2	11828	59.50	85.4
GEORGIA	GEORGIA	8684715	57918.7	1519	56.35	85.7

In this display you see the states listed in alphabetical order. Each state is a case in this aggregate data file. The first case is Alabama, the second case is Alaska, and the third case is Arizona. The first variable in this data file is the state's name, the second variable is the population, the third variable is the state's land area, and so on. The cases are then represented in each row. If you scroll down to the bottom, you will see that this data file has 50 cases in it. The 50th case is Wyoming.

Aggregate data are necessary for certain types of political research. If, for example, you wanted to determine how the forms of government in different nations are related to their economic development, you would need to use aggregate data, rather than individual data.

There is a rather significant danger associated with using the wrong data to test a hypothesis. It is often the case that one will find a significant relationship between variables at the aggregate level that do not exist in the same way at the individual level. For example, if we used the STATES data file to understand the relationship between divorce rates and electoral support for George W. Bush in the 2004 election, we would see the following:

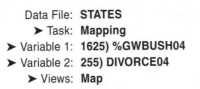

Data File: **STATES**
➤ Task: **Mapping**
➤ Variable 1: **1625) %GWBUSH04**
➤ Variable 2: **255) DIVORCE04**
➤ Views: **Map**

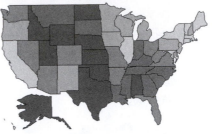

%GWBUSH04 -- 2004: PERCENT OF VOTES FOR GEORGE W. BUSH (REP.)

r = 0.428*

DIVORCE04 -- 2004: NUMBER OF DIVORCES PER 1000 POPULATION (NCHS)

Notice that many of the states that are lightly colored on the divorce rate map (low divorce rate) are also colored lightly on the support for Bush map (low support for President Bush). If you click on Illinois, you will see that it is ranked 42nd in its support for Bush and 44th in its divorce rate. Conversely, high-divorce-rate states seemed to have higher support for Bush. Idaho was ranked third in its support for Bush and has the fourth highest divorce rate. So it certainly seems to be the case that **divorced people are more likely to support Bush.** But think about the flaw in this reasoning. We have drawn a conclusion about **individual attitudes** based upon **aggregate data.** Let's analyze the relationship based upon individual data using the NES 04 file.

➤ Data File: **NES 04**
➤ Task: **Cross-tabulation**
➤ Row Variable: **312) WHO.VOTE?**
➤ Column Variable: **6) MARITAL**
➤ Views: **Column %**

WHO.VOTE? by MARITAL
Cramer's V: 0.152**

		MARITAL					
		MARRIED/P	WIDOWED	DIV/SEP	NVR MARR	Missing	TOTAL
WHO.VOTE?	KERRY	194	36	71	98	0	399
		42.4%	64.3%	53.4%	55.7%		48.5%
	BUSH	264	19	58	71	0	412
		57.6%	33.9%	43.6%	40.3%		50.1%
	OTHER	0	1	4	7	0	12
		0.0%	1.8%	3.0%	4.0%		1.5%
	Missing	190	36	62	100	1	389
	TOTAL	458	56	133	176	1	823
		100.0%	100.0%	100.0%	100.0%		

Research Methods in Political Science

To construct this table, return to the main menu and select the CROSS-TABULATION task, then select 312) WHO.VOTE? as the row variable and 6) MARITAL as the column variable. When the table is showing, select the [Column %] option.

When we test this hypothesis using individual data, we see a very different pattern than what we find using aggregate data. Look at the row containing those people who voted for Bush in the 2004 election. 57.6% of married individuals supported Bush, compared to only 43.6% of those who were divorced. Clearly, divorced people seem more likely to support Kerry than to support Bush.

From the comparison of the analysis of marital status and support for George W. Bush, you can see that we would have made a very serious error if we had drawn a conclusion about individual preferences in the 2004 election based upon aggregate data. This kind of error is known as an ecological fallacy.

APPROACHES TO DATA COLLECTION

Surveys

In political science, survey data are used more than any other kind. We collect survey data through face-to-face interviews, telephone interviews, mail questionnaires, or questionnaires given directly to groups of people. Thus, *survey data are collected through surveys and are data for which the individual is the unit of analysis*. Both parts of that definition are important. We can have data for individual persons that were not collected through a survey. For example, we would not consider the voting records of individual legislators to be survey data. We can also have data that were originally collected through surveys, but in which the individual is no longer the case. For example, census data are collected through surveys, but the case is no longer the individual person after the data have been aggregated into larger units (e.g., the percentage of a state's population living in urban areas).

Organizations collect survey data for a variety of purposes. You are probably most familiar with the surveys of commercial polling organizations (e.g., the Gallup Poll). Results from surveys by such organizations are sometimes presented on television or in newspapers or magazines. Though such surveys were not originally conducted for political science research, their results can be quite useful to political science researchers. You can find data from Gallup surveys from 1936 to the present in the reference section of your library in the multivolume *Gallup Poll*. Also, look in the periodicals section for *The Gallup Poll Monthly*. You can find a variety of results from other survey organizations in either *Public Opinion Quarterly* or *The Public Perspective*.

Though such survey results from commercial polling organizations are very useful, we cannot do additional analysis of the data. We can see the percentages of people who are for or against this or that, and the results might be broken down into several different categories (gender, race, region, party preference, religious preference, and so on). But we cannot do further analysis of the data because we have only these summary results—we do not have the actual data for each person.

There are several academic survey organizations that collect and maintain the actual data gathered from each person. Two of the major academic survey organizations are the National Opinion Research Center (NORC) and the Center for Political Studies (CPS).

NORC is known for its General Social Surveys (GSS). Almost every year since 1972, NORC has interviewed a national sample in the United States concerning a variety of political opinions, social opinions, background characteristics, personal habits, and so on. The GSS data files you have been using consist of selected variables from NORC's 2004 and 2006 GSS.

CPS is known for its American National Election Studies (NES). These surveys are conducted every two years, close to the times of the national elections, and include many questions about political attitudes, political behavior, socioeconomic background, and so on. The NES file that you have been using consists of selected variables from the 2004 and 2006 NES.

Experiments

There is little experimentation within political science. The problem is that experimentation requires that we be able to manipulate variables, and the kinds of variables we use in political research cannot be easily manipulated by researchers. We cannot, for example, actually control the environments in which people are raised to determine what effects different environments have on political attitudes and behavior. We cannot assign some countries to have democratic governments, some to have authoritarian governments, and some to have virtually no governments to determine what kinds of political systems are most likely to engage in war.

Although we don't do much experimentation in political science, it is possible to do some, and there have been a number of valuable studies that were based on experiments. Here's a simple example of what an experiment might look like. Consider this question: Does contacting registered voters increase the probability that they will actually vote on election day? Using public records, you could make a list of all registered voters in a precinct. Then you would randomly assign (e.g., by flipping a coin) people to the experimental group (those who will be contacted before election day) and the control group (those who will not be contacted). Close to the election, you contact people in the experimental group and urge them to vote on election day. (Note that you could also set up several experimental groups based on the type of communication—written vs. telephone vs. face-to-face.) After the election, you would need to check the public records to see who voted. Then you would determine whether there was a difference in voting turnout between the experimental group (contacted) and the control group (not contacted). If there is no substantial difference between the two groups in voting turnout, you would conclude that the contact made no difference. If there is a substantial difference, then you would conclude that the contact did make a difference.

Direct Observation

The direct observations used to gather data are made in a highly systematic fashion. Before undertaking the observations, the researcher develops a set of variables related to the content of the observations. Then the researcher systematically records data—gathered through observation—for these variables.

For example, suppose a researcher was interested in patterns of influence among state legislators and decided to observe interactions among legislators on the floor of the legislature while some important matters were being decided. A team of observers could systematically record observations that showed who interacted with whom, who initiated interactions, how much time was spent in interactions, who was isolated from the main patterns of interaction, and so on. This kind of data, especially in conjunction with other types of data such as voting records, can be very useful in examining patterns of influence in legislative bodies.

Content Analysis

Content analysis is systematic analysis of communications. The communications involved can be of any type—speeches, articles, books, letters to the editor, or conversations. The researcher develops an overall framework with a set of variables for the analysis. Typically, the researcher first goes through the communications quickly to develop a set of variables, then goes back through and classifies the parts of the communications into the variables that have been developed. Suppose you want to study the campaign speeches of candidates for public office to see what types of themes are stressed. The variables would be the themes, and each part of the speeches would be classified in terms of those variables.

To take another example, suppose you want to examine changes over time in the kinds of positions taken on political and social issues by the major newspapers in a given country. You could obtain copies of editorials from the major newspapers from various time periods, develop a set of variables, and classify the positions taken during different time periods to see whether there are any basic trends.

Extracting Data from Public Records

We will use the term **public records data** here as a broad category to include any data that can be obtained from publicly available records of any sort. Because it is such a broad category, this source of data can overlap with the other sources used.

In the United States, a wide variety of data is available through public records. This includes, for example, data on governmental agencies' expenditures on various programs (e.g., public assistance programs for the poor), statistics related to crime (e.g., arrests, rate of violent crime, sentencing of convicted criminals), and election results for various public offices.

Political scientists have given great attention to one kind of data in this category: roll-call votes. A *roll-call vote* is a vote by a public body (e.g., a state legislature or the U.S. House of Representatives) in which the votes of individual public officials are recorded by name. For example, if there is a roll-call vote on an issue in the House of Representatives, a record of the way each representative voted is kept in the *Congressional Record.* Congressional Quarterly, Inc., also compiles information about important votes in Congress and publishes this information in a convenient format in the *Congressional Quarterly Almanac.* Roll-call voting data are also available on the Internet.

LEVELS OF MEASUREMENT

Not only are there different sources of data in political research, there are also differences in the levels of measurement of data. *The level of measurement is very important, because we use different statistical techniques for data analysis depending on it.* Here we will discuss four levels of measurement: nominal, ordinal, interval, and ratio.

Nominal Measurement

Nominal measurement is classification of observations into a set of categories that have no direction.

In nominal measurement, we place observations in categories that have no direction—that do not fall into any order. *We cannot say that the observations in one category have more or less of the variable being measured than do the observations in a different category.* If we arrange the categories in an order, this arrangement is simply for convenience (e.g., alphabetical order) and does not reflect anything about the amount of the variable possessed by cases in the categories.

The variable *gender* provides a good example of nominal measurement. We classify people into categories (male or female) on the basis of gender. These categories do not have direction: We cannot say that males have more or less gender than do females. Race provides another good example. We classify people into racial categories on the basis of physical characteristics, but we cannot say that people in one of the racial categories have more race than people in another—for example, that whites have more race than African Americans.

Place of residence is another example. We could not say, for example, that those who live in Iowa have more or less state of residence than those who live in Texas. Nor could we say that those who live in Ireland have more or less nation of residence than those who live in Canada.

The set of categories must be *mutually exclusive.* That is, an observation can be placed in only one particular category. Also, the set of categories must be *exhaustive*—the categories must cover all possibilities.

Ordinal Measurement

Ordinal measurement is classification of observations into a set of categories that do have direction.

In both nominal and ordinal measurement, we place observations in categories on the basis of the characteristics of the observations. In ordinal measurement, however, the categories have direction, or order. *In ordinal measurement, we can say that observations in one category have more or less of the variable being measured than do observations in a different category.*

Let's say that we ask people how interested they are in politics: very interested, somewhat interested, not very interested, or not interested at all. We can say that those people who said *very interested* have more political interest than those who said *somewhat interested*. Those who are *somewhat interested* are more interested than those who are *not very interested,* and so on. To take another example, if we asked people whether they favored or opposed gun-control legislation, we could say that those who answered *favor* show greater support for gun-control legislation than those who answered *oppose*.

Suppose we classified people into one of the following categories based on their income levels: under $20,000; $20,000 to $30,000; $30,000 to $45,000; over $45,000. We can say that people in the *over $45,000* income category have more income than those in the *$30,000 to $45,000* category, those in the *$30,000 to $45,000* category have more income than those in the *$20,000 to $30,000* category, and so on.

For either nominal or ordinal measurement, we can assign numbers to the categories for the sake of convenience. For the income example above, we can let 1 stand for the lowest income category, 2 for the next lowest, and so on up to 4 for the highest. When we assign numbers to categories in either nominal or ordinal measurement, we do so only for the sake of convenience; we have not somehow increased the level or the precision of the measurement by this process.

It's important to recognize that all ranks are ordinal. Suppose we rank all nations in terms of how well they protect human rights. The most protective nation is number 1, the second most protective is number 2, and so on. Assuming reliable and valid measurements, we can say, for example, that the nation ranked 6 protects human rights more than the nation ranked 32.

Though ordinal measurement tells us more than nominal measurement, there is a limitation: We cannot assume that the intervals between categories are equal. For example, if we take one person from each of the political interest categories discussed above, can we assume that the difference in political interest between the *very interested* person and the *somewhat interested* person is the same as the difference between the *somewhat interested* person and the *not very interested* person? We cannot. If you examine the income categories discussed above, you will see that they are not equal in terms of the amount of income covered by each category. Further, within each category there will be variations in income among people. Thus, we cannot assume that the intervals are equal in ordinal measurement.

Interval Measurement

Interval measurement assigns real numbers to observations and has equal intervals of measurement but has no absolute zero point.

In interval measurement, we use real numbers—rather than simply letting numbers stand for categories—and the intervals of measurement are equal. However, political science does not use interval measurement much. Our measurement is usually either at a lower level than interval (nominal or ordinal) or at a higher level than interval (ratio). Therefore, we will demonstrate interval measurement with a common—but not politically relevant—example: the Fahrenheit thermometer.

On the Fahrenheit thermometer, the interval of measurement is the degree of heat. One degree of heat is one degree of heat no matter where it is on the thermometer. The difference between 80° and 70° is 10°; this 10° of heat is the same amount of difference as that between 30° and 20°. Thus, the intervals of measurement are equal.

A more common example in political research would be the years that a series of events took place. Imagine that you are collecting data on infant mortality in a country between the years 1917 and 2002. In this example the year would be an interval variable. The interval of measurement would be equal from one year to the next, and we can say with confidence that one unit change (the interval) all along this measurement is identical in meaning. We can also say that the difference between 1982 and 2002 (20 years) is twice that of the difference between 1917 and 1927 (10 years).

The problem with interval measurement is that the zero point—if there is one at all—is an arbitrary point. An arbitrary zero point does not indicate a complete absence of the variable being measured. Thus, on the Fahrenheit thermometer, the zero point does not indicate a complete absence of heat—we can go below zero. We also cannot say that the year 0 A.D. represents the absence (or even the beginning) of time. Human beings have assigned these numbers to mark the intervals between years, but this measure of time does not represent an absolute measure of time.

Ratio Measurement

Ratio measurement assigns real numbers to observations, has equal intervals of measurement, and has an absolute zero point.

If the zero point means *none* of whatever we're measuring, and if the intervals of measurement are equal, then we are conducting ratio measurement. An example of ratio measurement is population size by nation. The intervals of measurement are equal—one person is one person. A population of zero would mean that the nation had no population at all—although, of course, it might not be meaningful to refer to something as a nation if it had no population.

Let's say that you find out how many people in each state voted in the last presidential election. This is ratio measurement. If you converted each such number into a proportion or a percentage, it would still be ratio. All proportions and percentages are ratio because we start out with ratio measurements in order to derive them.

Sometimes a variable may be ratio or it may be some other level of measurement, depending on how we set up or categorize the variable. Income in dollars (e.g., $17,350) is ratio; income in terms of categories (e.g., under $15,000) is ordinal. Education in years is ratio; education in terms of a set of categories (e.g., high school degree or higher) is ordinal. In general, it is better to have ratio measurement for our variables than it is to have lower levels of measurement. Usually we can do better statistical analysis if we have higher levels of measurement. In specific circumstances, however, it is sometimes more convenient to use lower levels of measurement.

More Examples of Levels of Measurement

Example 1: Religious Preference

Let's examine several other examples of variables and specify the levels of measurement for these variables. However, because political research does not use interval measurement much, we will exclude it here and focus on nominal, ordinal, and ratio measurement. Let's begin with the frequency distribution and pie chart for variable 113) RELIGION in the GSS data file. This variable measures the concept of *religious preference*.

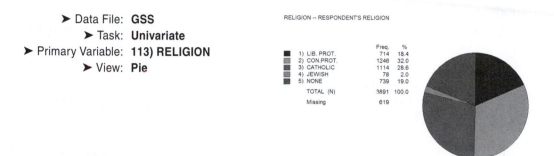

> Data File: **GSS**
>> Task: **Univariate**
> Primary Variable: **113) RELIGION**
>> View: **Pie**

First of all, this variable has a set of categories (Liberal Protestant, Conservative Protestant, Catholic, Jewish, None), which automatically means that it must be either nominal or ordinal. (**Note:** The frequencies and percentages presented for this variable concern the *results* rather than the values of the variable.) Ask yourself this question: Can we say that one of the categories represents more or less of the concept (religious preference) than another category? If we can, then the variable is ordinal. If we can't, then the variable is nominal.

In fact, it would not make sense to say that people in one category have more or less religious preference than people in another category (except perhaps for those who selected *no religion*). We cannot say, for example, that Liberal Protestants have more (or less) religious preference than do Catholics. Thus, this variable is nominal—a set of categories with no direction.

Example 2: Support for Capital Punishment

Let's look at the frequency distribution and pie chart for variable 107) EXECUTE? from the GSS data file.

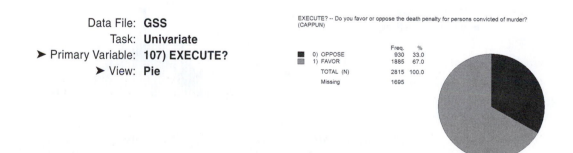

Data File: **GSS**
Task: **Univariate**
> Primary Variable: **107) EXECUTE?**
> View: **Pie**

Let's conceptualize that variable as support for capital punishment. The variable is set up in terms of two categories (oppose, favor), and so it must be either nominal or ordinal. Ask yourself this question: Do people in one of the categories have more of the concept (support for capital punishment) than people in the other category? If so, then the variable is ordinal. If not, then the variable is nominal. We can say that people who answered *favor* have greater support for capital punishment than those who answered *oppose*. Thus, the variable is ordinal. Be careful though, this variable is coded 40 thru 0 = oppose and 1 = favor, and so it suggests that 0 is the absence of the concept. Not all variables will be coded this way.

Example 3: Age

Now look at the frequency distribution and pie chart for variable 6) AGE from the HOUSE file.

➤ Data File: **HOUSE**
➤ Task: **Univariate**
➤ Primary Variable: **6) AGE**
➤ View: **Pie**

AGE -- Age Group

	Freq.	%
1) 45 or less	67	15.4
2) 46-55	141	32.4
3) 56-65	162	37.2
4) Over 65	65	14.9
TOTAL (N)	435	100.0

Again, we see that the variable is set up in terms of categories. Thus, it must be either nominal or ordinal. Can we say that representatives in any particular category have more or less age than representatives in the other categories? If so, then the variable is ordinal. If not, the variable is nominal. Obviously, we can say that representatives in a particular age category have more or less age than representatives in another age category. There is order to the categories. Representatives in the *over 65* age category have more age than those in the *56–65* age category, who in turn have more age than those in the *46–55* age category, and so on. Thus, this variable is ordinal.

Example 4: Age Again

Next look at the bar graph for variable 5) AGE (U) from the HOUSE file. (All variables in the HOUSE file that have [U] at the end of their names are ungrouped—not set up in categories.)

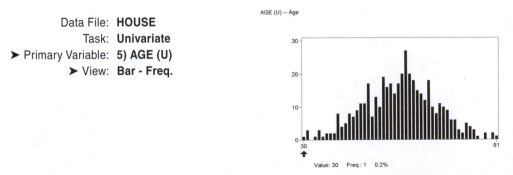

Data File: **HOUSE**
Task: **Univariate**
➤ Primary Variable: **5) AGE (U)**
➤ View: **Bar - Freq.**

AGE (U) -- Age

Value: 30   Freq.: 1   0.2%

This variable is not set up in terms of categories, so it must be either interval or ratio. It has equal intervals of measurement (years) and an absolute zero point (moment of birth). So here, age is ratio. In the previous example, the age variable had been grouped into a set of categories

Research Methods in Political Science

to make it more useful for certain types of analysis. When we collapse a ratio variable into categories, we reduce it from a ratio variable to an ordinal variable.

TERMS INTRODUCED IN THIS CHAPTER

Case (or unit of analysis)   Nominal measurement
Individual data   Ordinal measurement
Aggregate data   Interval measurement
Survey data   Ratio measurement
Public records data   Ecological fallacy

FOR FURTHER READING

Survey data are the basis of a substantial portion of the articles published in major political science journals. Additionally, the *Public Opinion Quarterly* is almost entirely based on survey research. Any issue of this journal contains articles about the methodology of survey research and the results of analysis based on survey research. For just one example, see Jeffrey W. Koch, "Political Rhetoric and Political Persuasion: The Changing Structure of Citizens' Preferences on Health Insurance During Policy Debate," *Public Opinion Quarterly* 62 (Summer 1998): 209–229.

For an interesting discussion of the role of survey research in political science, see Henry E. Brady, "Contributions of Survey Research to Political Science," *PS: Political Science and Politics* 33 (March 2000): 47–57.

For an example of experimental research in political science, see Thomas E. Nelson, Rosalee A. Clawson, and Zoe M. Oxley, "Media Framing of a Civil Liberties Conflict and Its Effect on Tolerance," *American Political Science Review* 91 (September 1997): 567–583. Another example of experimental research—one that embeds an experiment within a survey—is reported in James L. Gibson, "A Sober Second Thought: An Experiment in Persuading Russians to Tolerate," *American Journal of Political Science* 42 (July 1998): 819–850.

An example of content analysis is found in Kim Quaile Hill, Stephen Hanna, and Sahar Shafqat, "The Liberal-Conservative Ideology of U.S. Senators: A New Measure," *American Journal of Political Science* 41 (October 1997): 1395–1413.

For good examples of articles using different kinds of data, see Marcus E. Ethridge, *The Political Research Experience: Readings and Analysis,* 2nd ed. (Guilford, CT: Dushkin, 1994). Chapters 2 and 3 discuss, and provide selected readings for, aggregate data and individual data. Chapters 7 and 9 cover survey research and content analysis.

For an interesting collection of various types of data concerning American politics, see the latest edition of Harold W. Stanley and Richard G. Niemi, *Vital Statistics on American Politics* (Washington, DC: CQ Press).

worksheet

NAME: _____

COURSE: _____

DATE: _____

Workbook exercises and software are copyrighted. Copying is prohibited by law.

1. Let's start with the GLOBAL data file.

> ➤ Data File: **GLOBAL**
> ➤ Task: **Mapping**
> ➤ Primary Variable: **49) FERTILITY**
> ➤ View: **List: Rank**

Read the variable description for 49) FERTILITY. What kind of data is this? (Circle one.)

Survey   Experiment   Direct observation   Content analysis   Public records

What level of measurement is 49) FERTILITY? (Circle one.)

Nominal   Ordinal   Interval   Ratio

What was the source of data for 49) FERTILITY? Write the source below. (**Note:** The source is abbreviated as SOWC, 2005 in the variable description. To see what SOWC stands for, click on the notebook icon [just left of the printer icon] on the toolbar. The file notes for the GLOBAL file give you more information about the data sources.)

_____

_____

2. Now look at variable 421) TRUST?.

> Data File: **GLOBAL**
> Task: **Mapping**
> ➤ Primary Variable: **421) TRUST?**
> ➤ View: **List: Rank**

Read the variable description for 421) TRUST?. What was the source of data for 421) TRUST? Write the source below. (**Note:** The source is abbreviated as WVS in the variable description. To see what WVS stands for, click on the notebook icon [just left of the printer icon] on the toolbar.)

_____

_____

worksheet

How were the data for this variable originally collected? (Circle one.)

Survey   Experiment   Direct observation   Content analysis   Public records

What level of measurement is 421) TRUST? (Circle one.)

Nominal   Ordinal   Interval   Ratio

3. Obtain univariate statistics for 64) TRIBUNALS.

> ➤ Data File: **HOUSE**
> ➤ Task: **Univariate**
> ➤ Primary Variable: **64) TRIBUNALS**
> ➤ View: **Pie**

This variable refers to the representatives' vote on a bill to try enemy combatants and ban torture.

In terms of the unit of analysis, is it individual data or aggregate data? (Circle one.)

Individual data   Aggregate data

What is the case for this data file? That is, for what specific unit of analysis do we have data? (**Hint:** In this situation, the number of cases in this data file provides a clue as to what the cases are.)

There are different views on the best way to classify the level of measurement of a variable having just two categories. However, if we conceptualize this variable as support for a ban on torture, what level of measurement is this variable? (**Hint:** Those who voted yes showed more support for anti-abortion laws than those who voted no.) (Circle one.)

Nominal   Ordinal   Interval   Ratio

Look at the categories (no and yes) and the numbers (0 and 1) next to them. For this roll-call vote and for the other roll-call votes in this data file, a no vote is assigned the number 0 and a yes vote is assigned the number 1. In this situation, does the 0 represent an absolute zero point (here, a complete absence of any support for limiting abortion), or is it merely a number that has been assigned to the no category of this variable? (Circle one.)

It is an absolute zero point.   It is merely a number assigned to the no category.

Print this pie chart and attach it to your assignment. (**Note:** If you have been instructed not to use the printer, just skip this task.)

4. Look at the variable 22) DIST.HIS.

> Data File: **HOUSE**
> Task: **Univariate**
> ➤ Primary Variable: **22) DIST.HIS**
> ➤ View: **Pie**

What level of measurement is this variable in its present format? (Circle one.)

    Nominal   Ordinal   Interval   Ratio

5. Now look at 7) RELIGION.

> Data File: **HOUSE**
> Task: **Univariate**
> ➤ Primary Variable: **7) RELIGION**
> ➤ View: **Pie**

What level of measurement is this variable in its present format? (Circle one.)

    Nominal   Ordinal   Interval   Ratio

All the variables in some data files might have the same source of data—for example, all the variables in the GSS data file are from a survey. On the other hand, some data files might have data from various sources. The HOUSE data file contains data from several different sources (e.g., roll-call votes, election data, and U.S. Census data). Similarly, the GLOBAL and the STATES data files contain data from a variety of sources.

6. Let's examine some variables in the NES file.

> ➤ Data File: **NES**
> ➤ Task: **Univariate**
> ➤ Primary Variable: **8) AGE**
> ➤ View: **Statistics (Summary)**

Circle the source of the data in the NES file.

    Survey   Experiment   Direct observation   Content analysis   Public records

In terms of the unit of analysis, is it individual data or aggregate data?

    Individual data   Aggregate data

Given equal intervals of measurement (years), an absolute zero point (the moment of birth), and real numbers, what level of measurement is this age variable? (Circle one.)

    Nominal   Ordinal   Interval   Ratio

What percentage of people are 20 years old? _____%

This age variable can be quite useful in its present format for certain kinds of statistical analysis. However, there are also situations in which it would not be very useful in this format. Thus, we will sometimes collapse such a variable—reduce it to a smaller set of categories. (In a later chapter, you will see how to collapse variables.) Let's look at the collapsed variable for age that is included with this data set.

> Data File: **NES**
> Task: **Univariate**
> ➤ Primary Variable: **11) AGE CATEGR**
> ➤ View: **Pie**

What level of measurement is this variable? (Circle one.)

  Nominal   Ordinal   Interval   Ratio

What percentage of people are in the 50–64 age category? _____%

7. The NES 04 contains a composite index to operationally define the concept of political knowledge about public figures. This index is simply the sum of correct answers given to four identification questions asked of each respondent. A respondent who could not identify any of the four public figures (Dennis Hastert, Dick Cheney, Tony Blair, William Rehnquist) received a score of 0. A respondent who could identify all four received a score of 4. Let's look at the results.

> ➤ Data File: **NES 04**
> ➤ Task: **Univariate**
> ➤ Primary Variable: **527) POLITKNOW**
> ➤ View: **Pie**

If we conceptualize this variable as the number of correct identifications of these four public figures, what level of measurement is it? (Circle one.)

  Nominal   Ordinal   Interval   Ratio

We must be careful here in terms of how we treat the zero point for this variable. If a person received a 0, we can say that this person failed to identify any of these four public figures. Further, this strongly suggests that this person has a low level of political knowledge. However, despite the 0 for this variable, we cannot say that this person has an absolute zero level of political knowledge—that is, we cannot say that this person has no political knowledge whatsoever. Thus, in this situation, the zero point has meaning if we interpret this concept as number of correct identifications of four public figures, but we need to be cautious if we use this variable to operationalize the broader concept of political knowledge.

If we were to collapse this variable into low (those people who gave either zero or one correct responses), medium (those people who gave two correct responses), or high (those people who gave either three or four correct responses), what level of measurement would we have? (Circle one.)

  Nominal   Ordinal   Interval   Ratio

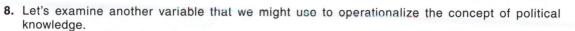
8. Let's examine another variable that we might use to operationalize the concept of political knowledge.

> Data File: **NES 04**
> Task: **Univariate**
> ➤ Primary Variable: **57) INFORMED?**
> ➤ View: **Pie**

Here the interviewers in the 2004 NES survey rated the respondents' levels of information about politics and public affairs. Write in the percentages for each level below.

Low = _____%

Average = _____%

High = _____%

What level of measurement is this variable? (Circle one.)

Nominal   Ordinal   Interval   Ratio

Thus, we have two different variables that we can use to operationally define the concept of political knowledge. In doing research, we might use both of those variables individually, combine them into one variable, or try to determine which one is the better indicator of political knowledge.

9. It is very important to know the levels of measurement of variables, because different levels of measurement require different statistical techniques (as you will see in later chapters). Using the NES 04 file, read the variable description for each of the following variables and circle the level of measurement for each variable.

2) RACE	Nominal	Ordinal	Interval	Ratio
3) INCOME	Nominal	Ordinal	Interval	Ratio
261) CHURCH_FRE	Nominal	Ordinal	Interval	Ratio
44) PBIRTH ABO	Nominal	Ordinal	Interval	Ratio
242) WHO_VOTE?	Nominal	Ordinal	Interval	Ratio
232) GUN_ACCESS	Nominal	Ordinal	Interval	Ratio
97) CROOKED?	Nominal	Ordinal	Interval	Ratio

10. We will now briefly examine the variables in the STATES file.

>   ➤ Data File: **STATES**
>   ➤ Task: **Mapping**

What is the case (the unit of analysis) for this data file? (**Hint:** There are 50
cases in this file.)   _____

Are the variables in this file based on individual or aggregate data?

    Individual data   Aggregate data

In the NES file, there were some nominal variables, some ordinal variables, and some ratio
variables. In the STATES file, however, all the variables except the state name are (circle
one)

    Nominal   Ordinal   Interval   Ratio

CHAPTER 4

Variables, Variation, and Explanation

Tasks: Univariate, Cross-tabulation, Mapping
Data Files: HOUSE, GSS 04, GSS, STATES, GLOBAL, NES 04

INTRODUCTION

The goal of political science is to *explain* aspects of political reality. In focusing on the key concept of explanation in political science, this chapter will:

- describe and demonstrate the different types of variables (dependent, independent, and so on)

- illustrate the concept of explanation in terms of relating variation in the dependent variable to variation in the independent variable

- distinguish between correlation and causality

- describe spurious relationships and their consequences for the strategy of political research

Explanation is crucial in political research. The goal is not just to *describe* political reality, but to *explain why* political reality is the way it is. Why do some people vote for one candidate and others vote for a different one? Why do some nations have democratic political systems and others have authoritarian systems? What accounts for differences in the voting behavior of U.S. senators? For each of these questions, what we are trying to do is account for *variation* in a political variable. Because the focus here is on explanation, we will begin this chapter by distinguishing different types of variables in political research on the basis of their roles in explanation.

VARIABLE TYPES, VARIATION, AND EXPLANATION

Dependent and Independent Variables

A **dependent variable** is a variable whose variation is to be explained in a study.

An **independent variable** is a variable that is used to explain variation in a dependent variable.

The terms *explain* and *explanation* are used in a special sense in this context. Thus, in the process of defining dependent and independent variables, we need to define *explanation* as well and reiterate the definition of *variation*.

Explanation means relating variation in the dependent variable to variation in the independent variable.

Variation means differences within a set of measurements of a variable.

Consider the observation that people have different attitudes about reverse gender discrimination in the workplace. In 2004 the GSS asked respondents to consider the chances that a man won't get a job or promotion while an equally or less qualified woman gets one instead.

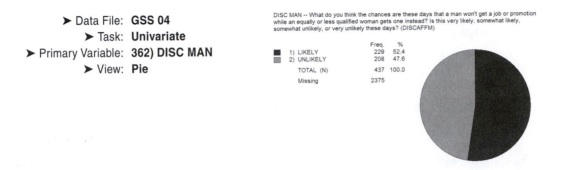

➤ Data File: **GSS 04**

➤ Task: **Univariate**

➤ Primary Variable: **362) DISC MAN**

➤ View: **Pie**

DISC MAN -- What do you think the chances are these days that a man won't get a job or promotion while an equally or less qualified woman gets one instead? Is this very likely, somewhat likely, somewhat unlikely, or very unlikely these days? (DISCAFFM)

	Freq.	%
1) LIKELY	229	52.4
2) UNLIKELY	208	47.6
TOTAL (N)	437	100.0
Missing	2375	

In this example you will notice that people do not feel the same way about this issue. Different people have differing levels of belief about the likelihood of reverse gender discrimination. Some people think that reverse gender discrimination against males is likely (52.4%), but others believe that it is unlikely (47.6%). Thus, there is *variation*, or differences, in the belief that discrimination against males for a job or promotion is unlikely.

Let's say that your research goal is to account for the variation in attitudes about reverse discrimination—you want to determine *why* some people believe that discrimination against males is likely and why others believe it is unlikely. In such analysis the 362) DISC MAN variable is the *dependent variable*—the variable whose variation you want to explain.

We might use one's gender (measured by the variable 38) SEX as one *independent variable* to help explain the dependent variable 362) DISC MAN. Gender also has variation: Different people have one of two genders. Our CROSS-TABULATION analysis below shows us that variation in 362) DISC MAN (dependent variable) is related to variation in 38) SEX (independent variable).

Data File:	**GSS 04**
➤ Task:	**Cross-tabulation**
➤ Row Variable:	**362) DISC MAN**
➤ Column Variable:	**38) SEX**
➤ Views:	**Column %**

DISC MAN   by   SEX
Cramer's V: 0.169**

		SEX		
		MALE	FEMALE	TOTAL
DISC MAN	LIKELY	120	109	229
		61.9%	44.9%	52.4%
	UNLIKELY	74	134	208
		38.1%	55.1%	47.6%
	Missing	1086	1289	2375
	TOTAL	194	243	437
		100.0%	100.0%	

To construct this table, return to the main menu and select the CROSS-TABULATION task, then select 362) DISC MAN as the row variable and 38) SEX as the column variable. When the table is showing, select the [Column%] option.

In this example there is a pattern connecting attitudes about discrimination against males to the sex of the respondent. If you read the table across from left to right, you can see that men are more likely to say that the chances are good that a man won't get a job or promotion (61.9%), and that women are less likely to say that a man won't get a job or promotion (44.9%). Thus, we can account for some of the differences in attitude toward reverse gender discrimination in terms of differences in gender. The independent variable 38) SEX helps to explain the dependent variable 362) DISC MAN.

In theoretical terms, we think of the independent variable as having an effect on the dependent variable. In everyday life and in theorizing in political research, we think in terms of causality: One factor (A) causes—or partly causes—another factor (B). There are problems in dealing with the notion of causality in research, however, and we will discuss them later.

It must make theoretical sense to suggest that a particular independent variable can affect a particular dependent variable. In the example above, does it make sense to think that people's gender could have an effect on their attitude toward reverse gender discrimination? Yes, it does. We could come up with several reasons why men are more likely than women to be concerned with reverse gender discrimination.

A variable that is a dependent variable in one study can sometimes be an independent variable in another study, and vice versa. For example, suppose a political researcher is interested in explaining variation in political knowledge among citizens; thus, political knowledge is the dependent variable here. Suppose another researcher wants to explain variation in support for democratic institutions and expects that people with more political knowledge will give more support to democratic institutions. In this case, political knowledge is an independent variable, whereas it was a dependent variable in the previous case.

In some situations, you simply must know the purpose of a particular study to determine which variables are dependent and which are independent. In all cases, however, keep this question in mind: *Does it make sense to think that this independent variable could affect this dependent variable?*

Sometimes the effects can occur either way, and the only way to determine which variable is dependent and which is independent is to know the purpose of the study. For example, suppose you were examining political participation and political knowledge. You could argue that political knowledge affects political participation, but you could also argue that political participation affects political knowledge. In some situations, however, it is clear that one variable could not affect another. For example, consider the relationship between political party preference and gender. Gender could have an effect on political party preference, but it would not make any sense to suggest that political party preference could affect gender.

Intervening and Antecedent Variables

In political research, we ordinarily focus on the effects of the independent variable on the dependent variable. What effect, for example, does education have on political tolerance? However, there are other types of variables that might affect the relationship between the independent variable and the dependent variable: *intervening variables* and *antecedent variables*.

An *intervening variable* is one that occurs between the independent variable and the dependent variable and affects the relationship between them.

We can diagram the connections between intervening, independent, and dependent variables as follows:

Independent→Intervening→Dependent

Several studies in political science have used education as an independent variable to explain the dependent variable *political tolerance*. It is not likely, however, that the simple number of years spent in school has a direct impact on political tolerance. Rather, it is more likely that time and experiences in school lead to the development of other characteristics, which in turn foster political tolerance. One specific example is that the more time people spend in school, the more likely it is that they will be exposed to diverse people and ideas. Exposure to social diversity can in turn lead to greater political tolerance. Thus, the number of years of school (independent variable) affects exposure to social diversity (intervening variable), which in turn affects political tolerance (dependent variable).

An *antecedent variable* is one that occurs before the independent variable and the dependent variable.

If there is a causal effect here, it might take either of two patterns. *First, the antecedent variable might affect the independent variable and alter its relationship to the dependent variable.* We can diagram this situation as follows:

Antecedent→Independent→Dependent

For example, suppose you want to study the relationship between the policy decisions of U.S. senators (dependent variable) and the sources of their campaign contributions (independent variable). Specifically, you expect that senators would tend to support policies favorable to the interest groups that gave them campaign contributions. If you carried out this research, you would probably find the expected relationship. However, there is a problem here in saying that the campaign contributions (independent variable) affected the decisions of the representatives (dependent variable). An interest group is most likely to make campaign contributions to candidates who already share its views. Thus, the views of the candidate would constitute an antecedent variable affecting the independent variable (campaign contributions), which might or might not affect the dependent variable (representative's policy decisions).

Second, the antecedent variable might affect both the independent variable and the dependent variable, without the independent variable affecting the dependent variable. This is a *spurious relationship,* which we will discuss in the next section. It can be diagrammed as follows:

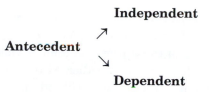

Antecedent or intervening variables can affect relationships between dependent variables and independent variables in various ways. Such relationships might become weaker, or stronger, or different in kind or direction, or disappear altogether. Thus, whenever we examine a relationship between a dependent variable and an independent variable, we need to consider possible antecedent and intervening variables that could affect that relationship. In the process of including such variables, we further develop our explanations of political reality.

CORRELATION, CAUSALITY, AND SPURIOUS RELATIONSHIPS

When we theorize about relationships between variables, we think in terms of causality: One variable affects another variable. When we do research, we seek to demonstrate that there is a relationship between variables: Variation in one variable is related to variation in the other variable. In this sense, one variable explains the other variable.

The term ***correlation*** broadly refers to any relationship between two variables. However, just because two variables are related or correlated (when variation in one variable is related to variation in the other), this does not necessarily mean that one variable *causes* the other or even *affects* it in any manner. In theorizing, we *think* in terms of causality, but in doing our actual research, we must be careful in dealing with causality.

Suppose that variables A and B are related. What might account for this correlation? Let's list four basic possible reasons for it.

- Variable A causes variable B.

- Variable B causes variable A.

- It is simply a coincidence.

- Some other variable, C, causes both variable A and variable B.

The last possibility given above is a major problem in political research—or any other kind of scientific research. Let's look at that problem: spurious relationships.

A *spurious relationship* is an apparent causal relationship between two variables that is actually due to one or more other variables.

In a spurious relationship, two variables are correlated and it *appears* that their relationship is *causal*—it appears that one variable is having an effect on the other. However, the correlation between the two variables actually exists only because an antecedent variable is affecting both. Variable A appears to cause variable B only because another variable, C, is affecting both A and B in certain ways.

For example, in large cities, there is a correlation between ice cream sales and the rate of violent crime. As ice cream sales go up, so does violent crime. As ice cream sales go down, so does violent crime. Does consumption of ice cream cause people to commit violent crimes? Obviously, this is not the case. Another variable is involved—the weather. As the temperature increases, ice cream sales go up. Likewise, warm weather increases the likelihood that people interact with each other, which has the unfortunate outcome that some of these interactions result in murder. As the temperature decreases, ice cream sales go down—and so does the rate of violent crime.

Based on the correlation between ice cream sales and rate of violent crime, you are not likely to conclude that eating ice cream causes people to commit violent crimes. However, other spurious relationships are not always this obvious. It may seem very plausible that variable A was causing variable B when both were actually being affected by variable C in such a way that A *appeared* to be causing B.

For example, suppose we found that in an election campaign, those with a college degree were more likely to support candidate Smith, and those without a college degree were more likely to support candidate Jones. We might conclude that education has an effect on candidate preference. In fact, Smith's supporters might argue that the more educated, brighter people came to the conclusion that Smith was the better candidate. However, education may have had nothing to do with this choice. Perhaps Smith appealed to those who were financially better off and candidate Jones appealed to those who were relatively worse off. Thus, financial situation could be the key variable determining people's voting preferences. Further, financial situation is correlated with education: People with higher education usually have higher incomes. Going one step further, people who have a college degree are much more likely to have come from a family that was relatively well off financially, because people with higher incomes are more likely to send their children to college.

Thus, it is possible in this situation that any relationship between education level and voting preference is spurious. Economic variables (either the person's present economic situation or his or her family background) might have determined *both* that person's education level and his or her voting preference.

The possibility of spuriousness has important implications for the strategy of political research. We begin political research with a theory (an explanation of the aspects of political reality with which we are concerned), and then we undertake research to test that theory. When theorizing, we think in terms of causality. However, because of the possibility that the relationships we find are spurious, we cannot absolutely prove causality. We cannot prove that variable A causes variable B because it is always possible that some other variable, C, is actually affecting A and B in such a way that it simply *appears* that A is causing B.

Consequently, we need to be careful to include in our research other variables that might affect the relationships between our dependent and independent variables. We also need to make sure that our relationships make sense theoretically. Finally, the possibility of spuriousness means that our strategy of research will be oriented toward *disproof* rather than *proof.* We will discuss this idea in the next chapter.

VARIATION AND EXPLANATION: FURTHER ILLUSTRATION

This section presents a hypothetical example to further demonstrate the concepts we have been discussing. Suppose you measured three variables for a sample of 16 people: support for sexual equality, education, and gender. To make this example easier to understand, we have categorized people as either *high* or *low* in terms of support for sexual equality. Further, we have categorized people as either *high* or *low* in terms of education level.

The hypothetical data for these three variables are shown in Table 4.1. Note that there is *variation* in each variable. Some people show high support for sexual equality; some show low support. Some people have high education, and some have low education. Some people are male; some are female. Thus, each of the three variables has variation.

Suppose you believe that the *independent variable* education affects the *dependent variable* support for sexual equality. That is, you believe that variation in education at least partly accounts for variation in support for sexual equality. Your theoretical reasons for this belief might be that people with higher education are more likely to understand the arguments in favor of sexual equality, whereas people with lower education might be less likely to challenge traditional social norms. At the same time, however, you suspect that the relationship between education and support for sexual equality might be different for females than it is for males. Thus, you will use gender as an antecedent variable.

The patterns in Table 4.1 are difficult to read, so Table 4.2 collapses the information into a cross-tabulation (or contingency table). Note the pattern: Those with high education are more likely to support sexual equality than those with low education. For the eight cases with high education, six had high support for sexual equality. For the eight cases with low education, six had low support for sexual equality. Thus, there is a clear pattern. Variation in support for sexual equality is strongly related to variation in education—education helps to *explain* support for sexual equality.

Table 4.1 Hypothetical Data to Illustrate Variables, Variation, and Explanation

Support for Sexual Equality	Education Level	Gender
High	High	Female
High	High	Female
High	High	Female
High	High	Female
High	High	Male
High	Low	Male
High	High	Male
High	Low	Male
Low	Low	Female
Low	Low	Female
Low	Low	Female
Low	Low	Female
Low	High	Male
Low	Low	Male
Low	High	Male
Low	Low	Male

Table 4.2 Support for Sexual Equality By Education Level

	High Education	Low Education
High Support for Sexual Equality	6	2
Low Support for Sexual Equality	2	6

Now, however, we need to determine whether gender has any effect on this relationship. So, to control for this variable, we set up two separate tables: one for males and one for females. Tables 4.3 and 4.4 present these results for males and females separately.

Table 4.3 Support for Sexual Equality By Education Level—Males Only

	High Education	Low Education
High Support for Sexual Equality	2	2
Low Support for Sexual Equality	2	2

Table 4.4 Support for Sexual Equality By Education Level—Females Only

	High Education	Low Education
High Support for Sexual Equality	4	0
Low Support for Sexual Equality	0	4

Among females, there is a *perfect relationship*. All females who have high education have high support for sexual equality; all females who have low education have low support for sexual equality. Thus, among females, the independent variable education completely explains the dependent variable *support for sexual equality*. Putting this differently, among females, if we know a woman's education level, we can perfectly predict where she stands on sexual equality.

The situation is different for males—there is *no relationship at all* between education and support for sexual equality. Half the males who have high education have high support for sexual equality, but the other half have low support. Half the males who have low education have low support for sexual equality, but the other half have high support. Thus, variation in education is not related to variation in support for sexual equality among males. In this hypothetical example, if we were trying to predict a man's level of support for sexual equality, it would not help us to know his education level.

TERMS INTRODUCED IN THIS CHAPTER

Dependent variable   Intervening variable
Independent variable   Antecedent variable
Explanation   Correlation
Variation   Spurious relationship

FOR FURTHER READING

Political party identification is a dependent variable in some research *(What explains why different people have different party identifications?)* and an independent variable in other research *(What effects does party identification have on the political behavior of people?)*. One very readable book that combines both aspects is by William H. Flanigan and Nancy H. Zingale, *Political Behavior of the American Electorate,* 10th ed. (Washington, DC: CQ Press, 2003). In Chapter 4 and part of Chapter 6, the authors ask what effect party identification has on such variables as political participation or stands on political issues. In Chapter 5, the authors in essence ask what social characteristics of people lead them to become Democrats, Republicans, or Independents.

What explains why American Jews are more liberal on certain political issues than Protestants or Catholics? For an interesting example of research that uses American Jewish liberalism as a dependent variable and controls for the effects of sociodemographic characteristics (antecedent or intervening variables), see Steven M. Cohen and Charles S. Liebman, "American Jewish Liberalism: Unraveling the Strands," *Public Opinion Quarterly* 61 (Fall 1997): 405–430.

For a related but somewhat different discussion of types of variables, see Chapter 3 of Fred N. Kerlinger, *Foundations of Behavioral Research,* 3rd ed. (New York: Holt, Rinehart and Winston, 1986).

For an interesting example of research that demonstrates different types of variables, see John Lynxwiler and David Gay, "Reconsidering Race Differences in Abortion Attitudes," *Social Science*

Quarterly 75 (March 1994): 67–84. This research reviews and expands the explanation of the relationship between abortion attitudes (dependent variable) and race (independent variable) while controlling for certain other variables that might affect the relationship.

For another interesting example of research that demonstrates explanation and different types of variables, see James L. Guth et al., "Faith and the Environment: Religious Beliefs and Attitudes on Environmental Policy," *American Journal of Political Science* 39 (May 1995): 364–382.

For two examples that not only demonstrate explanation and different kinds of variables but also demonstrate that a dependent variable in one study might be an independent variable in another, first see the use of public opinion variables as *dependent variables* in Benjamin Page, Robert Shapiro, and Glenn Dempsey, "What Moves Public Opinion?" *American Political Science Review* 81 (March 1987): 23–43. Then see the use of public opinion variables as *independent variables* in Benjamin Page and Robert Shapiro, "Effects of Public Opinion on Public Policy," *American Political Science Review* 77 (March 1983): 175–190.

worksheet

CHAPTER

4

NAME: _____

COURSE: _____

DATE: _____

1. Let's begin with some analysis of a roll-call variable from the HOUSE file.

➤ Data File: **HOUSE**

➤ Task: **Univariate**

➤ Primary Variable: **58) TAX CUTS**

➤ View: **Pie**

Look at the results for this vote in the U.S. House of Representatives on a bill that would cut taxes in 2006. Let's label this variable support for tax cuts. Write in the percentages of representatives who voted yes and no on this bill.

Percentage of representatives who voted yes   _____%

Percentage of representatives who voted no   _____%

The maximum variation for a variable that has only two categories is a 50-50 split. The minimum variation for such a variable is the situation in which 100% of the cases are in just one of the categories.

In the situation above, does this variable have high variation (closer to the maximum) or low variation (closer to the minimum)?

      High variation   Low variation

2. We want to explain variation in this variable: Why did some representatives vote for this bill and others vote against it? So, we will treat support for tax cuts as a dependent variable—the variable whose variation we want to explain. One variable that might help explain variation in support for tax cuts is the political party affiliations of representatives. In general, the Republican Party has favored tax cuts and the Democratic Party has opposed tax cuts.

First, however, we need to see if there is sufficient variation in the independent variable. If we are to explain the variation in a dependent variable in terms of variation in an independent variable, then there must be variation in both the dependent variable and the independent variable. In this particular situation, we know, of course, that there were both Democrats and Republicans in the 109th Congress and, therefore, there is variation in the party-affiliation variable. But let's look at the degree of variation anyway.

Data File: **HOUSE**
Task: **Univariate**
➤ Primary Variable: **11) PARTY**
➤ View: **Pie**

Write the percentage of representatives who are Democrats. _____%

Write the percentage of representatives who are Republicans. _____%

Does this variable have relatively high variation or relatively low variation?

High variation   Low variation

3. There is variation both in the dependent variable (support for tax cuts) and in the independent variable (party affiliation). Now the question is this: Is variation in support for tax cuts related to variation in party affiliation?

To answer this question, we will examine selected results from a cross-tabulation (or contingency) table. A later chapter will provide fuller instruction on reading and interpreting such tables, but the briefer instructions here will carefully guide you through the selection of relevant information from such tables.

Data File: **HOUSE**
➤ Task: **Cross-tabulation**
➤ Row Variable: **58) TAX CUTS**
➤ Column Variable: **11) PARTY**
➤ View: **Tables**
➤ Display: **Column %**

> To construct this table, return to the main menu and select the CROSS-TABULATION task, then select 58) TAX CUTS as the row variable and 11) PARTY as the column variable. When the table is showing, select the [Column %] option.

This table presents the dependent variable (tax cuts) along the side and the independent variable (political party affiliation) across the top. Each cell of this table now presents two numbers. The first is the cell frequency—the number of cases in that particular cell. Look at the upper left cell of the table. The number 182 in this cell means that there were 182 Democrats who voted no on this bill. The second number in each cell is the column percentage. Write these column percentages in the table below. (I have provided the first one to get you started.)

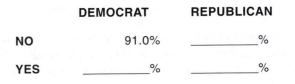

	DEMOCRAT	REPUBLICAN
NO	91.0%	_____%
YES	_____%	_____%

4. Let's interpret the first column percentage—the one that was provided for you. This percentage means that 91.0% of the Democrats voted no on this bill. Thus, almost no Democrats voted for the bill. Now look at the percentages for the Republicans. Almost all of the Republicans voted yes on the bill.

> Is variation in the dependent variable (tax cuts) related to variation in the independent variable (political party affiliation)? That is, does the independent variable political party affiliation help to explain variation in the dependent variable support for tax cuts?   Yes   No

5. A variable that is a dependent variable in one study might be an independent variable in a different study, depending on the goals of the researcher. In the preceding analysis, we treated party affiliation as an independent variable to explain support for tax cuts. Now let's treat party affiliation as a dependent variable.

What accounts for variation in the party-affiliation variable? More specifically, what explains why some congressional districts elected Democrats and some elected Republicans? There are, of course, many variables that we could use as independent variables. For now, let's look at the percentage of the district's population that is African American. Beginning with Roosevelt's New Deal coalition in the 1930s, African Americans have been one of the core parts of the coalition making up the Democratic Party. Thus, we might expect that congressional districts with higher percentages of African Americans would be more likely to elect Democrats and that congressional districts with lower percentages of African Americans would be less likely to elect Democrats. Let's test this proposition.

Data File:	**HOUSE**
Task:	**Cross-tabulation**
➤ Row Variable:	**11) PARTY**
➤ Column Variable:	**20) DIST.AFRAM**
➤ View:	**Tables**
➤ Display:	**Column %**

This table presents the dependent variable (political party affiliation) along the side and the independent variable (percentage of the district's population that is African American) across the top. Write the column percentages in the table below. (Again, one value has already been filled in for you.)

	0 TO 5.9%	6 TO 14.9%	15% OR +
DEMOCRAT	37.3%	_____%	_____%
REPUBLICAN	_____%	_____%	_____%

6. The goal here is to determine whether the independent variable (percentage of the district's population that is African American) helps to explain whether the district elected a Democrat or a Republican to Congress. That is, is variation in party affiliation of the representative related to the percentage of his or her district's population that is African American?

Let's look first at the row for Democrats. Compare the column percentages as you read across this row. The first percentage (the one provided for you) shows that, of those congressional districts where less than 6% of the population is African American, 37.3% of those districts elected Democrats to Congress.

As you read across the row, notice that the percentage increases (more Democrats elected) as the percentage of the district's population that is African American increases. Among districts where at least 15% of the population is African American, 72.0% of the districts elected a Democrat to Congress.

Now look at the Republican row and you see exactly the opposite pattern: Districts that had a smaller percentage of African Americans were more likely to elect Republicans to Congress.

Is there a relationship between the dependent variable (party affiliation of the district's representative) and the independent variable (percentage of the district's population that is African American)? That is, if we know what percentage of the district's population is African American, does this help us to predict whether the district will elect a Democrat or a Republican to Congress?   Yes   No

7. Using the NES 04 data file, let's examine the relationship between presidential voting choice in 2004 and ideological identification.

> ➤ Data File: **NES 04**
> ➤ Task: **Cross-tabulation**
> ➤ Row Variable: **312) WHO.VOTE?**
> ➤ Column Variable: **25) IDEOLOGY**
> ➤ View: **Tables**
> ➤ Display: **Column %**

There is variation in presidential voting choice (some voted for Gore, some for Bush, and some for Nader or other candidates), and there is variation in ideological identification (some are liberals, some are moderates, and some are conservatives).

The question is whether variation in presidential voting preference is related to variation in ideological identification. We would expect that ideological identification would help a great deal to explain presidential voting choice.

Write the column percentages in the table below. (The first column percentage has been filled in for you.)

	LIBERALS	MODERATES	CONSERVATIVES
KERRY	89.6%	_____%	_____%
BUSH	_____%	_____%	_____%
OTHER	_____%	_____%	_____%

worksheet

CHAPTER 4

Does ideological identification help to explain presidential voting choice?
That is, if we know the ideological identification of a person, does that help
us to predict who that person voted for in the 2004 presidential election?   Yes   No

8. Now let's switch to the 2006 GSS file and examine the following proposition: Religious attitudes
and political attitudes are sometimes related differently for African Americans and white Americans. Thus, we are proposing that race is an antecedent variable that sometimes affects relationships between religious variables and political variables. First, using the GSS data file, let's
examine a relationship without taking race into consideration. Then we will examine this same
relationship separately for whites and for blacks.

> Data File: **GSS**
> Task: **Cross-tabulation**
> Row Variable: **190) ABORT SING**
> Column Variable: **127) BIBLE**
> View: **Tables**
> Display: **Column %**

Here we see the relationship between the dependent variable (willingness to allow an abortion
for a woman who is not married) and the independent variable (view of the Bible). To simplify
this analysis, let's just examine the Yes row—the row based on those who would allow an abortion in this situation. Because there are only two rows, we can see the basic pattern in the
results by looking at either row. Write in the column percentages for the Yes row below.

	ACTUAL	INSPIRED	ANCIENT BOOK
YES	_____ %	_____ %	_____ %

Which of these three groups was most supportive of allowing abortion in this situation?
(Circle one.)

Actual   Inspired   Ancient Book

Print this table and attach it to your assignment. (**Note:** If you have been instructed not to use
the printer, just skip this task.)

Does the independent variable (view of the Bible) help to explain the
dependent variable (willingness to allow an abortion for a woman who
is not married)?   Yes   No

9. Next we will look at the same relationship for African Americans and white Americans separately.
That is, we will use race as a control variable to see whether it affects the relationship between
the dependent variable (willingness to allow an abortion for a woman who is not married) and
the independent variable (view of the Bible).

Chapter 4   Worksheet

81

worksheet

Data File: **GSS**
Task: **Cross-tabulation**
Row Variable: **190) ABORT SING**
Column Variable: **127) BIBLE**
➤ Control Variable: **38) RACE**
➤ View: **Tables (White)**
➤ Display: **Column %**

The option for selecting a control variable is located on the same screen that you use to select other variables. For this example, select 38) RACE as a control variable and then click [OK] to continue as usual. Separate tables for each of the 38) RACE categories will now be shown for the 190) ABORT SING and 127) BIBLE cross-tabulation. Thus, here we will have one table for white respondents and another table for African American respondents. Chapter 12 will give you more detailed instructions on doing such analyses.

The first table shows you the results for white respondents. Note the line that reads "Controls: RACE: White."

Write in the column percentages for the Yes row of this table.

CONTROL CATEGORY: WHITE

	ACTUAL	INSPIRED	ANCIENT BOOK
YES	_____%	_____%	_____%

Now go to the next table by clicking the right arrow under the box labeled "Control 1 of 2" on the left of the screen. Using this procedure, you can move forward to the next table, and then you can go back to a previous table.

Data File: **GSS**
Task: **Cross-tabulation**
Row Variable: **190) ABORT SING**
Column Variable: **127) BIBLE**
Control Variable: **38) RACE**
➤ View: **Tables (Black)**
➤ Display: **Column %**

Note that the "Controls" line now reads "RACE = Black." Write in the column percentages for the Yes row of this table.

CONTROL CATEGORY: BLACK

	ACTUAL	INSPIRED	ANCIENT BOOK
YES	_____%	_____%	_____%

worksheet

Compare the results for the white respondents and for African American respondents.

Among whites, which category of people (on the basis of their view of the Bible) is most willing to allow an abortion for a woman who is not married? (Circle one.)

Actual   Inspired   Ancient Book

Among African Americans, which category of people (on the basis of their view of the Bible) is most willing to allow an abortion for a woman who is not married? (Circle one.)

Actual   Inspired   Ancient Book

With regard to the comparison of whites and African Americans in terms of the relationship between attitudes toward abortion and views of the Bible, which of the following statements is most accurate? (Circle one.)

a. The relationship among whites is almost exactly the same as it is among African Americans.

b. The relationship among whites is not exactly the same as it is among African Americans, but the basic pattern is very similar: The Actual category is the least likely to allow the abortion, and the Ancient Book category is the most likely to allow the abortion.

c. The relationship among whites is very different (the pattern is different) from that among African Americans.

10. We cannot use cross-tabulation for the type of variables in the STATES file or the GLOBAL file. Those variables are ratio variables and many of them contain decimal points. For now, we will use MAPPING to look at relationships between such variables. We will begin with a variable from the STATES file.

> Data File: **STATES**
> Task: **Mapping**
> Variable 1: **1233) VCRIME02**
> View: **Map**

By looking at this map, we can see that there are some geographic patterns to the violent crime rate. For example, the violent crime rate generally seems to be higher in the southern tier of the United States than in the north.

Next, let's examine a variable that might help to explain variation in the violent crime rate.

Data File: **STATES**
Task: **Mapping**
Variable 1: **1233) VCRIME02**
> Variable 2: **35) %URBAN00**
> View: **Map**

At this point, the screen shows maps of the violent crime rate and the percent urban—the percentage of the state's population living in urban areas. If these two variables are related to one another, then there will be some correspondence between the two maps. Do the two maps seem to be similar to each other (dark states on one map are dark on the other map, light states on one map are light on the other), opposite of one another (dark states on one map are light on the other map), or unrelated? (Circle one.)

Similar   Opposite   Unrelated

Does it appear that there is at least some pattern here—that variation in the dependent variable (rate of violent crime) is at least partly explained by variation in the independent variable (percentage of the state's population living in urban areas)?   Yes   No

11. On the right side of the screen, just below the line that separates the two lists or maps, is the phrase r = .365**. This is a **correlation coefficient;** it measures the extent to which two interval or ratio variables are related. Chapter 13 will give a fuller discussion of correlation coefficients, but let's take a quick look at them now.

A correlation coefficient of zero means that there is no relationship at all between the two variables. A correlation coefficient of 1.0 means that there is a perfect correlation. Thus the higher the correlation coefficient, the more the independent variable explains the dependent variable.

In this situation, the correlation between the violent crime rate and the percentage of the population living in urban areas is .365**, which is a moderately strong relationship. This again indicates that the more urban states have higher crime rates. Which of the following is the better conclusion? (Circle the letter of your choice.)

    a. There is little or no relationship between these two variables.
    b. There is an important relationship between these two variables.

12. We will now examine a relationship from the GLOBAL data file.

> ➤ Data File: **GLOBAL**
> ➤ Task: **Mapping**
> ➤ Variable 1: **314) CIV LIBS04**
> ➤ Variable 2: **133) ECON DEVEL**
> ➤ View: **Map**

Here we see two maps showing the dependent variable, extent of civil liberties in nations, and the independent variable, level of economic development. Compare the two maps. Do they seem to be similar, opposite of one another, or unrelated? (Circle one.)

Similar   Opposite   Unrelated

Look at the correlation coefficient. In general, the absolute value (ignoring the positive or negative sign) of this correlation coefficient should be at least .30 for it to be of any importance.

Write the value of the correlation coefficient.   r = _____

Which of the following would be the better conclusion? (Circle the letter of your choice.)

a. There is little or no relationship between these two variables.

b. There is an important relationship between these two variables.

13. Now look at the relationship between the extent of civil liberties in nations and their population densities.

Data File: **GLOBAL**
Task: **Mapping**
Variable 1:   **314) CIV LIBS04**
➤ Variable 2:   **20) POPDENSITY**
➤ View: **Map**

Compare the two maps. Do they seem to be similar, opposite of one another, or unrelated? (Circle one.)

Similar   Opposite   Unrelated

In general, the absolute value (ignoring the positive or negative sign) of the correlation coefficient should be at least .30 for it to be of any importance.

Write the value of the correlation coefficient.   r = _____

Which of the following would be the better conclusion? (Circle the letter of your choice.)

a. There is little or no relationship between these two variables.

b. There is an important relationship between these two variables.

14. For the final exercise, let's make things a bit more challenging. Using the kinds of analyses you've just been doing, continue the analysis of variable 314) CIV LIBS04 by selecting another variable that you think helps to explain variations in the extent of civil liberties in nations.

Please write the variable number and name here: _____

What is the basic concept involved in the variable you selected?

_____

Do the analysis that is needed to determine whether this variable helps to explain the extent of civil liberties in nations, and print and attach the relevant results, and discuss them as you explain your conclusion in the space provided below.

_____

_____

_____

That's all for this lesson.

Hypotheses

Tasks. Mapping, Cross-tabulation
Data Files: GLOBAL, NES 04, HOUSE, GSS

INTRODUCTION

Hypotheses play an important role in the efforts of political scientists to explain political reality. They provide the bridge between theorizing and research. Building on explanation as a key concept in political research, this chapter will

- describe what a hypothesis is and relate hypotheses to theory

- demonstrate how to state hypotheses

- describe what a null hypothesis is and discuss its role in the research process

WHAT IS A HYPOTHESIS?

A **hypothesis** is a testable statement of relationship, derived from a theory.

That definition of a hypothesis has three parts, and each is important.

1. A hypothesis must be testable. (As we will see later, however, what we actually test is the *null hypothesis.*)

2. A hypothesis is a statement of relationship. That is, a hypothesis specifies that there is a certain kind of relationship between a dependent variable and an independent variable; it might also include antecedent or intervening variables.

3. A hypothesis is derived from a theory.

Political research should be guided by theory. We begin with a theoretical explanation of whatever aspects of political reality we are investigating, then we test our theory by deriving one or more hypotheses from it and testing those hypotheses. On the basis of the results, we draw conclusions about the theoretical explanation with which we started.

Thus, a hypothesis is a prediction derived from a theory. We can say, "If this theory is correct, we will find this type of relationship between these variables." That prediction must be stated in such a way that it can be tested *empirically* (through sensory observations of reality). The test of the hypothesis might either disprove the theory or add support to it.

Strictly speaking, we can never prove a theory. As indicated in the previous chapter, we cannot absolutely prove that anything causes anything else: It is always possible that the relationship we think is a causal relationship is actually a *spurious relationship*. Because theories contain causal statements, and causality cannot be proven, we cannot ever prove a theory beyond any possible doubt. However, a theory that has a great deal of evidence to support it—from different studies by different people—might be treated in virtually the same way as if it had been proven.

Sometimes political researchers begin with theories that are well developed, and they can logically derive hypotheses from them. But often in actual research, they begin with theories that are loosely formulated.

HOW TO STATE A HYPOTHESIS

Hypothesis Format for Directional Variables

There are various ways to state hypotheses, but here we will discuss just one approach. We begin with a hypothesis format for the situation in which all variables have direction (order). Thus, all variables involved are ordinal, interval, or ratio. If all the variables involved in a hypothesis have direction, then the hypothesis will specify a direction for the relationship. On the other hand, if either the independent variable or the dependent variable is nominal, then the hypothesis cannot have direction and we must use a different hypothesis format. Later, we will discuss a format for the situation in which at least one variable is nominal and, therefore, has no direction. For now, let's look at the format for directional variables as shown in Figure 5.1.

In this format, we are stating that there is a certain type of relationship between the dependent variable and the independent variable. When both variables have direction, we must specify the direction of the relationship between them. The direction of the relationship in a hypothesis will be either *positive* or *negative*.

Figure 5.1 How to State a Hypothesis When Both Variables Are Ordinal or Higher

Format: There is a _____ relationship between
(direction)

_____ and _____.
(dependent variable)   (independent variable)

Examples: There is a *positive* relationship between *political tolerance* and *education*.

There is a *negative* relationship between *support for sexual equality* and *age*.

Positive (or Direct) Relationships

In a ***positive*** (or ***direct***) ***relationship,*** two variables vary together in the same direction.

A *positive* relationship is also called a *direct* relationship; in this context, the terms *positive* and *direct* mean the same thing, so you can use either term. In a positive relationship, as one variable increases, the other increases, and as one decreases, the other decreases.

The first example in Figure 5.1—"There is a *positive* relationship between *political tolerance* and *education*"—means that people with less education have less political tolerance and that people with more education have more political tolerance. Individuals who have lower values on one variable will tend to have lower values on the other variable; those who are higher on one variable will be higher on the other variable.

Here is another example of a hypothesized positive relationship: *There is a positive relationship between per capita expenditures of nations on social welfare programs and their per capita income.* That means that countries with higher per capita income will spend more money on social welfare programs and, conversely, that countries with lower per capita income will spend less on social welfare programs.

Negative (or Inverse) Relationships

In a ***negative*** (or ***inverse***) ***relationship,*** two variables vary together in opposite directions.

A *negative* relationship is also called an *inverse* relationship. In this context, the terms *negative* and *inverse* mean the same thing, so you can use either term. In a negative relationship, as one variable *increases,* the other variable *decreases.* (The cases that have high values on one variable will have low values on the other variable.)

The second example in Figure 5.1—"There is a *negative* relationship between *support for sexual equality* and *age*"—means the older that people are, the lower their support for sexual equality, and the younger they are, the higher their support for sexual equality.

Here is another example of a hypothesized negative relationship: *There is a negative relationship between racism and education.* This means that people with more education are less racist and people with less education are more racist.

Hypothesis Format for Nondirectional Variables

If *either* variable involved in a hypothesis is *nominal* (a set of categories with no direction), the preceding hypothesis format will not work, because we cannot state a direction for a relationship if one or both of the variables are nondirectional (nominal). For example, it wouldn't make sense to say that there is a positive relationship between gender and political knowledge. This would mean that people with more gender have more political knowledge, and that does not make any sense.

If either variable is nominal, the hypothesis format says nothing about a positive or negative direction. Instead, it specifies the type of relationship between the variables in terms of how differences in the dependent variable are linked with differences in the independent variable. Figure 5.2 presents three types of situations in which at least one variable is nominal. In this situation, the examples will probably increase your understanding more than the abstract descriptions will.

Figure 5.2 How to State a Hypothesis When One Variable Is Nominal

- If the independent variable is nominal, but the dependent variable is at least ordinal, compare the categories of the independent variable in terms of their relative values on the dependent variable.

  Example: Whites have greater support for capital punishment than do African Americans.

- If the independent variable is at least ordinal, but the dependent variable is nominal, specify how the relative values of the independent variable are related to the categories of the dependent variable.

  Example: People with higher incomes are more likely to be Republicans than are people with lower incomes.

- If both variables are nominal, specify which categories of the independent variable are related to which categories of the dependent variable.

  Example: Women are more likely to be Democrats, and men are more likely to be Republicans.

Stating Hypotheses with Antecedent or Intervening Variables

If there is a *control variable* (either an antecedent variable or an intervening variable) to be taken into account in a hypothesis, we simply add it to the basic hypothesis statement. The way in which this is done varies depending on the levels of measurement of the variables involved. *If all variables involved (dependent, independent, and control) are at least ordinal, then we can simply add the phrase "while controlling for" and specify the control variable.*

> *Example:* There is a positive relationship between political tolerance and education, while controlling for income.

If the control variable is nominal, then we can specify the kind of relationship we expect to find among different categories of the control variable. This could require at least two hypothesis statements. For example, if we were hypothesizing a relationship between two variables and using gender as a control variable, then we would have two statements. The first hypothesis would begin "Among males . . ." and the second would begin "Among females . . . ."

Let's look at another example. Suppose you are doing survey research in several different nations to investigate the relationship between education level and support for democratic principles. You expect to find that this relationship differs depending on the nations' *types* of government. In democratic political systems, you think that the better educated will be more likely than the less educated to support democratic principles. However, in authoritarian political systems, you expect to find that the better educated (the relatively privileged class) are less supportive of democratic principles. We would state these hypotheses as follows:

- In *democratic* political systems, there is a *positive* relationship between support for democratic principles and education.

- In *authoritarian* political systems, there is a *negative* relationship between support for democratic principles and education.

Note that this is not a spurious relationship. Instead, it is a conditional relationship, in which the relationship between the dependent variable and the independent variable depends on the control variable.

THE NULL HYPOTHESIS

A **null hypothesis** states that there is *no relationship* between the variables in a hypothesis.

As mentioned before, we actually test the null hypothesis rather than the hypothesis. Because we cannot prove causality, the basic strategy of scientific research focuses on *disproof* rather than on *proof*. We test the null hypothesis and draw implications about the hypothesis—and about the theoretical explanation from which it was drawn.

Let's return to the relationship between political tolerance and education. The hypothesis and the null hypothesis are as follows:

> *Hypothesis:* There is a positive relationship between political tolerance and education.

> *Null hypothesis:* There is no relationship between political tolerance and education.

On the basis of our research, we would decide either to *reject* or to *fail to reject* the null hypothesis. If we fail to reject the null hypothesis, we are deciding that there is *no relationship* between the dependent variable and the independent variable. This would not support our hypothesis—or our theory. Provided that we had adequately tested the null hypothesis, we would then need to revise the theory (or develop a new one), formulate new hypotheses, and conduct new research to test the new hypotheses.

If our research leads us to reject the null hypothesis, we have decided that there is a real relationship between the dependent variable and the independent variable. This supports our hypothesis and adds evidence to support our theory. *It does not, however, prove the theory.* When we derive a hypothesis from a theory, we are saying that if the theory is correct, we will find this relationship between variables. If we do not find this relationship, the theory is not correct. If we do find the relationship, this supports the theory—but the theory may still be wrong.

Suppose, for example, that we have a theory concerning political participation and its relationship to people's economic situation. One important hypothesis that we derive from this is: *There is a positive relationship, among individuals, between political participation and increase in annual income from the previous year.* We test the null hypothesis: *There is no relationship between political participation and increase in annual income from the previous year.* There are two basic outcomes:

- If we *fail to reject* the null hypothesis, we have decided that *there is no relationship* between political participation and increase in annual income from the previous year. Therefore, the results do not support the theory.

- If we *reject* the null hypothesis, we have decided that *there is a relationship* between political participation and increase in annual income from the previous year. This supports the theory. However, even though this relationship exists, the theoretical explanation for the relationship's existence may still be wrong. Thus, the research *supports* the theory but does not *prove* it.

In later chapters, we will focus on actually testing hypotheses. When we do research, we develop the theoretical explanation first and then test it through the process of formulating and testing hypotheses.

THEORY AND HYPOTHESIS: AN EXAMPLE

For an actual example of theorizing and hypothesizing, let's briefly examine the following article:

Mark N. Franklin and Wolfgang P. Hirczy de Miño, "Separated Powers, Divided Government, and Turnout in U.S. Presidential Elections," *American Journal of Political Science* 42 (1998): 316–326.

Franklin and Hirczy de Miño note that past research has done a good job in explaining why some individuals vote while others do not. However, such research has not explained why the United States has lower voting turnout than other countries.

The authors extract from theories of voting the idea that individuals are more likely to vote when the election is salient to them—they care about the election's outcome and believe that it will have an impact on public policy or practices. Anything that increases the electoral salience increases the motivation for people to vote. In general, electoral salience is increased when the results of the election might have a substantial impact on public policy. When the electoral salience is reduced, then voting turnout is reduced. Thus, any factor that reduces the possibility of the election results having a policy impact reduces the salience of the election and reduces voter turnout.

Franklin and Hirczy de Miño hypothesize that a divided government can reduce voting turnout. In comparison with 25 other countries with readily available electoral statistics, the United States is the only one with a strict separation of powers between the legislative and executive branches. Sometimes the executive branch and the legislative branch are controlled by the same party, and sometimes they are not. When both the executive and legislative branches are controlled by the same party, it is easier to enact policies and easier for the public to assess where to place the responsibility for policy decisions. Thus, the electoral salience should be higher.

When the presidency is controlled by one party but Congress is controlled by a different party (or split), it is more difficult to enact policies and more difficult for the public to assess responsibility. It also increases the "information costs"—it is more difficult for people to understand what's happening and to act on that knowledge. The increase in information costs reduces the motivation of people to vote.

Thus, the dependent variable here is voter turnout and the independent variable is whether the government is divided or not. Although Franklin and Hirczy de Miño did not state their hypothesis in the following manner, we can paraphrase their hypothesis as follows: *A divided government leads to a lower voter turnout rate than does a nondivided government.*

Conversely, the null hypothesis would be: *There is no relationship between voter turnout and whether or not the government is divided.*

Franklin and Hirczy de Miño used the U.S. results from presidential elections between 1840 and 1992 to test their hypothesis. We also need to note that the authors took into account another variable that might affect the hypothesized relationship—the closeness of the electoral race. Thus, when this variable is added, we have this hypothesis: *A divided government leads to a lower voter turnout rate than does a nondivided government, while controlling for the closeness of the electoral race.*

This would make the null hypothesis: *There is no relationship between voter turnout and whether the government is divided or not, while controlling for the closeness of the electoral race.*

The results of the study supported the hypothesis and thus the theory. Although the closeness of the electoral race has an effect on voter turnout, divided government reduces voter turnout even when controlling for the effects of closeness of the electoral race. Thus, the null hypothesis is rejected.

TERMS INTRODUCED IN THIS CHAPTER

Hypothesis

Positive (direct) relationship

Negative (inverse) relationship

Null hypothesis

FOR FURTHER READING

Any issue of most major political science journals in your library will have articles in which researchers test hypotheses. Some authors of political science studies are explicit about their hypotheses and the way they derived them from a particular theory. In the work of other researchers, the hypotheses and the process of deriving them from some theory is less explicit.

An example of a study that is very explicit about hypotheses and the theory from which they are derived is C. Richard Hofstetter, "Political Talk Radio, Situational Involvement, and Political Mobilization," *Social Science Quarterly* 79 (June 1998): 273–286.

An example of a study that does not explicitly state any hypothesis (although there is an implicit hypothesis that you can recognize as you read the article) is Benjamin Highton, "Easy Registration and Voter Turnout," *Journal of Politics* 59 (May 1997): 565–575. Although there are no explicit hypotheses in this study, the author is explicit about the theory that forms the basis of his research.

For an example of the process of deriving explicit hypotheses from a particular theory (social judgment theory, in this case) and then testing the hypotheses, see Jon Hurwitz, "Issue Perception and Legislative Decision Making: An Application of Social Judgment Theory," *American Politics Quarterly* 14 (July 1986): 150–185.

For an example in which the hypothesis formulation is less explicit, see Fay Lomax Cook et al., "Media and Agenda Setting: Effects on the Public, Interest Group Leaders, Policy Makers, and Policy," *Public Opinion Quarterly* 47 (Spring 1983): 16–35.

For an example of integrating and testing several different hypotheses based on more than one theory, see Steven E. Finkel and Karl-Dieter Opp, "Party Identification and Participation in Collective Political Action," *Journal of Politics* 53 (May 1991): 339–371.

worksheet

NAME: _____

COURSE: _____

DATE: _____

1. You will learn more fully about the process of testing hypotheses in Chapter 10, but we will test some hypotheses here. Let's begin with this question: In the nations of the world, what kind of relationship would you expect between the degree of individual freedom and newspaper availability (the extent to which newspapers are available to people)?

Before stating your hypothesis, use the GLOBAL file to examine variable descriptions for the two variables (degree of individual freedom and newspaper availability) to determine whether both variables have direction (ordinal measurement or higher).

It is important to pay close attention to how the variable FREEDOM is coded. A freedom rating of one is the most free, while a rating of three is not free. So, as the degree of freedom increases, nations have lower freedom ratings.

> ➤ Data File: **GLOBAL**
> ➤ Task: **Mapping**
> ➤ Variable 1: **311) FREEDOM**
> ➤ Variable 2: **213) NEWS/CP**
> ➤ Views: **Map**

Is the variable *degree of individual freedom* ordinal or higher? (Circle one.)   Yes   No

Is the variable *newspaper availability* ordinal or higher? (Circle one.)   Yes   No

Do you need to use the hypothesis format for directional variables or a hypothesis format for nondirectional variables? (Circle one.)

  a. Hypothesis format for directional variables

  b. Hypothesis format for nondirectional variables

State your hypothesis. (Please review the section on stating hypotheses so that you set up the hypothesis properly.)

_____

_____

_____

_____

_____

_____

State the null hypothesis for the preceding hypothesis. (Please review the section on null hypotheses so that you set up the null hypothesis properly.)

_____

_____

_____

_____

In the following space, explain why you expect to find the relationship you hypothesized. This hypothesis presumably came from some theory you have involving the concepts with which you are dealing. Don't let the term "theory" make you nervous—just explain why you think that the newspaper availability of nations will have the kind of effect on degree of individual freedom that you hypothesized. (Attach an additional sheet if you need more room.)

_____

_____

_____

_____

Now let's test the hypothesis. Compare the two maps on the screen. If these two maps are very similar, then the relationship between the two variables is positive. If the two maps are opposites (light-colored nations on one map are dark on the other, and vice versa), then the relationship is negative. If there is no pattern of similarities or pattern of differences between the two maps, then there is no relationship.

On the basis of your comparison of the two maps, which of the following would you conclude? (Circle one.)

a. There is a positive relationship between the degree of individual freedom in nations and newspaper availability in those nations.

b. There is a negative relationship between the degree of individual freedom in nations and newspaper availability in those nations.

c. There is no relationship between the degree of individual freedom in nations and newspaper availability in those nations.

On this basis, would you reject the null hypothesis?   Yes   No

Write the value of the correlation coefficient.   r = _____

If this correlation coefficient is positive, then the relationship between the two variables is positive. If it is negative, then the relationship between the two variables is negative. In terms of strength of the relationship, let's say that this correlation should be .30 or above (either positive or negative) for the relationship to be strong enough to be of much importance.

On that basis, which of the following would you conclude? (Circle one.)

a. There is not an important relationship between the degree of individual freedom in nations and newspaper availability in those nations.

b. There is an important positive relationship between the degree of individual free-dom in nations and newspaper availability in those nations.

c. There is an important negative relationship between the degree of individual free-dom in nations and newspaper availability in those nations.

2. State below a hypothesis to express the relationship between the degree of individual freedom in nations and urbanism (the percentage of the population living in urban areas).

_____

_____

_____

State the null hypothesis for the preceding hypothesis.

_____

_____

_____

Let's test the hypothesis.

Data File:	**GLOBAL**
Task:	**Mapping**
Variable 1:	**311) FREEDOM**
➤ Variable 2:	**22) URBAN %02**
➤ Views:	**Map**

Compare the two maps on the screen. If these two maps are similar, then the relationship between the two variables is positive. If the two maps are opposites (light-colored nations on one map are dark on the other, and vice versa), then the relationship is negative. If there is no pattern of similarities or pattern of differences between the two maps, then there is no relationship.

On the basis of your comparison of the two maps, which of the following would you conclude? (Circle one.)

a. There is a positive relationship between the degree of individual freedom in nations and urbanism in those nations.

b. There is a negative relationship between the degree of individual freedom in nations and urbanism in those nations.

c. There is no relationship between the degree of individual freedom in nations and urbanism in those nations.

On that basis, would you reject the null hypothesis?   Yes   No

3. Formulate a hypothesis to express the relationship between the birthrate in nations and the level of economic development.

_____

_____

_____

Briefly explain why you expect to find the relationship you hypothesized above. Theorize—explain why you think the level of economic development of a nation could have the kind of impact on the birthrate that you hypothesized. (**Hint:** Think of life in the United States a hundred years ago. Where did the typical family live and what did it do for a living? How did this change when the United States became more industrialized?)

_____

_____

_____

State the null hypothesis for the preceding hypothesis.

_____

_____

_____

Test your hypothesis.

Data File:	**GLOBAL**
Task:	**Mapping**
➤ Variable 1:	**28) BIRTHRATE**
➤ Variable 2:	**133) ECON DEVEL**
➤ Views:	**Map**

On the basis of the correlation coefficient and your comparison of the two maps, would you reject the null hypothesis?   Yes   No

Which of the following conclusions is most appropriate? (Circle one.)

a. There is not an important relationship between the birthrate in nations and the level of economic development in those nations.

b. There is an important positive relationship between the birthrate in nations and the level of economic development in those nations.

c. There is an important negative relationship between the birthrate in nations and the level of economic development in those nations.

4. Using the NES 04 data file, let's test the following hypothesis: *There is a negative relationship between approval of President Bush's job performance and conservative identification.* We would expect that people who are politically conservative would give higher approval to Bush, moderates would be in the middle, and liberals would give the lowest approval to Bush.

Write the null hypothesis below.

_____

_____

_____

_____

Now test the hypothesis.

➤ Data File: **NES 04**
➤ Task: **Cross-tabulation**
➤ Row Variable: **121) BUSH_APPR?**
➤ Column Variable: **25) IDEOLOGY**
➤ View: **Tables**
➤ Display: **Column %**

Write the column percentages in the table below.

	LIBERAL	MODERATE	CONSERVATIVE
APPROVE	_____%	_____%	_____%
DISAPPROVE	_____%	_____%	_____%

For the moment, we can conceptualize the independent variable as conservative identification. Those who classified themselves as conservatives have the most conservative identification, moderates are in the middle, and liberals have the least conservative identification.

Because there are only two rows in this table, we can see the pattern (if any) by examining just one row. For the Approve row, read the column percentages going across the row. As you move from the Liberal category on the left to the Conservative category on the right, what happens to the percentage of people who approve of Bush's job performance? (Circle one.)

    a. The percentage increases.

    b. The percentage decreases.

    c. There is no particular pattern of increases or decreases.

Which of the following statements best describes the results in the preceding table? (Circle one.)

    a. There is no relationship between approval of Bush's job performance and conservative identification.

    b. There is a positive relationship between approval of Bush's job performance and conservative identification.

    c. There is a negative relationship between approval of Bush's job performance and conservative identification.

Should we reject the null hypothesis? (Circle one.)   Yes   No

5. In the preceding example, both variables were ordinal. Now let's test a hypothesis that has a nominal variable in it. The following hypothesis was briefly mentioned earlier in this chapter: Whites have greater support for capital punishment than do African Americans.

Write the null hypothesis below. (**Hint:** What is the independent variable here? Don't just think in terms of categories of the independent variable.)

_____

_____

_____

Let's look at the results.

    ➤ Data File: **GSS**
    ➤ Task: **Cross-tabulation**
    ➤ Row Variable: **107) EXECUTE?**
    ➤ Column Variable: **38) RACE**
    ➤ View: **Tables**
    ➤ Display: **Column %**

Write the column percentages in the following table.

	WHITE	BLACK
OPPOSE	_____%	_____%
FAVOR	_____%	_____%

On the basis of those results, which of the following statements is correct? (Circle one.)

a. White Americans favor capital punishment more than African Americans do.

b. African Americans favor capital punishment more than white Americans do.

c. There is no relationship between support for capital punishment and race.

Should we reject the null hypothesis?   Yes   No

Print this table and attach it to your assignment. (**Note:** If you have been instructed not to use the printer, just skip this task.)

6. Let's examine a hypothesis based on the HOUSE data file. 77.7% of the representatives in the 109th Congress were incumbents who had also served in the 109th Congress. Why is there so little turn-over in the House? Open the HOUSE file and read the variable description for 28) %OF VOTE. Let's call the concept measured by this variable *district competitiveness for members of Congress*. Members with highly competitive districts would have won less than 55% of the votes in that district, while members in districts that are not competitive would have won more than 65% of the votes in their district. Every ten years, districts are drawn up by state legislatures, but the new district boundaries are usually drawn up with input from standing members of Congress from those districts. The way that the district boundary is drawn influences the district's competitiveness. Read the variable description for 13) #TERMS2. Let's call this variable *terms of service*. Would you expect a positive or a negative relationship between the number of terms served by a member and the competitiveness of a member's district?

Formulate a hypothesis to express your expectation concerning the relationship between terms of service and the competitiveness of a member's district.

_____

_____

_____

State the null hypothesis for the preceding hypothesis.

_____

_____

_____

➤ Data File: **HOUSE**
➤ Task: **Cross-tabulation**
➤ Row Variable: **13) #TERMS2**
➤ Column Variable: **28) %OF VOTE**
➤ View: **Tables**
➤ Display: **Column %**

Write the column percentages in the following table.

	UNDER 55%	55%–65%	OVER 65%
ONE	_____%	_____%	_____%
2 TO 4	_____%	_____%	_____%
5 OR MORE	_____%	_____%	_____%

Who is more likely to have served 5 or more terms? (Circle one.)

  a. Representatives who come from competitive districts

  b. Representatives who come from districts that are not competitive

Do these results indicate that you should reject your null hypothesis?   Yes   No

7. Do Democrats and Republicans in Congress differ on whether or not their districts are competitive? Formulate a hypothesis for the relationship between political party affiliation and district competitiveness, and state it below. (**Hint:** Treat political party affiliation as a nominal variable here.)

State the null hypothesis for this situation.

_____

_____

worksheet

Perform the following analysis:

> Data File: **HOUSE**
> Task: **Cross-tabulation**
> ➤ Row Variable: **11) PARTY**
> ➤ Column Variable: **28) %OF VOTE**
> ➤ View: **Tables**
> ➤ Display: **Column %**

Write the column percentages in the table below.

	UNDER 55%	55%–65%	OVER 65%
DEMOCRAT	_____%	_____%	_____%
REPUBLICAN	_____%	_____%	_____%

Who is more likely to come from competitive districts? (Circle one.)

       Democrats   Republicans   No difference between them

Who is more likely to come from districts where the representative won between 55% and 65% of the vote? (Circle one.)

       Democrats   Republicans   No difference between them

Who is more likely to come from districts where the representative won more than 65% of the vote? (Circle one.)

       Democrats   Republicans   No difference between them

Do those results indicate that you should reject your null hypothesis?   Yes   No

Print these results and attach them to your assignment. (**Note:** If you have been instructed not to submit the printout, just skip this task.)

How did you come to the conclusion that you should accept (or reject) the null hypothesis? On what evidence is this conclusion based?

_____

_____

_____

_____

That's all for this lesson.

CHAPTER 6

Sampling

Tasks: Univariate, Cross-tabulation
Data Files: GSS, NES 04, GSS 04

INTRODUCTION

This chapter will

- describe three general kinds of sampling (haphazard, quota, and probability) and explain why probability sampling is the most useful

- discuss sampling error and sample sizes in surveys

- explain how certain types of probability samples are selected

- describe sources of error (other than sampling error) in surveys

In many political studies—especially in survey research—we use a sample of cases, rather than all possible cases. Thus, it is important for you to understand the basic ideas about sampling. Further, given the widespread use of public opinion polls in many democratic political systems, it is important for you to understand the sampling procedures behind the poll results. Certain aspects of sampling are fairly simple and straightforward; others are complex. This chapter will provide a fair degree of detail about certain aspects but will give only a general description of those that are more complex.

TYPES OF SAMPLES

In the United States, the historical development of sampling has moved from *haphazard sampling* to *quota sampling* to *probability sampling*. Today, political scientists who use samples consider probability sampling to be the most scientific form of sampling. However, to put probability sampling into its proper context, we need to see what was wrong with other types of sampling.

Haphazard Sampling

A ***haphazard sample*** is a sample selected in such a way—usually convenience or self-selection—that certain people within a population are more likely to be included than are others.

Haphazard samples are based on either *convenience* or *self-selection*. When convenience is involved, researchers choose people for the sample based on how convenient it is to select them—within the limits of the situation. The street-corner interview is the classic example of the haphazard sample. For example, a television crew might set up its camera at a particular location and interview people who pass by that location. When interviewers stop people in malls to interview them, this procedure is called a *mall intercept interview.*

Convenience is also involved when a professor administers a questionnaire to a class. Another example is the situation in which a researcher uses a convenient list of people in a population (e.g., a particular city) even though that list (e.g., a list of newspaper subscribers) has been generated in such a way that certain people would be included and others would not.

When self-selection is involved, people basically decide for themselves whether they are part of the sample or not. A good example of this is the television call-in survey. Someone on a television show invites people to call a certain number if they take one side on an issue and call a different number if they take a different side. Self-selection is involved in questionnaires published in newspapers or magazines. Self-selection is also involved in the surveys found on many Internet sites.

Whether a haphazard sample is selected through convenience, self-selection, or a combination of these, we cannot trust the results. Too many biases are built in to haphazard samples. Let's use the street-corner interview and the television call-in survey to demonstrate.

When someone conducts a street-corner survey, the presumption is that the views of the respondents will reflect the views of the population in the surrounding area. However, we cannot assume that the people passing a particular street corner are representative of the people in that area. Further, the types of people passing a particular street corner might be different at different times of day (e.g., 10 A.M. vs. 7 P.M.) or different days of the week (e.g., weekdays vs. weekends). Thus, the location and timing of street-corner surveys can affect the selection of people for the sample, and that can affect the results.

Moreover, in street-corner interviews or in mall intercept interviews, the interviewers tend to select certain people on the basis of their appearances. People who look unusual might be excluded, people who are not at least fairly well dressed might be excluded, and people who do not look friendly might be excluded. People's appearance might be related to characteristics that are relevant to their political views. For example, those who don't look friendly might be unemployed; that could affect the way they perceive the political situation. Biases in selecting the particular respondents for the sample add to the biases that already result from the particular place and time.

For the television call-in survey, people select themselves to participate or not to participate. Certain kinds of people are more likely to participate; that causes bias in the results. For example, people with more education and more income are more likely to participate—especially when there will be some sort of charge for the telephone call. People who are more interested in the particular topic—or in politics in general—are more likely to respond to a television call-in poll about political matters. Those who feel intensely about a topic might be more likely to call, and they might call more than once to try to affect the results of the survey.

The best-known haphazard survey in the United States is a straw poll conducted by a magazine organization during the 1936 presidential campaign. The *Literary Digest* had conducted such polls during two previous elections and had correctly predicted the winners. In 1936, the *Literary Digest* sent out more than 10 million questionnaires, primarily to people listed in telephone directories or on automobile registration lists. More than 2 million people returned the questionnaires. In October, the *Literary Digest* published its final results—which indicated that Roosevelt would lose by a landslide. In fact, Roosevelt won by a landslide!

The basic problem was that the people listed in telephone directories and on automobile registration lists at this time—during the Depression of the 1930s—were not representative. Those who could afford a car or a telephone during this time were much better off economically—and were much more likely to prefer the Republican candidate—than was the average person. Thus, the results were biased because of the selection process.

Today, you can still find many examples of haphazard sampling in magazines, books, television, and radio shows and on the Internet. Although haphazard sampling is still used, responsible pollsters no longer consider it to be an adequate sampling technique. The famous *Literary Digest* debacle in 1936 discredited such sampling. (It also contributed to the demise of the magazine soon thereafter.)

Quota Sampling

A *quota sample* tries to obtain a group representative of the population by setting quotas for selecting various categories of people based on their proportions in the population.

In 1936, the *Literary Digest* had a haphazard sample of more than 2 million respondents, and its results were very inaccurate. However, George Gallup's newly formed organization surveyed a quota sample of only about 2,000 people and correctly predicted the winner. Consequently, quota sampling became the preferred method of the emerging professional polling organizations.

When an organization takes a quota sample, it first divides the population into categories on the basis of variables from census data. Then it sets sample selection quotas for each category based on its proportion in the population. For example, suppose census data show that 53% of the population is female and 47% is male. The researcher sets quotas such that 53% of the sample must be female and 47% must be male. Suppose that 86% of the population is white and 14% is African American. Then 86% of the people selected for the sample must be white and 14% must be African American. To set all the quotas, an organization will usually use about six to eight such demographic variables. After the quotas are set, those who do the survey basically can survey whomever they want—within certain guidelines—as long as they are filling the quotas.

Quota sampling produces a more representative sample than does haphazard sampling, but quota sampling is not without its own shortcomings. The biggest problem is that interviewers have too much discretion in selecting people to interview. For face-to-face interviews, for example, the survey organization sends interviewers to a certain area and gives them instructions on how to select households. However, interviewers may skip certain areas if they don't feel comfortable interviewing people in them. Interviewers might, for example, skip areas they think are dangerous. They are likely to skip poor neighborhoods and very rich neighborhoods. In general, interviewers would be most comfortable interviewing people who are similar to themselves; that, of course, would create biases in the survey results.

As a result of the interviewer-discretion problem and other problems (e.g., problems involved in getting accurate, current data on the proportions of different categories of people in the population), quota sampling was ultimately discredited. In the presidential election of 1948, the pollsters' predictions corresponded to the prevailing public opinion that Dewey would defeat Truman. In fact, Truman won. The poll results were wrong partly because of the problems involved in quota sampling. As a result, quota sampling is no longer considered to be an adequate sampling technique by itself.

Probability Sampling

A **probability sample** is a sample of a population in which each person has a known chance of being selected.

The important principle in probability sampling is that each person in the population has a known chance of being selected—basically an equal chance at the start of the process. That removes bias from the sample selection process and makes probability samples more representative than haphazard or quota samples. No type of person is overrepresented or underrepresented. Further, when you have a probability sample, you can use probability theory to make estimates of the accuracy of the sample.

After 1948, survey research turned to probability sampling. Most of the rest of this chapter concerns probability sampling as applied specifically to survey research. However, the same basic ideas also apply to sampling of other types of cases (e.g., cities, counties, or newspaper editorials).

Probability sampling does work, but we are dealing with probabilities here. Provided that a probability sample has been selected properly and there are enough people in the sample, the probability sample will produce results that are within a certain margin of error a certain proportion of the time. What does that mean? The next section will discuss it.

SAMPLING ERROR AND SAMPLE SIZE

How many people would you need for a probability sample? To answer that question, you would first need to know three things:

1. How much accuracy do you need in the survey results?
2. How much confidence do you want that your results are actually within the specified range of accuracy?
3. How much variability is there in the variable?

Accuracy

The degree of **accuracy** is also called the margin of error. How close to the true population results do you need the sample results to be? The degree of accuracy is usually stated in plus-or-minus percentage terms: ±1 percentage points, ±2 percentage points, ±3 percentage points, and so on.

Let's say that a national survey had a margin of error of ±3 percentage points, and the survey indicated that 68 percentage points favored gun control legislation and 32 percentage points opposed it. That means that the true percentage (the percentage that would be obtained if the entire population, rather than just a sample, were surveyed) favoring gun-control legislation could be anywhere between 65 percentage points and 71 percentage points. Similarly, the true percentage opposing gun-control legislation could be anywhere between 29 percentage points and 35 percentage points.

Researchers must decide how much accuracy they require for a particular survey. That decision depends on the purposes of the survey and the resources available for it. Typically, national surveys in the United States specify ±3 percentage points as the level of accuracy, but some of the smaller ones—especially surveys that are conducted immediately after some national event—use the ±5 percentage points level.

Confidence

Because sampling is based on probability, we cannot be completely sure that the results are actually within the level of accuracy we have specified. However, probability theory allows us to specify the **confidence level**—the probability that the results are outside the specified level of accuracy.

The confidence level is stated in probability terms: .01, .02, and so on. A confidence level of .01 means there is 1 chance out of 100 that the survey results are outside the specified range of accuracy. A confidence level of .05 means there are 5 chances out of 100 that the survey results are outside the specified range of accuracy. National survey researchers usually select the .05 confidence level.

For example, what does it mean if we say that a survey uses the ±3 percentage points accuracy level and the .05 confidence level? It means that there are 5 chances out of 100 that the sample results are more than 3 percentage points away from the results that would be obtained if the entire population were surveyed. Similarly, there are 95 chances out of 100 that the sample results are within 3 percentage points of the results that would be obtained if the whole population were surveyed.

Variability

So far, we have assumed that the same standards apply to all variables within a survey. In fact, the accuracy of results might vary from one variable to another depending on the amount of variability within the variables. We have discussed variation before; here, **variability** means basically the same thing. The general principle can be stated as follows: All other things being equal, the greater the variability within a variable, the lower the survey accuracy. Of course, the lower the variability within a variable, the more accurate the results.

Suppose that *everyone* within a particular population was Protestant. There would be no variability at all in this particular variable. How difficult would it be to obtain accurate results for this particular variable? It would not be difficult—a sample of just one person would accurately represent the population for this particular variable. At the other extreme, suppose that for a particular population, each person had a different view of how much money should be spent on the space program. How difficult would it be to obtain accurate results for this particular variable? It would be very difficult because the variability would be so high.

To compute the sample size needed for a particular survey, researchers need to decide how much variability is involved. Researchers usually just make an *assumption* about variability: *They assume maximum variability for a binomial variable*. A binomial variable is one that can take just two values—for example, the variable gender can be male or female. Maximum variability in this case would be 50% for each of the two values. After making this assumption of maximum variability for a binomial variable, researchers select a formula that reflects this assumption and also incorporates the desired levels of accuracy and confidence.

Determining Sample Size

So, how many survey respondents are necessary for a probability sample? Once decisions have been made regarding accuracy, confidence levels, and variability, a formula can be used to determine how many people are needed in the sample. Although the formula must be adjusted if your requirements change (that is, if you change the required level of accuracy, the confidence level, etc.), it is useful to start with some basic assumptions. For the rest of this discussion, let's assume the following: The population from which we are sampling is relatively large (say, more than 80,000), the confidence level is .05, and there is maximum variability for a binomial (two-category) variable. As it happens, if the population from which we are drawing our sample is relatively large (as we're going to assume for this example), the only matter that really must be decided is the required level of accuracy. Given the above assumptions, Table 6.1 shows the various levels of accuracy from which we can choose, along with the required sample size to meet each level of accuracy.

Thus, for example, if a researcher wants to be 95% sure (the .05 confidence level) of being within 3 percentage points of the true results for a binomial variable for a large population, the sample size would need to be 1,067 people. You may notice that this is smaller than the usual national sample, which typically includes about 1,500 people to claim a 3 percentage points margin of error. We will shortly explain the reason for that in the section on multistage cluster sampling.

Table 6.1 Required Sample Sizes for Different Levels of Accuracy

Desired Accuracy	Required Sample Size
±1 percentage points	9,604
±2 percentage points	2,401
±3 percentage points	1,067
±4 percentage points	600
±5 percentage points	384

Research Methods in Political Science

SAMPLE SELECTION

How does one go about selecting a probability sample? The selection process depends on the type of probability sample involved. Let's look at the selection of two types of probability samples. First we will describe the process for selecting a simple *random sample* in detail. Then we will describe the general idea for the more complex *multistage cluster sample*.

Random Sampling

A ***random sample*** is a sample in which each person in the population has an equal chance of being selected throughout the selection process.

There is a popular misconception about what a random sample is: Many people think that a random sample is a haphazard sample. In fact, a random sample gives each person in the population an equal chance of being selected. This process removes any bias from sample selection and makes it the opposite of a haphazard sample.

There is one important requirement for a random sample: *There must be a list of everyone in the defined population.* We do not have a list for most large populations (e.g., all U.S. adults), but there are certain populations for which we can obtain complete lists. For example, suppose you are going to survey all registered voters in a particular city. The population here would be defined as the registered voters in this city, and you can obtain a list of such registered voters from the official voter registration records. To take another example, suppose you are doing research on the political attitudes of students at your college. The population here consists of the students at your college, and you could probably obtain a list of all students from the college records.

Given a list of all persons in a particular population, the process of selecting a random sample is fairly simple, although it can be tedious and time consuming. To demonstrate the steps in this process, let's use a hypothetical example.

> *Problem:* You have a list of all 80,000 registered voters in a city. You want a random sample of 1,200 of those registered voters.
>
> *Step 1:* Assign each voter on the list a unique number with the same number of digits.

In this situation, each person will have a five-digit number, because there are five digits in the highest number (80000). Each number will be unique—no two people will have the same number. The first person is number 00001, the second person is number 00002, and so on.

> *Step 2:* Obtain a table of random digits and randomly point to a location in the table to obtain a starting point.

A table of random digits is a table of digits set up so that there is no pattern to the digits. The probability of a particular digit appearing at a particular point is the same as the probability of any other digit being there. If you randomly choose a starting point and select the first five digits starting from that point, the probability of *any* five-digit number appearing is the same as the probability of any other five-digit number being there. Thus, there is no pattern—no bias—in the order of the numbers.

Where do you get a table of random digits? Most statistics textbooks and many research methods books have tables of random digits in the back. There are also computer programs that will generate lists of random digits. Table 6.2 contains a series of four-digit random numbers generated by a computer program. Note that the number 5516 is in bold type and underlined. Let's suppose that this is where your finger landed when you chose the starting point.

Table 6.2 Table of Random Digits

5551	5412	3765	4953	0455	9710	2164	8634
7361	5427	2956	7405	3914	1084	4300	1221
2605	0815	8612	8995	7925	1856	3096	6139
3666	**<u>5516</u>**	9467	2205	2370	0047	1760	7761
0344	6338	2301	5586	3207	2432	2307	9833
4457	3231	2771	9421	1477	7301	9410	1487
1312	7180	1243	4936	6459	4632	5090	6230
8704	5116	3620	5997	6908	1230	3803	6223
5473	8580	6266	1238	5358	7831	0054	4935

Step 3: From the starting point, select numbers that have the same number of digits as the numbers assigned to the population.

In this situation, you need five-digit numbers. From the starting point (5516), read across and regroup digits into five-digit numbers—it doesn't matter that the numbers in the columns are now set up in terms of four digits. Therefore, we form five-digit numbers as follows:

55169   46722   05237   00047   17607   76103   44633   . . .

Step 4: If a particular five-digit number falls within a range of numbers assigned to the population, the person with that number becomes part of the sample. If the number is outside the range of numbers assigned to the population, skip it and go to the next number. Continue this process until you have the number of people you need for the sample.

Thus, the first person we select for the sample is the one who has the number 55169. The second person has the number 46722; the third, 05237; and so on. We would continue until we had the number of people we needed for the sample—although, of course, the small table of random digits here would not be adequate. Alternatively, if you had access to a computer program that generates random digits, you could set it up to generate 1,200 random numbers between 00001 and 80000.

Using this process, there is no bias in the list of people to be included in this sample. Each person on the population list has exactly the same chance (1 out of 80,000) of being selected for the sample.

Research Methods in Political Science

Multistage Cluster Sampling

Multistage cluster sampling is a sampling procedure in which smaller units are sampled from larger units through two or more stages until the sample of people is clustered into a fairly small number of areas.

How does an organization select a probability sample for a nation? There is no list of the entire population. Therefore, we cannot select a simple random sample of everyone in the nation. One way to obtain a national sample—especially when the survey requires face-to-face interviews—is to select a multistage cluster sample. As its name implies, this process involves sampling at more than one stage, and it ultimately clusters the sample into a relatively small number of areas for the sake of practicality in carrying out the actual survey.

Selecting a multistage cluster sample is extremely complex. Further, different organizations go about the selection process in somewhat different ways. Therefore, we will present only a simplified, general outline of the process here.

> *Step 1:* Select the primary sampling units.

The primary sampling units are simply the first units selected. Such units might be counties, cities, congressional districts, or some other type of unit. Let's say for our present purposes that a survey organization selects 100 counties.

> *Step 2:* From the list of primary sample units, take a sample of smaller units.

In this example, given the list of 100 counties, the researcher would make a list of city blocks (or rural equivalents) within each of those counties. Then the researcher would take a sample of those city blocks or rural equivalents.

> *Step 3:* Make a list of smaller units and take a sample of them.

Here the researcher would make a list of the households for each city block or rural equivalent included in the sample. Then the researcher would select a sample of households.

> *Step 4:* Select a sample of persons.

At this point, one person would be randomly selected from each household. This process would be set up in such a way that the interviewer would have no choice about the particular person selected. Further, this particular person would be the only one in the household to be surveyed. If that particular person were not there, the interviewer would check back later.

One problem with multistage cluster sampling is that sampling error occurs at each stage of the sampling process. To compensate for this, researchers who use multistage cluster sampling need to select more people than they would if they were using a simple random sample. Thus, although the sample-size table (Table 6.1) shows that we would need a sample of 1,067 people to represent a large population with a 3 percentage points margin of error, researchers would select about 1,500 people for a multistage cluster sample to achieve a 3 percentage points margin of error.

RECENT DEVELOPMENTS

This discussion of sampling would be incomplete without a brief discussion of two relatively recent developments: random-digit dialing and exit polls.

Random-Digit Dialing

Random-digit dialing (RDD) is a method of selecting a national sample for a telephone survey by using random digits for the telephone numbers. Collecting telephone directories for a national telephone survey is a massive problem, although tremendous collections of telephone numbers are now available on CD-ROM. Further, telephone directories are somewhat out of date by the time they are printed, and they become more out of date as time goes by. Moreover, some people have unlisted telephone numbers. All of those problems are solved by RDD.

A survey organization that wants to use RDD to select a national sample first obtains certain information from the telephone companies: how many telephone numbers there are within a particular area code, what the three-digit prefixes are, and how many numbers there are for the three-digit prefix. Given this information, the researcher computes the number of people needed for particular area codes and particular prefixes, then uses random digits for the last four digits of each telephone number.

Let's suppose that a researcher compiling a national sample has determined that ten numbers are to be selected for area code 765, prefix 289 (in Muncie, Indiana). The researcher then selects a series of four-digit random numbers to complete the telephone numbers. Suppose, for example, that the first four-digit random number is 2511. The telephone number to be dialed is (765) 289-2511. The interviewer will call and ask whether it is a residential number. If it is, the interviewer proceeds with the interview. If it is not, the interviewer goes on to the next randomly generated number.

Random-digit dialing gives every household with a telephone a basically equal chance of being selected. That includes people with unlisted numbers and people who obtained their telephone numbers that day. Although the process works well, there are a few problems such as the situation in which a household has more than one telephone number.

Exit Polls

In an *exit poll,* researchers survey people on election day as they leave the polling place. In the United States, each television network does an exit poll (or cooperates in a joint exit poll conducted by the Voter News Service) during a presidential election. Exit polls have the advantage of producing immediate results. Also, the total sample sizes are usually at least 10,000 people, and that allows for substantial analysis of subgroups of the sample and the reasons they voted the way they did. Another advantage for analyzing voting behavior is that we know for sure that the people included in exit polls actually did vote. In other types of national surveys, some people who did not vote will say that they did, because they don't want to look bad.

Exit polls are based on probability sampling. Within each state, the researcher selects precincts through probability sampling, then selects individual voters within the precinct through probability sampling. Those sampling procedures involve other aspects of probability sampling, which we will not discuss here.

SOURCES OF ERROR IN SURVEYS

We have already looked at sampling error, which arises because we are using a sample rather than the entire population. Let's briefly examine some other sources of error in surveys.

Problems in Survey Execution

In sample selection or in carrying out a survey, mistakes can occur and create errors in the results. Some mistakes are fairly harmless because they create only *random error* in the results. Other mistakes, however, are more serious because they create *systematic error* in the results. Although all surveys have such problems, professional polling organizations minimize the occurrence of these errors. Nonprofessional surveys may have them to a much greater extent.

Dishonesty

Dishonesty in surveys can occur at various points. For example, an unethical survey organization might manipulate survey results by various means—although such organizations generally do not last long. Also, interviewers have practiced dishonesty by faking interviews, but professional polling organizations now have techniques to check for faking.

The biggest source of dishonesty in surveys is dishonesty on the part of the respondents. There are basically two types of lying by respondents. *First, a very small percentage of people lie to interviewers just for the sake of lying—they apparently obtain some psychological satisfaction from fooling someone.* Such lying is not a major problem in surveys, partly because few people do it. Also, lying seems to create random error rather than systematic error—one person's lie is canceled by another person's lie rather than adding up to a systematic pattern.

The second type of lying by respondents is more serious and can create systematic error in the results: lying to protect one's image. People might give a false answer to the interviewer because they think the true answer would make them look bad in some way. For example, some people say they voted in an election even when they didn't. Professional polling organizations use various techniques to minimize the motivation for respondents to lie to protect their images. Interviewers are skilled at making respondents feel comfortable during the interview. It is also important that the questions be phrased in such a way that people feel comfortable giving true responses.

Nonresponse

Nonresponse can occur in two basic ways in surveys; both ways cause error. *First, those who are selected for the sample may refuse to take part in the survey.* We cannot replace those people in the sample. We compute the response rate for a survey by dividing the number of respondents by the sample size. If we selected a sample of 1,500 people and 1,200 of them took part in the survey, our response rate would be 1200/1500, or 80%.

The response rate must be as high as possible, because those who do not take part in a survey are often different from those who do. For example, research has shown that those who refuse to take part in surveys usually have less education, income, and political interest. Therefore, survey organizations put a great deal of effort into maximizing the response rates. Traditionally, there has been great success (70% response rates or above) for telephone surveys and face-to-face interviews, and with substantial effort, mail surveys have achieved good response rates. In recent times, however, response rates have been declining, which has become a concern for survey researchers.

The second form of nonresponse occurs when people do not answer particular questions. If people have no opinion on some matter, there is no problem if they don't answer or if they give a "don't know" response. In fact, this is what we want them to do if they do not have an opinion. However, error results when a respondent who has an opinion does not give it. Again, such people may think their opinion would make them look bad in some way. And again, this kind of problem can usually be resolved by wording questions in a nonthreatening way and by the interviewer's skill in making the respondent feel comfortable.

Question-Wording Problems

Badly worded questions create problems for respondents and create error in the survey results. Here are a few types of problems to avoid.

Leading Questions

Leading questions are worded in such a way that the respondent is led to select a particular response. Examples: *Should the courts be allowed to continue coddling criminals? Do you support Senator Smith's fight for honest and efficient government?*

Social Desirability

Social desirability affects survey results when there is a socially accepted response for a question and the respondent selects that response to avoid looking bad. Examples: *Did you vote in the last presidential election? Do you agree or disagree that everyone should have an equal opportunity to get ahead in life?*

Vagueness

When a question is *vague,* different people can interpret it in different ways; that leads to error. Example: *Do you watch the news on television frequently?* Here the word *frequently* is vague; different people will interpret it differently.

Double-Barreled Questions

A *double-barreled question* asks more than one question. The respondent gives a single response, which might or might not be appropriate for both parts of the question. Examples: *Do you agree or disagree that government spending and taxes should be reduced? Do you agree or disagree that people have a right to own guns and that there should be no government regulation of gun ownership?*

TERMS INTRODUCED IN THIS CHAPTER

Haphazard sample	Multistage cluster sampling
Quota sample	Random-digit dialing (RDD)
Probability sample	Exit poll
Accuracy (margin of error)	Leading question
Confidence level	Social desirability
Variability	Double-barreled question
Random sample	Vagueness

FOR FURTHER READING

Textbooks on public opinion usually contain good discussions of sampling that are very readable. For example, see Chapter 2 in Robert S. Erikson and Kent L. Tedin, *American Public Opinion: Its Origins, Content, and Impact,* 6th ed. (Boston: Allyn and Bacon, 2000). Also see Carroll J. Glynn, Susan Herbst, Garrett J. O'Keefe, and Robert Y. Shapiro, *Public Opinion* (Boulder, CO: Westview Press, 1999).

For another readable discussion of sampling, see Chapter 4 in Herbert Asher, *Polling and the Public: What Every Citizen Should Know,* 4th ed. (Washington, DC: CQ Press, 1998). Another readable, helpful, and relevant book is Michael W. Traugott and Paul J. Lavrakas, *The Voter's Guide to Election Polls,* 2nd ed. (Chatham, NJ: Chatham House Publishers, 2000). An interesting treatment of the general topic of survey research—including sampling—is Sondra Miller Rubenstein's *Surveying Public Opinion* (Belmont, CA: Wadsworth, 1995).

Any issue of *Public Opinion Quarterly* (in the periodicals section of your library) contains articles about survey methodology and the results of surveys.

worksheet

CHAPTER 6

NAME: _____

COURSE: _____

DATE: _____

Workbook exercises and software are copyrighted. Copying is prohibited by law.

1. There are many online surveys on the Internet in which people can express their opinions about various political or social issues. After the user completes the survey and clicks [Submit], most of the surveys present immediate results based on those who have taken it so far.

A lot of people take online surveys, but are the "samples" involved in that process representative of the general public? There are at least two questions here. First, are the people who have access to the Internet representative of the general public? Second, are the people who take part in online polls representative of the general "Internet public"? Let's consider the first question.

The 2004 NES survey includes the question "Do you have access to the Internet or the World Wide Web ('the Web')?" Take a look at the results for that question.

> ➤ Data File: **NES 04**
> ➤ Task: **Univariate**
> ➤ Primary Variable: **421) WWW_ACCESS**
> ➤ View: **Pie**

The population represented by the NES sample consists of adults aged 18 and over in the United States. What percentage of adults in the United States said that they did have access to the Internet? _____%

Are the people who lack access to the Internet similar to the people who have access? Let's start by comparing those two groups in terms of age.

> Data File: **NES 04**
> ➤ Task: **Cross-tabulation**
> ➤ Row Variable: **421) WWW_ACCESS**
> ➤ Column Variable: **7) AGE**
> ➤ View: **Tables**
> ➤ Display: **Column %**

Write in the column percentages in the following table:

	< 30 YEARS	30–39	40–49	50-64	65 and UP
YES	_____%	_____%	_____%	_____%	_____%
NO	_____%	_____%	_____%	_____%	_____%

Chapter 6 Worksheet

119

worksheet

Among adults in the United States, are younger people or older people more likely to have Internet access? (Circle one.)

   a. Younger people

   b. Older people

Now let's consider whether education is related to Internet access.

> Data File: **NES 04**
> Task: **Cross-tabulation**
> Row Variable: **421) WWW_ACCESS**
> ➤ Column Variable: **4) EDUCATION**
> ➤ View: **Tables**
> ➤ Display: **Column %**

Write in the column percentages in the following table:

	NO HS DG	HS GRAD	SOME COLLE	COLL GRAD
YES	_____%	_____%	_____%	_____%
NO	_____%	_____%	_____%	_____%

Which of these education groups are least likely to have Internet access?(Circle two.)

   a. No high school degree

   b. High school graduate

   c. Some college

   d. College graduate

Now let's examine the link between family income and Internet access.

> Data File: **NES 04**
> Task: **Cross-tabulation**
> Row Variable: **421) WWW_ACCESS**
> ➤ Column Variable: **3) INCOME**
> ➤ View: **Tables**
> ➤ Display: **Column %**

Write in the column percentages in the following table:

	<$35,000	$35K–$69.9K	>$70,000
YES	_____%	_____%	_____%
NO	_____%	_____%	_____%

On the basis of those results, which of the following statements is most accurate? (Circle one.)

    a. There is no relationship between household income and Internet access.

    b. There is a negative relationship between household income and Internet access.

    c. There is a positive relationship between household income and Internet access.

On the basis of all the preceding analyses, would it be safe to conclude that people who have Internet access are very similar to people who do not have Internet access? (Circle one.)   Yes   No

2. Now let's explore the question of whether people who have Internet access are different from those who do not, in terms of views on political issues. First, read the variable description for 38) ABORTION. Then do the following analysis and fill in the column percentages in the table that follows.

> Data File: **NES 04**
> Task: **Cross-tabulation**
> ➤ Row Variable: **72) ABORTION**
> ➤ Column Variable: **421) WWW_ACCESS**
> ➤ View: **Tables**
> ➤ Display: **Column %**

Write in the column percentages in the following table:

	YES	NO
NOT PERMIT	_____ %	_____ %
LIMITED	_____ %	_____ %
NO RESTRIC	_____ %	_____ %

Which group is more liberal on the abortion issue? (Circle one.)

    a. Neither—the two groups are very similar on this issue

    b. Those who have Internet access

    c. Those who lack Internet access

Given those results, an online Internet survey might give the impression that the public is (circle one)

    a. more liberal on the abortion issue than it actually is.

    b. more conservative on the abortion issue than it actually is.

Abortion is a noneconomic issue. Let's now analyze the relationship between Internet access and an economic issue. First, read the variable description for 42) GOVJOBS. Then do the indicated analysis and fill in the column in the table that follows. We'll also assume that the response "Government should let each person get ahead on their own" represents a conservative response.

worksheet

Data File: **NES 04**
Task: **Cross-tabulation**
➤ Row Variable: **42) GOVJOBS**
➤ Column Variable: **421) WWW_ACCESS**
➤ View: **Tables**
➤ Display: **Column %**

	YES	NO
GUARANTEE	_____%	_____%
IN BETWEEN	_____%	_____%
ON OWN	_____%	_____%

Which group is more conservative on the job/standard of living issue?
(Circle one.)

    a. Neither—the two groups are very similar on this issue

    b. Those who have Internet access

    c. Those who do not have Internet access

Given those results, an online Internet survey might give the impression that
the public is (circle one)

    a. more liberal on the job/standard of living issue than it actually is.

    b. more conservative on the job/standard of living issue than it actually is.

3. The NES 04 data file is a selection of variables from the 2004 American National Election Study, and the GSS 04 data file is a selection of variables from the 2004 National Opinion Research Center's General Social Survey. Both surveys use national probability samples, but they differ in the processes by which they select the samples. Because of those sampling differences, the results of the surveys can differ too. Let's compare the two surveys, starting with the gender variable from the NES.

Data File: **NES 04**
➤ Task: **Univariate**
➤ Primary Variable: **1) SEX**
➤ View: **Pie**

In the NES section of the following table, write in the percentages of males
and females.

	NES RESULTS	GSS RESULTS
MALES	_____%	_____%
FEMALES	_____%	_____%

Now obtain the results for the gender variable from the GSS data file and write those results in the GSS section of the table.

> ➤ Data File: **GSS 04**
> ➤ Task: **Univariate**
> ➤ Primary Variable: **38) SEX**
> ➤ View: **Pie**

Print this pie chart and attach it to your assignment. (**Note:** If you have been instructed not to use the printer, just skip this task.)

Compare the results for this gender variable for these two national surveys. Do both surveys seem to have very similar results for this gender variable?   Yes   No

In both surveys, there are more females than males. There actually are more females than males in the United States, but not to the extent indicated by these results. Write below any reasons you can think of to explain why there are more female than male respondents in these surveys.

_____

_____

_____

4. If a sample overrepresents some kinds of people and underrepresents other kinds of people, it can affect the results. Although both the NES and the GSS are excellent surveys, we saw that females are somewhat overrepresented among the respondents. What effect might this have on the results? For example, would the results concerning a political issue be distorted because there are somewhat more females than there should be in the sample? To check that, let's use one of the political issues on which there seems to be the greatest difference between males and females: pornography.

Using the GSS 04 file, obtain cross-tabulation statistics for the pornography issue. In addition to writing the percentages for males and females, be sure to write the percentages for each category in the TOTAL% column of the following table.

> Data File: **GSS 04**
> ➤ Task: **Cross-tabulation**
> ➤ Row Variable: **197) PORN.LAW?**
> ➤ Column Variable: **38) SEX**
> ➤ View: **Tables**
> ➤ Display: **Column %**

	MALE	FEMALE	TOTAL
YES:ALL	_____%	_____%	_____%
YES:<18	_____%	_____%	_____%
NO LAWS	_____%	_____%	_____%

Compare the results for this pornography issue for males and females to the TOTAL% column. Just look at the *YES:ALL* category. Who is more likely to favor outlawing all pornography?

　　　　Males　　　　Females

In this situation, females are somewhat overrepresented in the sample. However, the degree of overrepresentation is slight. Which of the following statements seems more accurate? (Circle one.)

a. Because females are overrepresented in the sample, the results show slightly greater support for outlawing pornography than would be the case if females and males were each represented completely accurately in the sample.

b. Because females are overrepresented in the sample, the results show substantially greater support for outlawing pornography than would be the case if females and males were each represented completely accurately in the sample.

5. Let's compare the results from the NES and GSS national samples for another variable.

　　　　　　Data File:　**GSS 04**
　　　　　➤ Task:　**Univariate**
　➤ Primary Variable:　**562) PRES00**
　　　　　　➤ View:　**Pie**

In the GSS section of the following table, write in the percentages who voted for Gore, Bush, and Nader.

	NES RESULTS	GSS RESULTS
GORE	_____%	_____%
BUSH	_____%	_____%
NADER	_____%	_____%

Now obtain the results from the NES survey and write the percentages in the NES section of the table.

　　➤ Data File:　**NES 04**
　　　　➤ Task:　**Univariate**
　➤ Primary Variable:　**12) PRES 00**
　　　　➤ View:　**Pie**

Compare the results from these two national samples. Which of the following seems to be the most accurate statement based on that comparison? (Circle one.)

    a. The results for the two surveys are substantially different from one another.

    b. The results for the two surveys are almost exactly the same.

    c. The results for the two surveys show the same basic patterns of results, but there are small differences between them because of sampling error and differences in sample selection processes.

6. If a sampling procedure were set up in such a way that people with higher education were heavily overrepresented in the sample, how might that affect the results? For example, let's say that someone selected a sample in such a way that only college graduates were included in the sample. How might that affect the results? Let's use the issue of religious observances in the public schools as an example. Begin by obtaining univariate statistics for this issue for the whole GSS sample.

    ➤ Data File: **GSS**
    ➤ Task: **Univariate**
  ➤ Primary Variable: **126) SCHOOLPRAY**
    ➤ View: **Pie**

What percentage of the respondents approved of the Supreme Court's rulings on religious observances in the public schools?   _____%

Would you expect that people with a college education would be more likely or less likely than the general public to approve of the Supreme Court's ruling that state and local governments could not require religious observances in the public schools? Circle the statement below that is closest to your own expectation on this. Then explain in one sentence why you think it is correct.

    a. People with college degrees are more likely to approve of the Supreme Court's ruling on religious observances in the public schools.

    b. People with college degrees are less likely to approve of the Supreme Court's ruling on religious observances in the public schools.

    c. There is not much difference on this issue between those with college degrees and the general public.

Reason:

_____

_____

_____

_____

Now obtain the results for just those respondents who have completed four or more years of college.

> Data File: **GSS**
> Task: **Univariate**
> Primary Variable: **126) SCHOOLPRAY**
> ➤ Subset Variable: **34) EDCAT**
> ➤ Subset Category: **Include: 3) COLL EDUC**
> ➤ View: **Pie**

> **The option for selecting a subset variable is located on the same screen you use to select other variables. For this example, select 34) EDCAT as a subset variable. A window will appear that shows you the categories of the subset variable. Select 3) COLL EDUC as your subset category and choose the [Include] option. Then click [OK] and continue as usual. With this particular subset selected, the results will be limited to the college graduates in the sample. *The subset continues until you exit the task, delete all subset variables, or clear all variables.***

Among the respondents who have finished four or more years of college, what percentage approves of the Supreme Court rulings on religious observances in the public schools?   _____%

Compare the results for those with four or more years of college with the previous results for the total sample. Is there a substantial difference between the two sets of results?   Yes   No

If college-educated people were heavily overrepresented in a sample, how would that affect the conclusion that might be reached about public opinion on this issue?

_____

_____

_____

7. If a survey oversamples people with higher incomes, what kind of effect might that have on survey results? We might expect that would have the greatest impact on results concerning economic issues. Let's examine the univariate statistics for an economic issue from the NES 04 data file.

> ➤ Data File: **NES 04**
> ➤ Task: **Univariate**
> ➤ Primary Variable: **411) SS$_PRIV**
> ➤ View: **Pie**

What percentage of respondents would like the government to privatize a portion of their social security?   _____%

Now let's see what might happen if a sample had been selected in which those with higher incomes were heavily overrepresented.

Data File:	**NES 04**
Task:	**Univariate**
Primary Variable:	**411) SS$_PRIV**
➤ Subset Variable:	**3) INCOME**
➤ Subset Category:	**Include: 3) $70,000+**
➤ View:	**Pie**

Here we have selected those cases that are in the (roughly) upper third in terms of family income. Among those cases, what percentage would favor the privatization of social security?   _____%

Now let's compare this to the views of those with lower incomes.

Data File:	**NES 04**
Task:	**Univariate**
Primary Variable:	**411) SS$_PRIV**
Subset Variable:	**3) INCOME**
➤ Subset Category:	**Include: 1) <$35,000**
➤ View:	**Pie**

Here we have selected those cases that are in the (roughly) bottom third in terms of family income. Among those cases, what percentage would favor the privatization of social security?   _____%

On the basis of those results, if a sample heavily overrepresented upper-income people, which of the following would likely occur? (Circle one.)

   a. It would somewhat overestimate the extent to which people support social security privatization.

   b. It would somewhat underestimate the extent to which people support social security privatization.

   c. It wouldn't make any difference at all in the results.

8. Let's look at the wording of two questions in the GSS data file.

➤ Data File:	**GSS**
➤ Task:	**Univariate**

Look at the variable description for 98) COMMUN.SP. It reads: Suppose an admitted Communist wanted to make a speech in your community. Should he be allowed to speak or not?

Look also at the variable description for 104) HOMO. SP. It reads: Consider a man who admits that he is a homosexual. Suppose this admitted homosexual wanted to make a speech in your community. Should he be allowed to speak or not?

 **worksheet**

 **CHAPTER 6**

These two questions have a wording problem that might lead some people to be more likely to give a negative response to the questions than they would be if the wording problem did not exist. (**Note:** Although survey researchers recognize that this wording problem exists, they still use the original wording in order to make comparisons with the results of earlier studies.) What is the wording problem for those two questions?

_____

_____

_____

_____

_____

_____

That's all for this lesson.

Research Methods in Political Science

CHAPTER 7

Data Preparation and Entry

Tasks: New File, Define & Edit Variables, Enter Data, Univariate
Data Files: SENATORS (created by student)

INTRODUCTION

This chapter will show you how to create a MicroCase data file. The major steps in this are

- organizing and coding the data

- creating the file

- defining the variables

- entering the actual data

We have looked at several topics related to the collection of data in one way or another, and you are now familiar with the MicroCase data files. But let's say you have a collection of data—such as a set of questionnaires you have administered to people, or information you have collected about cities in the United States, or roll-call votes from your state legislature. How do you move this data into a computer data file so that you can analyze it? To fully understand research methods in political science, you must know how to get the original raw data into a data file.

This chapter will take you through the process of creating an actual data file in a step-by-step fashion. However, to show you how to create a data file without taking up too much of your time, we will use just a few variables for a small number of cases. Specifically, we will use just 6 variables for 10 U.S. senators from the 109th Congress (2005–2006). Even though you will be creating just a small file, if you understand these step-by-step instructions, then you will also understand how to create a huge data file with thousands of variables and cases.

After you have been through the process of learning how to create a MicroCase data file, your instructor may want you to create a larger data file. For this purpose, Appendix B includes many variables for all 100 senators from the 109th Congress. Alternately, you can collect information for more-recent votes on bills in Congress from publications such as the *Congressional Record,* the *Congressional Quarterly Weekly Report,* and the *Congressional Quarterly Almanac.* You can also find information on the World Wide Web. Another alternative is to collect a different kind of data (e.g., from a survey of students) and create a data file with those data.

With your Student Version of MicroCase, you can create a data file with as many as 50 variables for as many as 100 cases. After you have created a data file—such as the small file you will create to learn the process—you can create a new data file, which will replace the old one. Keep in mind that the new file you create will replace any previous file you have created—so make sure that you don't replace a file that you've created until you're finished with it. The data entry option will not affect the original data files (GSS, and so on) that you received with Student MicroCase—you cannot accidentally (or intentionally) replace one of those files using the data entry feature.

ORGANIZING AND CODING THE DATA

No matter what kind of data you are using—survey data, aggregate data, public records data, or any other kind—you need to organize it before creating a data file. You need to know what variables you will be using and how you are going to *code* (assign numbers to) those observations that are not already in numeric form.

Coding is the assignment of numbers to the categories or values of a variable.

For example, if you have a question that asks whether people favor or oppose gun-control legislation, you need to assign a number to the *favor* response and a number to the *oppose* response. You also must assign numbers to those who don't answer the question and to those who give the "don't know" response. Interval and ratio variables are already in numeric form (e.g., education measured as the actual number of years of school), but categoric (nominal and ordinal) variables must be coded.

You also need to decide what to treat as *missing* for each variable. For example, if you have a question concerning political party preference, you would certainly treat the *No Answer* category as missing, but what about those who said "don't know" and those who identify with an extremely small political party? If you specify certain observations as missing for a particular variable, then those observations will be excluded from the analysis of that particular variable.

For some variables, you must decide whether to truncate the values. For example, if you had data for states, would you want to use actual population size or population in thousands? How do you handle a variable whose values have decimal points? For example, if you have for each state the number of abortions per 1,000 people, do you round off each one to the nearest whole number, treat it as a proportion, treat it as a percentage, or what? You must make decisions about what will be most useful.

Once you have made those decisions and coded the data, you need to make sure that they are organized in a convenient format so that, when the time comes to do so, it will be relatively easy to enter the data into the file. For purposes of the file you are about to create, we will use the data in Table 7.1. We have already coded the party affiliation of the senators as

     1 = Democrat   2 = Republican

Further, the two roll-call votes are coded as

     0 = No   1 = Yes

Table 7.1 Data for Selected Variables for 10 Senators for the 109th Congress (2005–2006)

Name	Party	Percent of Total Vote Received in Most Recent Election	State	Resolution Calling for a Phased Withdrawel from Iraq	Amendment for a Program to Reduce Greenhouse Gas Emissions
Bayh	Dem	62	14	Y	Y
Bond	Rep	56	25	N	N
Boxer	Dem	58	5	Y	N
Cantwell	Dem	49	47	Y	Y
Dodd	Dem	66	7	Y	Y
Gregg	Rep	66	29	N	Y
Inouye	Dem	76	11	Y	Y
McCain	Rep	77	3	N	Y
Stevens	Rep	77	2	N	N
Voinovich	Rep	64	35	N	N

After the data are organized, you are ready to go through the three stages of creating a data file: creating the file, defining the variables, and entering the data.

After a data file has been set up and the data have been entered, you will need to check the data for errors and correct any that appear. That process is called *data cleaning*.

Data cleaning is the process of checking a data file for errors and correcting the errors.

In the instructions that follow, we will indicate how certain types of data entry errors can be either avoided or detected. Please go to the computer that you will be using. We will go through the process of creating a MicroCase data file in a step-by-step fashion.

INSTRUCTIONS FOR CREATING A MICROCASE FILE

Student MicroCase allows you to create a data file with as many as 50 variables for as many as 100 cases. You can create only one data file at a time. If you create a second data file, the second file replaces the first one. It is important to note that if you replace a data file, that must be done within Student MicroCase using the NEW FILE option. *Do not* use the <Delete> key or the recycling bin (or any other Windows operation) to delete a MicroCase file. We will return to that task in the section "How to Replace a File You Created with a Newer File."

Step 1: Create a New Data File

From the DATA MANAGEMENT menu, select the NEW FILE task. The File Description box asks for a description (as many as 80 characters long) of the data file. For this example, type **Data for U.S. Senators in the 109th Congress.** Then press <Enter> or click [Next] and then [Finish] to return to the main menu.

Now press the <Tab> key to go to the File Description box. If you accidentally pressed <Enter> instead of using the <Tab> key, the program will ask whether you want to give a file description.

You have now created a MicroCase file. Note that the new file name appears on the top line of the screen. In the following steps, you will define the variables and enter the data.

Step 2: Define the Variables

For each variable, you need to provide certain information (e.g., a variable name). Select the DEFINE & EDIT VARIABLES task. The cursor is in the Variable Name box, and the term *undefined* is highlighted. The program is asking for a name for the first variable in the data file. *A variable name consists of 1–10 characters, including any blank spaces in the name.* A variable name should give a quick idea of what the variable is all about. You have already seen many examples of names (e.g., EDUCATION, POLPARTY) used in the data files.

For the first variable, we will give each senator a case identification number: 1 for the first senator, 2 for the second senator, and so on, to 10 for the last senator. Let's call this first variable CASE ID. So, type **CASE ID** in the Variable Name box and press the <Tab> key to continue to the Variable Description box. **Note:** If you accidentally press <Enter> here instead of the <Tab> key, the program will operate on the assumption that you are finished with the first variable, and it will take you to the second variable. If you accidentally do that, simply click the left arrow under the Current Variable Number in order to return to Variable 1. Then move to the Variable Description box.

The variable description indicates what the variable is all about—you have seen many variable descriptions in the MicroCase data files by this point. For this first variable, type **Case identification number for senators** and press the <Tab> key to go to the next box. Again, if you accidentally press <Enter> rather than <Tab>, you can return to Variable 1 by clicking the left arrow under the Current Variable Number box.

The program now asks for the minimum and the maximum values for the variable. This can help you to avoid errors when you enter the data, because if you type a value outside the possible range, the program will alert you. For the CASE ID variable, we have 10 senators and will assign the first senator the number 1 and the last senator the number 10. Thus, for the minimum, type **1** and press the <Tab> key. For the maximum, type **10** and press the <Tab> key.

The program then asks how many digits there are to the right of the decimal point. That is not relevant here, so press the <Tab> key again to go to the next box.

Now you can give a 1–10 character label for each category of the variable. Student MicroCase allows you to label any categoric variable that has 10 or fewer categories. For the labels, we will use the names of the senators (note that we would need to abbreviate any name that exceeded 10 characters). For the first category label, type **Bayh** and press either <Enter> or <Tab>. For the second category label, type **Bond** and press either <Enter> or <Tab>. Continue that process until you reach the last one, **Voinovich.**

At this point, you have finished defining Variable 1 and are ready for the next variable. Before moving on, however, check the information on the screen for accuracy. If there is a mistake, simply position the cursor over the mistake and correct it. Then, to continue to the next variable, click the [Continue] button in the upper right area of the screen.

The second variable is the political party affiliation of the senator. Let's call this variable PARTY. Type **PARTY** in the Variable Name box and press the <Tab> key. For the variable description, type **Senator's political party affiliation,** and then press the <Tab> key.

This variable is coded as 1 for Democrat and 2 for Republican. So, for the minimum value, enter **1** and press the <Tab> key. For the maximum value, enter **2** and press the <Tab> key.

Press the <Tab> key again to skip the prompt about decimal digits. Then type **Democrat** for the first category label, press the <Tab> key, type **Republican** for the second category label, and check the information on the screen for accuracy. If everything is accurate, click [Continue] to go to Variable 3.

The third variable is the percentage of the total vote received by the senator in his or her most recent election. Let's call this variable PCT VOTE. So type **PCT VOTE** in the Variable Name box and press the <Tab> key. For the variable description, type **Percentage of the total vote received by the senator in his or her most recent election,** and press the <Tab> key.

For the third variable the numbers might vary quite a bit, and it might be difficult to determine the minimum and maximum values if we were working with a large data file. So, press the <Tab> key twice to skip the questions about the minimum and maximum values.

This variable has no digits to the right of the decimal point. So, type **0** in the Decimal Digits box and press the <Tab> key. Note that the program does not ask for category labels—there are no categories involved in this ratio variable. So, press [Continue] to go to Variable 4.

Variable 4 is an identification number for the senator's state. The states were arranged alphabetically and numbered from 1 to 50. For the variable name, type **STATE** and press the <Tab> key. For the variable description, type **State identification number (1 = Alabama, 2 = Alaska, 3 = Arizona,** etc.) and press the <Tab> key.

For the minimum, type **1** and press the <Tab> key. For the maximum, type **50** and press the <Tab> key.

There is no decimal point here, so the next box is not relevant. Further, you cannot assign names to the categories (state names) of this variable. Student MicroCase does not allow you to assign category names to variables that have more than 10 categories. Although we have only 10 cases (senators) here, we indicated that there could be 50 categories (senators' state names). So, click on [Continue] to go to Variable 5.

Variable 5 consists of the senators' votes on a resolution calling for a phased withdrawel of troops from Iraq. Let's call this variable TROOPS OUT. Type **TROOPS OUT** and press the <Tab> key.

For the description, type the following: **A vote on a resolution calling for a phased withdrawal of troops from Iraq (6/22/05).** This roll-call vote and the next one are both coded 0 for *no* and 1 for *yes*. So, type **0** for the minimum, press <Tab>, type **1** for the maximum, and press <Tab> *twice* to skip the decimal digits box.

For the value 0, type the category label **No** and press <Tab>. For the value 1, type the category label **Yes** and press <Tab>. After checking the information on the screen for accuracy, click on [Continue] to go to the next variable.

The last variable (number 6) is a vote on an amendment to reduce greenhouse gas emissions. For the variable name, type **GREENHOUSE** and press <Tab>. For the variable description, type **GREENHOUSE—An amendment to provide for a program to accelerate the reduction of greenhouse gas emissions in the United States. (5. Amendment 826 to HR 6 failed 6/22/05).** Press <Tab>.

Enter **0** for the minimum and **1** for the maximum. Skip the decimal digits box, enter **No** for the category name for the value 0, and enter **Yes** for the value 1. Then check the information for accuracy.

At this point you have finished defining all the variables. To return to the main menu, click the [Menu] button.

Step 3: Enter the Data
You are now ready to enter the data. Click the ENTER DATA task, note that the format option is set for Grid Entry, and click [OK].

The screen presents a data entry matrix. Click on the cell in the upper left to position the cursor there. That cell is for Variable 1 (CASE ID) for the first case. We are simply assigning a number to each senator, ranging from number 1 for the first senator to number 10 for the last senator. So, type **1** (for Senator Bayh) and press <Enter>.

The cursor moved to the next cell, which represents the second variable (PARTY) for the first case. Referring back to Table 7.1, you will see that Senator Bayh is a Democrat. We coded Democrats as 1 and Republicans as 2. So, type **1** (for Democrat) and press <Enter>.

For variable 3 (PCT VOTE), Senator Bayh received 62% of the vote. So, type **62** and press <Enter>. (**Note:** Do not type the percentage sign.)

For Variable 4 (STATE), Senator Bayh is from Indiana, which is state number 14 (listed alphabetically). So, type **14** and press <Enter>.

For Variable 5 (TROOPS OUT), Senator Bayh voted *yes*. We are coding a *no* vote as 0 and a *yes* vote as 1. So, type **1** and press <Enter>.

For Variable 6 (GREENHOUSE), Senator Bayh voted *yes*. So, type **1** and press <Enter>.

At this point, you have entered all data for the first case, Senator Bayh. Check the data for accuracy. If you made a mistake, you can position the cursor over the mistake and correct it.

Now we are ready for the second case, Senator Bond. Make sure the cursor is in the cell for Variable 1 (CASE ID), case number 2. For the case identification number, type **2** and press <Enter>.

Senator Bond is a Republican, so enter **2** for PARTY. For PCT VOTE, type 56 and press <Enter>. Senator Bond is from state number 25 (Missouri). So, for STATE, type **25** and press <Enter>.

Senator Bond voted *no* on TROOPS OUT, so type **0** and press <Enter>. Senator Bond voted *no* on GREENHOUSE, so type **0** and press <Enter>.

At this point, you should understand the process, so read the rest of this paragraph first and then enter the data for all the other cases except the last one (Senator Voinovich). If any of the senators did not vote, indicate this by leaving it blank. *Do not enter data for the last case (Senator Voinovich), because we will use this last case to demonstrate another feature of data entry in MicroCase.*

When you have finished entering all the data (except for Senator Voinovich), click [Menu] to return to the main menu. Then click the [Save] button to save your data file.

Question Entry
At this point you should be back on the main menu. Now let's enter the data for the last senator, Senator Voinovich, but we will do it somewhat differently to demonstrate another possibility. Select the ENTER DATA task again and note that the default format is Grid Entry. This time we will use Question Entry. So select the [Question Entry (with grid)] option and click [OK].

Note that the cell for Variable 1, case number 10, is emphasized. If that is not the situation, please click in the cell to select it. You will also see that a box in the upper area of the screen contains the names of the senators. Instead of typing in the case identification number for Senator Voinovich, simply double-click his name. His case identification number is entered for Variable 1, and the cursor moves to the next variable. Senator Voinovich is a Republican. Instead of typing **2** in the cell, simply double-click the *Republican* category in the box. The program will automatically enter the code 2 in the cell for Variable 2.

The next variable does not consist of categories, so that method does not help us here. Simply type in Senator Voinovich's percentage of the vote, 64, in this box, and it is immediately entered into the cell for Variable 3. Press <Enter> and type in the state number, 35, and press <Enter> again.

For the last two variables, the two roll-call votes, you can enter the data for this case by double-clicking *No* for Senator Voinovich's vote on the Iraq resolution and double-clicking *No* for his vote on greenhouse gas emissions. The program automatically inserts the 1 for the *yes* vote and the 0 for the *no* vote.

This questionnaire method of data entry can be quite convenient for entering data from questionnaires or for other situations in which the data are set up in categories.

We have now finished entering all the data for the data file. So click [Menu] to return to the main menu. Then click [Save] to save your modified data file.

Rekey Verification

When you enter data, there is always the possibility that you might make mistakes. In rekey verification, simply reenter the data and the program checks these data against the original data that you entered. If you made a mistake in entering the data the first time, you will likely discover your mistake by using this method.

Let's demonstrate this by reentering the data for the first case, Senator Bayh. Select ENTER DATA again, select the [Enable Rekey Verification] option, and click [OK].

Click in the first cell (Variable 1, case 1) and enter **1** for Variable 1, the case identification number. Because that is the same value that you originally entered for Senator Bayh, the program will simply continue to the next data entry when you press <Enter>. Senator Bayh is a Democrat and you entered 1 for the PARTY variable before. However, to see how the rekey verification process works, type **2** and press <Enter>. Note that the program informs you that there is a mismatch between the value that you originally entered (1) and the value that you just entered (2). The program asks you to choose between the existing value and the new value. If this were a real error, you would check to see which value is correct and select the correct value. For this example, select the existing value and click [OK].

For the next variable, type **55.5** and press <Enter>. The program alerts you of the mismatch between the original, existing value (62) and the value you just typed (55.5). Again, select the correct value (62).

After you finish reentering the data for the first case, click the [Menu] button to return to the main menu. Although we have not made any changes (unless you actually did make errors in entering the data for the first case), you would usually click [Save] to save the changes at this point.

Modifying the File You Created

After creating a data file, you might need to modify it in some way. For example, you might need to correct errors, add new variables, or add data.

Adding Data or Changing Data

To add new data or to change the data already in the file, make sure the file is open and then select the ENTER DATA task. Select the format (Question Entry or Grid Entry) that you want to use and click [OK]. The program will automatically take you to the end of the data file, and if you are adding new data (more cases), you are ready to continue. If you are changing data (e.g., to correct errors), then you can move about in the data file by clicking on the scroll bar and then placing the cursor wherever you want it to be. When you are finished, click the [Menu] button. Then click the [Save] button to save your modified data file.

Modifying a Data File

If you need to modify a MicroCase data file (e.g., adding variables or correcting errors in variable descriptions or labels), begin by selecting the DEFINE & EDIT VARIABLES task. The program will automatically take you to the next variable to be created. If you are adding new variables, you can simply continue from this point. However, if you need to modify existing variables, select the variable you want to modify by clicking on the arrow buttons under the Current Variable Number box. Thus, if you wanted to select Variable 4 (STATE), you would click on the left arrow under the Current Variable Number box until the number 4 appeared.

After finishing any modifications, click the [Menu] button to return to the main menu. Then click the [Save] button to save your modified data file.

How to Replace a File You Created with a Newer File

At this point you have created a demonstration file called SENATORS which you will use in the following worksheet section. When you are ready to create a file of your own, how do you replace the SENATORS file with your own file? Simply create a new file by clicking on the NEW FILE option and answering yes to the question "Do you want to replace the existing file?" The new file will replace the old file.

Student MicroCase allows you to create only one new file at a time. To create a second file, you must replace the first file you created using Student MicroCase's NEW FILE option.

TERMS INTRODUCED IN THIS CHAPTER

Coding   Data cleaning

FOR FURTHER READING

A very readable discussion of coding and data files is Chapter 5 in Larry D. Hall and Kimball P. Marshall, *Computing for Social Research: Practical Approaches* (Belmont, CA: Wadsworth, 1992).

Further information on coding can be found in pages 311–319 in Charles H. Backstrom and Gerald Hursh-César, *Survey Research,* 2nd ed. (New York: John Wiley & Sons, 1981).

worksheet

NAME: _____

COURSE: _____

DATE: _____

Now you are ready to take a look at the data file you created in the preliminary part of this chapter and answer some easy questions about it.

1. Let's first look at PCT VOTE.

    > Data File: **SENATORS**
    > Task: **Univariate**
    > Primary Variable: **3) PCT VOTE**
    > View: **Statistics (Summary)**

    What was the mean percentage of the vote received by these senators?   _____%

    Were there any missing cases for this variable?   Yes   No

2. Now obtain univariate statistics for the PARTY variable.

    Data File: **SENATORS**
    Task: **Univariate**
    > Primary Variable: **2) PARTY**
    > View: **Pie**

    How many of the senators are Democrats?   _____

    What percentage of the senators are Republicans?   _____%

3. Look now at the vote on the resolution to withdraw the troops from Iraq.

    Data File: **SENATORS**
    Task: **Univariate**
    > Primary Variable: **5) TROOPS OUT**
    > View: **Pie**

    How many senators voted in favor of this resolution?   _____

    What percentage of the senators voted in favor of this resolution? _____%

4. The last variable in the file represents the vote on the amendment to reduce greenhouse gasses.

> Data File: **SENATORS**
> Task: **Univariate**
> ➤ Primary Variable: **6) GREENHOUSE**
> ➤ View: **Pie**

How many senators voted in favor of this amendment?   _____

How many senators have missing data (did not vote) on this amendment?   _____

5. So far you have been examining the data for the variables one at a time. Student MicroCase also allows you to look at the data for all the variables.

From the FILE & DATA MENU, make sure that the SENATORS file is open and then select the LIST DATA task. Click [OK] in response to the pop-up screen that says that all cases and variables will be listed. The data matrix will appear on the screen. Print this data matrix. When the **Print** screen appears, look at the print range options, select All if it is not already selected, and click [OK]. (**Note:** If your computer is not connected to a printer, or if you have been instructed not to use the printer, just skip this task.) Attach this printout to your assignment.

You can also obtain a codebook for any or all of the variables in your data file. A codebook lists summary information for each variable. From the FILE & DATA menu, click the CODEBOOK task. On the screen that appears, you can elect to obtain the codebook for all variables, or you can select a list of variables. For our purposes, click [OK] to accept the default (all variables). The screen will show you the name, description, range, and distribution for the first variable. Click on the right arrow underneath the Variable Number box on the left side of the screen, and the screen will now show you information for the second variable. Click the right arrow again and the screen presents information for the third variable. Select the option to print this codebook. When the program asks you to select the variables you want to print, select the option for all variables and click [OK]. (**Note:** If you have been instructed not to use the printer, just skip this task.) Attach this printout to your assignment.

That's all for this lesson.

CHAPTER 8

Descriptive Statistics

Tasks: Univariate, Mapping
Data Files: NES 04, GSS, GLOBAL, NES

INTRODUCTION

To demonstrate further the statistical description of variables, this chapter will

- provide additional demonstration of the presentation of frequency distributions

- examine measures of central tendency (averages)

- describe measures of variability within a variable

In political research, we are engaged in *description* and *explanation* of political reality. This chapter focuses on the statistical description of variables. In examining bar graphs, pie charts, and frequency distributions, you have already begun the statistical description of variables. We will elaborate on this process and will look at two types of summary statistics used in describing a variable: measures of *central tendency* (averages) and measures of *variability*.

Although this chapter and several others deal with statistical concepts, we will not go into detail about the *mathematical* aspects of these topics. The purpose of this book is to help you understand research methods in political science, not to give you a course in statistics. Thus, although we will deal with statistical ideas and techniques, we will limit discussion of the mathematical aspects of these topics to what is needed for a basic understanding of them.

THE PRESENTATION OF FREQUENCY DISTRIBUTIONS

A *frequency distribution* is a listing of the values of a variable along with the number (and/or percentage) of cases for each value.

You have already seen frequency distributions in MicroCase, and you have seen how a frequency distribution can be presented graphically in a bar graph or pie chart. Here we will first demonstrate how tables are usually set up to present frequency distribution results in reports. Then we will demonstrate that more than one frequency distribution might be reported in a single table. At the end of this discussion, you will understand frequency distributions better and will be able to set up a frequency distribution table for a report.

A Table with a Single Frequency Distribution

How interested are Americans in political campaigns? The graphic below shows the summary view from the UNIVARIATE task for a frequency distribution for the variable 60) INTEREST? from the NES file. We will use this as an example to demonstrate how to present a frequency distribution for a single variable in a table for a report.

➤ Data File: **NES 04**
➤ Task: **Univariate**
➤ Primary Variable: **60) INTEREST?**
➤ View: **Statistics (Summary)**

INTEREST? -- Some people don't pay much attention to political campaigns. How about you? Would you say that you have been VERY MUCH interested, SOMEWHAT interested or NOT MUCH interested in the political campaigns so far this year?

Mean:	1.568	Std.Dev.:	0.654	N:	1066
Median:	1.000	Variance:	0.428	Missing:	146

99% confidence interval +/- mean: 1.516 to 1.619
95% confidence interval +/- mean: 1.528 to 1.607

Category	Freq.	%	Cum.%	Z-Score
1) VERY	558	52.3	52.3	-0.868
2) SOMEWHAT	411	38.6	90.9	0.661
3) NOT MUCH	97	9.1	100.0	2.190

The *Frequency* column shows how many respondents said "very much interested," how many said "somewhat interested," and how many said "not much interested." The % column shows what percentage said "very much interested," what percentage said "somewhat interested," and so on. The *Cum. %* (cumulative percentage) column adds the percentages as you move from one row down to the next. The other information is not important for our present purposes. Let's go through the steps to use this information from this view to set up a table in a typical format used for a report.

Labels

If a table is part of a series of two or more tables, it needs a label to distinguish it from the other table or tables. Such a label can be simply Table 1, or Table A, or Table 5.1 (to stand for Table 1 of Chapter 5). For this example, we will create a table and label it Table 8.1 to show that it is the first table in Chapter 8.

Title

A table needs a title that describes its contents so that the reader can see quickly what information the table presents. Let's title this particular table *Americans' Interest in Political Campaigns.*

A Column for the Values of the Variable

We need a column to list the values of the variable. Usually we use frequency distributions only for variables that have categories (nominal or ordinal variables) or that have a relatively small set of numeric values (e.g., a ratio variable, measuring political knowledge, that ranges from 0 to 6.)

In our present example, the column for the values of the variable will contain three categories: *Very much interested, Somewhat interested,* and *Not much interested.* Such a column may or may not have a label at the top, depending on whether a label is needed to make it clear. In this particular example, we do not need a label.

Table 8.1 Americans' Interest in Political Campaigns

	Frequency	Percentage
Very much interested	558	52.3%
Somewhat interested	411	38.6%
Not much interested	97	9.1%
Totals	1,066	100.0%

Source: 2004 American National Election Study (NES).

Question: *Some people don't pay much attention to political campaigns. How about you? Would you say that you have been very much interested, somewhat interested, or not much interested in the political campaigns so far this year?*

Column for Frequency and Percentage

We need one column to list the frequency—the number of cases—for each value of the variable and another column that converts this frequency into a percentage.

A Totals Row

Below the frequencies and percentages, we need a row that lists the totals. This will show the total number of cases included in the table, and it will show the total of the percentages, which will add up to 100% plus-or-minus a small amount that represents rounding error.

Source and Other Information

We usually need to specify the source of the data in the table so that others can easily identify it. Also, we might need to give other information about the data. For example, if we are using survey data, we usually need to present the exact survey question in the table. Whatever the type of data, we should give readers enough information in the table or in the text (or both) to easily determine what the data represent.

In this example, we need to specify the source: the 2004 American National Election Study (NES). We also need to present the question that was used. Our final table is Table 8.1.

A Table with More Than One Frequency Distribution

Sometimes we present more than one frequency distribution in the same table. Besides saving room, that makes it convenient to compare frequency distributions for different variables. For this example, let's use several questions from the GSS file that are concerned with attitudes toward spending on certain areas or problems in society.

Note first that the following table is labeled Table 8.2 to show that it is the second table in Chapter 8. The title specifies the content of the table. Note also that below the table, we have specified the source of the data and the wording of the question. In this table, we have presented frequency distributions for three spending areas. For each variable, the table presents the three response categories (*Too much, About right, Too little*), the percentage of the survey respondents selecting each response category, and the N (number of cases) for each response category.

Table 8.2 Distribution of Attitudes toward Spending on Certain Problems in the United States

Problem	Too much		About right		Too little	
	Percentage	N	Percentage	N	Percentage	N
Defense	40.8%	588	32.9%	475	26.3%	379
Crime	6.6%	95	31.5%	456	61.9%	897
Health	5.2%	75	19.4%	282	75.4%	1094

Source: 2006 National Opinion Research Center (NORC) General Social Survey (GSS).

Question: *We are faced with many problems in this country, none of which can be solved easily or inexpensively. I'm going to name some of these problems, and for each one, I'd like you to tell me whether you think we're spending too much money on it, too little money, or about the right amount.* The three areas included in this table are the military, armaments, and defense; halting the rising crime rate; and improving and protecting the nation's health.

Given that table, we can easily compare results for the different spending areas. We can see, for example, that a large majority thinks that more money should be spent on health and dealing with crime. On the other hand, only 26.3% think that too little is being spent on defense.

That is only one of various ways in which more than one frequency distribution can be presented in a single table. It is important that the table be readable, that it provide adequate information on its content, and that it not be set up in such a way that it is misleading.

MEASURES OF CENTRAL TENDENCY

A frequency distribution (where appropriate) is usually the first way in which we describe a variable. The second way is to provide one or more measures of central tendency (averages) for the variable. There are three kinds of averages: the *mode,* the *median,* and the *mean.* Each type of average gives somewhat different information. There are also limitations—depending on the level of measurement of the data—on the situations in which a given kind of average can be used.

Mode

The ***mode*** of a variable is the value that occurs most often in the data for that variable.

The mode is the simplest of the three averages. In a set of data for a variable, the mode is the value (either a category or a numeric value) associated with the most cases. For an example, turn back to Table 8.1. For this political campaign interest variable with three categories (*Not much interested, Somewhat interested,* and *Very much interested*), the category that survey respondents chose the most is the *Very much interested* category. Thus, the *Very much interested* category is the mode. If that category were assigned a number, then we would normally use that number as the mode.

Let's take another example. Suppose you have the following set of political knowledge scores for a small sample of people: 8, 9, 3, 5, 6, 5, 5, 4, 5, 7, 5, 1, 5, and 2. In this situation, more cases have the number 5 than any other number. Thus, the mode is 5.

The mode can be used with all levels of measurement. However, it is most useful for nominal and ordinal variables. *Of the three measures of central tendency, the mode is the only measure that appropriately can be used when the variable is nominal.* In many situations, the mode is not helpful in describing interval or ratio variables because of the large number of different values these variables can take.

Median

The **median** for a variable is the value of the variable that has 50% of the cases above it and 50% below it.

The median shows where the central tendency is for the distribution of the cases. The median can be used for ordinal, interval, and ratio variables but not for nominal variables.

Let's take a simple example. Suppose you've measured political knowledge for a sample of people based on the number of questions about politics they answered correctly. Each person has a score between 1 and 10. Suppose we have the following scores for these people: 4, 6, 7, 8, and 9. The median here is 7, the middle score. Suppose, however, that we add a score to this set. We now have the following scores: 3, 4, 6, 7, 8, and 9. There is no actual middle score in this situation, so we compute the median as the midpoint between the two middle scores. Thus, the median here is 6.5.

Mean

The **mean** for a variable is computed by adding the values of the variable for all the cases and dividing this sum by the number of cases.

The mean gives the mathematical average for interval and ratio variables, but sometimes we bend the rules and use it for ordinal variables as well. It can be useful to look at both the mean and the median for interval and ratio variables. The median may give us a better idea of the typical case, whereas the mean gives us a mathematical average of all the values. The difference is that the mean can be affected by extreme cases. Suppose you have a sample of 1,200 people, and some of them are millionaires. In that situation, the mean income would give us information about the sample, but the median might be more appropriate if we wanted to know about the typical member of the group.

Let's say you have the following set of political knowledge scores for five people: 8, 5, 6, 9, and 7. To compute the mean here, we first find the sum of the scores—here it is 35. Then we divide that sum by the number of cases—here we have 5 cases. Thus, $35 \div 5 = 7$, and the mean is 7.

In some situations (e.g., the *normal distribution,* which we will discuss shortly), the mean, median, and mode are all the same for a variable. In most situations, however, each of those averages will provide a somewhat different perspective on the data. For that reason, it is useful to have a frequency distribution to examine along with the averages.

MEASURES OF VARIABILITY
In describing a variable, we want to know the central tendency, but we also want to know how much variability (variation) there is in the variable. Suppose, for example, that we measure political knowledge for a group of people. We want to know the average score, but we also want to know how much variation there is in the scores.

Let's say that the mean score for a political knowledge test is 6 (out of a possible 10). How much variation is there in the scores? Did just about everyone get a score of 6? Were there two clusters of scores—one cluster very low and the other cluster very high—that simply averaged out to 6? Was there something approaching a *normal distribution* (the bell-shaped curve)? In response to such questions, we need to describe statistically the degree of variation within variables. For this, we use measures of variability, also called measures of dispersion.

Usually we do not describe statistically the variation within nominal or ordinal variables, although it can be done to some degree. Typically, we can just look at the frequency distribution to get a good idea of the degree of variation within a nominal or ordinal scale variable. *Variation is low for a nominal or ordinal variable to the extent to which the cases cluster in just one category.* For example, if you ask people whether they approve or disapprove of murder, just about everyone will disapprove; thus, there will be virtually no variation in this variable.

Conversely, variation in a nominal or ordinal variable is at its maximum when the cases are equally divided among the set of categories. For example, let's say that you asked a sample of college students whether they thought of themselves as liberals, moderates, or conservatives, and that exactly one-third of the students placed themselves in each of these three categories. Thus, we would have maximum variation for this variable: The cases would be equally distributed among the possible categories. Having said that about variation within nominal or ordinal variables, we will focus on describing variation within interval or ratio variables in the rest of this discussion.

Range

The ***range*** of a variable is determined by subtracting the lowest value of the variable from the highest.

For the ABORT TOT variable in the GSS data file, the lowest value is 0 and the highest value is 7—thus, the range is 7. To give another example, in the STATES file, the highest value for the variable MED.AGE 04 is 40.7 (Maine) and the lowest value is 28.0 (Utah). Thus, the range is 12.7 years.

Although the range gives us some information, it is limited in terms of what it can tell us about the amount of variation within a variable. Two variables might have exactly the same range and yet have different variation within them. Thus, the range is not very useful for describing variation within variables.

Variance and Standard Deviation

The ***variance*** and the ***standard deviation*** are related measures that express the degree of variation within a variable on the basis of the average deviation from the mean.

We use the variance or the standard deviation to measure the degree of variation within interval or ratio variables. These two measures are related: The standard deviation is the square root of the variance. The basic idea is that we measure the average *deviation* of cases from the mean: The deviation is the difference between the value of a variable for a particular case and the mean of that variable.

For example, using the PUPIL$05 variable from the STATES file, the mean annual expenditure per pupil in average daily attendance in public elementary and secondary schools in the states is $8,511. We could compute the deviation for individual states by subtracting the mean ($8,511) from each state's per pupil spending. For example, Indiana's per pupil spending was $8,734, which is a deviation of $223 from the mean.

Using a hypothetical political knowledge variable, Table 8.3 shows how the variance and the standard deviation are computed, so that you will know how these measures are derived. We will go through the steps briefly.

1. List the values of the variable X, and compute the mean of the variable. Here the mean is $35 \div 5$, which is 7. The mean is designated by an X with a bar across the top of it, referred to as "bar X." It looks like this: $\overline{X}$

2. Compute the deviations from the mean. For each value of the variable X, subtract that value from the mean. The sum of the deviations from the mean equals 0.

3. Square the deviations from the mean.

Table 8.3 Computation of the Variance and Standard Deviation

Value of the Variable Political Knowledge	Deviation from the Mean: the Value of the Variable Minus the Mean	Square of the Deviation from the Mean
X	$(X - \bar{X})$	$(X - \bar{X})^2$
8	1	1
5	−2	4
7	0	0
6	−1	1
9	2	4

Sum = 35   0   Variation = 10
Mean = 35 ÷ 5 = 7

Variance = (variation ÷ number of cases) = (10 ÷ 5) = 2

Standard deviation = (square root of the variance) = $\sqrt{2}$ = 1.41

4. In statistics, the term *variation* refers to the sum of the squared deviations from the mean. (Note that this is different from the broader sense in which we have been using the idea of variation with a variable.) Here the variation is 10. This doesn't mean much, because it doesn't take the number of cases into account.

5. Compute the variance by dividing the variation by the number of cases N when using a whole population (or $N - 1$ when using a sample of cases). Thus, the variance is basically the average squared deviation from the mean. Here the variance is 2.

6. Compute the standard deviation by taking the square root of the variance. Here the standard deviation is 1.41.

We can use either the variance or the standard deviation to indicate the amount of variation within a variable, but we usually use the standard deviation. These measures help us to understand the distribution of the values for a particular variable and can be very helpful when we are comparing two or more groups of cases.

Suppose that the per capita income for a sample of citizens of Country A is $8,000 and the per capita income for a sample of citizens of Country B is also $8,000. We might say that the income levels of people in those two countries are very similar, because the two countries have the same per capita income. Suppose, however, that the standard deviation for per capita income is $1,000 in Country A and $4,000 in Country B. This shows that the income is distributed in very different ways in the two countries.

- Within Country A (with a standard deviation of $1,000), people's incomes are similar to each other—there is a great deal of income equality. This is why the standard deviation is relatively low.

- Within Country B (with a standard deviation of $4,000), there is a great deal more variation in income—income inequality is much higher. This is why the standard deviation is relatively high.

The standard deviation shows us how much variation there is within a variable. For a variable, when there is little difference from one case to another, the standard deviation will be low. Conversely, when there is a great deal of diversity among the cases for a variable, the standard deviation will be high. When the distribution of values of a variable approaches a *normal distribution* (the bell-shaped curve), the standard deviation tells us even more.

The Normal Distribution

A line graph for a **normal distribution** is popularly called a *bell-shaped curve* because it resembles a bell. The mean, median, and mode are all at the highest point in the middle of a symmetrical distribution. As you move away from the middle of the distribution in either direction, there are fewer and fewer cases. When a variable is normally distributed, the range encompassed between the mean plus one standard deviation and the mean minus one standard deviation includes approximately two-thirds (more specifically, 68%) of all the cases. Further, the range between two standard deviations below the mean and two standard deviations above it includes 95% of all cases. Figure 8.1 demonstrates the approximate percentages of cases encompassed by standard deviations of the normal curve.

For example, let's say that we gave a political knowledge test to a national sample of people and it turned out that political knowledge was normally distributed with a mean of 50 and a standard deviation of 10. What would that mean?

- Approximately 68% of all respondents were within 1 standard deviation of the mean. Here, approximately 68% of all respondents would have scores between 40 and 60. This is the mean of 50 ±10.

- Approximately 95% of respondents would be within 2 standard deviations of the mean. Thus, here, approximately 95% of respondents would have scores between 30 and 70.

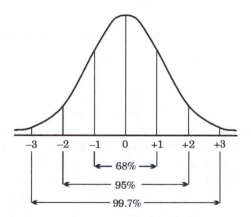

Figure 8.1 Approximate Percentages of Cases Included within Areas of the Normal Curve

- About 99.7% of all respondents would be within 3 standard deviations of the mean. Thus, approximately 99.7% of all respondents would have scores between 20 and 80.

Z-Scores

Let's say you earn a score of 84% on an exam, and you wonder how your score compares with other students' scores on the exam. After all, a score of 84% is spectacular if the average score is 55%, but it is not so impressive if most people scored 100% on the exam. To make such a comparison, it would be helpful for you to have your Z-score for the exam. *Z-scores* *are standardized scores for a variable (usually a variable that is normally distributed or fairly close to being normally distributed).* For a particular variable, a Z-score for a specific case tells us how many standard deviations above or below the mean that case is for that variable. For example, if your 84% score on the exam had a Z-score of 1.5, that would mean your score was 1.5 standard deviations above the mean. If your Z-score were 0.0, then you would have exactly the mean score on the exam. On the negative side, if your Z-score were –2.0, this would mean that your score was 2 standard deviations *below* the mean.

How do you compute Z-scores? If you have the mean and the standard deviation for a variable, the process is simple. For your exam, let's say the mean was 75% and the standard deviation was 6%. Follow these two steps:

1. Subtract the mean of the variable from the score for a particular case. In this example, subtract the mean (75%) from your score (84%); the result is 9%.

2. Divide the result by the standard deviation for the variable. In this example, divide 9% by the standard deviation (6%); the result is that the Z-score equals 1.5. Thus, your exam score is 1.5 standard deviations above the mean. Not bad! Let's take another example.

Based on the variable PUPIL$05 in the STATES file, we can determine that Pennsylvania had an annual per pupil spending of $9,638. Recall that the mean for all states was $8,511. The standard deviation is $1,755. Let's compute the Z-score for Pennsylvania.

1. Subtract the mean ($8,511) from Pennsylvania's score ($9,638). The result is $1,127.

2. Divide the result above ($1,127) by the standard deviation ($1,755). The result is .64.

That means that Pennsylvania's per pupil spending was .64 standard deviation above the mean for all 50 states. We could proceed to do that for all 50 states and then use those scores for the variable in lieu of the original scores; we would then call that variable a *standardized variable*. Z-scores give us more comparative information at a glance. Further, this standardization of variables makes it easier to compare information from more than one variable. If a case has a Z-score of 1.5 for one variable and a Z-score of 1.8 for another variable, then that immediately tells us this particular case is substantially above average on both variables. Instead of having to compare apples and oranges, we can compare standard deviations.

In this chapter we have examined the *description* of a variable—through frequency distributions, measures of central tendency, and measures of variability. The concept of variation is very important; we will return to it again and again. The chapters that follow focus more on *explanation,* and the basic meaning of explanation concerns relating variation in one variable to variation in another variable—we explain a variable by showing how variation in it relates to variation in another variable.

TERMS INTRODUCED IN THIS CHAPTER

Frequency distribution	Variance
Mode	Standard deviation
Median	Normal distribution
Mean	Z-score
Range	

FOR FURTHER READING

For more information on frequency distributions and descriptive statistics, see Chapters 2 through 4 in William Fox, *Social Statistics Using MicroCase,* 4th ed. (Belmont, CA: Wadsworth, 2003).

Another good source of information on frequency distributions and descriptive statistics is Chapter 2 in George W. Bohrnstedt and David Knoke, *Statistics for Social Data Analysis,* 3rd ed. (Itasca, IL: F. E. Peacock, 1994).

If you want to see many examples of frequency distributions in various formats, look in the periodicals section of your library for any issue of the *Gallup Poll Monthly, Public Perspective,* or *Public Opinion Quarterly. Public Perspective* also has many examples of bar graphs, pie charts, and other graphic representations of frequency distributions.

worksheet

NAME:

COURSE:

DATE:

1. Let's begin by examining descriptive statistics for some variables from the GSS file.

> ➤ Data File: **GSS**
> ➤ Task: **Univariate**
> ➤ Primary Variable: **62) PARTY**
> ➤ View: **Statistics (Summary)**

The MicroCase program does not list the mode because you can determine the mode simply by looking at the frequency distribution.

Which category of this political party identification variable is the mode? _____

What percentage of the respondents are in the political party identification category you named above? _____%

What level of measurement is this political party identification variable?
(Circle one.)

Nominal   Ordinal   Interval   Ratio

Given the level of measurement of this political party identification variable, would it be appropriate to use the mean for it?   Yes   No

2. Recall that when a variable is set up in terms of categories (either nominal or ordinal), minimum variation exists when all the cases are in one particular category, and maximum variation exists when the cases are evenly divided among the categories. Look at the variation in the family income variable.

> Data File: **GSS**
> Task: **Univariate**
> ➤ Primary Variable: **57) FAM.INCOME**
> ➤ View: **Bar - Freq.**

Before proceeding, be aware that this family income variable was collapsed into a smaller set of categories than what was originally used in the GSS. Collapsing a variable can, in itself, alter the variation in the variable. Nevertheless, let's examine the variation in this variable. Note that we can quickly grasp certain information about the distribution of this variable with just a glance at the bar graph. If variation in this family income variable is low, then one of the bars will be much higher than the rest. If variation in this variable is high, then all the bars will be similar to one another in height. Which is it?

Is variation in this variable fairly high or fairly low? (Circle one.)

Fairly high   Fairly low

3. Look at the descriptive statistics for the region variable.

> Data File: **GSS**
> Task: **Univariate**
> ➤ Primary Variable: **61) REGION**
> ➤ View: **Pie**

This pie chart is also a graphic representation of a frequency distribution. In this situation, if variation in region of residence is very high, then all the slices of the pie will be similar in size. If variation is very low, then one of the slices will be very large and the others will be very small.

In this situation, is variation closer to the low end or closer to the high end?

Low end   High end

Let's look at the averages for this variable.

> Data File: **GSS**
> Task: **Univariate**
> Primary Variable: **61) REGION**
> ➤ View: **Statistics (Summary)**

Which region is the mode? (Circle one.)

North   Midwest   South   West

Note that the program lists the mean for this variable as 2.680. Does it make any sense to say that the average region of residence is 2.680?   Yes   No

Which of the averages is the only one that is appropriate to use for nominal variables such as region? (Circle one.)

Mode   Median   Mean

Important: Statistical analysis programs compute all the descriptive statistics for a variable because they cannot determine which particular statistics are the most appropriate. It is up to us to choose—depending on the levels of measurement of variables—the appropriate statistics from among those that are listed.

4. Let's switch to the NES data file and look at the univariate results for RACE.

> ➤ Data File: **NES**
> ➤ Task: **Univariate**
> ➤ Primary Variable: **3) RACE**
> ➤ View: **Pie**

Is variation in this variable low or high?   Low   High

5. Look at the univariate results for the political knowledge variable–POLITKNOW–from the 2004 National Election Study.

> ➤ Data File: **NES 04**
> ➤ Task: **Univariate**
> ➤ Primary Variable: **527) POLITKNOW**
> ➤ View: **Statistics (Summary)**

Specify the mean, median, and mode for this variable.

Mean = _____   Median = _____   Mode = _____

If we interpret this variable simply as the number of correct political identifications, would it be appropriate to use the mean as an average for this variable?   Yes   No

What is the standard deviation for this variable? _____

6. Aside from having different averages for a variable, different groups might also have different degrees of variation for a variable. Let's compare education levels and variation for Democrats, Independents, and Republicans. Let's begin with Democrats.

> Data File: **NES 04**
> Task: **Univariate**
> ➤ Primary Variable: **4) EDUCATION**
> ➤ Subset Variable: **5) PARTY**
> ➤ Subset Category: **Include: 1) Democrat**
> ➤ View: **Statistics (Summary)**

> **The option for selecting a subset variable is located on the same screen you use to select other variables. For this example, select 5) PARTY as a subset variable. A window will appear that shows you the categories of the subset variable. Select 1) Democrat as your subset category and choose the [Include] option. Then click [OK] and continue as usual. With this particular subset selected, the results will be limited to the Democrats in the sample. The subset selection continues until you exit the task, delete all subset variables, or clear all variables.**

In the Democrats row of the table below, write the mean and the standard deviation for the education variable. Then we will proceed to obtain this information for Independents and Republicans.

	MEAN	STANDARD DEVIATION
DEMOCRATS	_____	_____
INDEPENDENTS	_____	_____
REPUBLICANS	_____	_____

Now obtain the information for Independents.

Data File: **NES 04**
Task: **Univariate**
Primary Variable: **4) EDUCATION**
Subset Variable: **5) PARTY**
➤ Subset Category: **Include: 2) Independ.**
➤ View: **Statistics (Summary)**

The easiest way to change the subset category to Independents (from Democrats) is to first delete the subset variable, 5) PARTY. Then reselect 5) PARTY as the subset variable. Include 2) Independ. as your subset category. Then click [OK] and continue as usual.

In the Independents row of the preceding table, write the mean and the standard deviation for education for Independents. Then we will obtain information for Republicans.

Data File: **NES 04**
Task: **Univariate**
Primary Variable: **4) EDUCATION**
Subset Variable: **5) PARTY**
➤ Subset Category: **Include: 3) Repub.**
➤ View: **Statistics (Summary)**

Again, the easiest way to change the subset category to Republicans (from Independents) is to first delete the subset variable, 5) PARTY. Then reselect 5) PARTY as the subset variable. Include 3) Repub. as your subset category. Then click [OK] and continue as usual.

In the Republicans row of the preceding table, write the mean and the standard deviation for education for Republicans.

7. Based on the previous analyses, consider the following propositions: Republicans have higher average education than do Democrats because Republicans have higher incomes and can better afford to send their children to college. However, Democrats who go to college are more likely to choose higher education as a career path; thus, among those with Ph.D.'s, a substantial percentage are Democrats.

While there are some ideas here that would require additional analysis, let's examine two parts of these ideas.

First, is the mean number of years of schooling completed higher for Republicans than for Democrats?   Yes   No

Second, if Democrats are more likely to come from both ends of the educational spectrum (people with lower education and people with higher education), then we would expect that variation in education would be greater among Democrats than among Republicans. Examine the standard deviations for education for Democrats and Republicans in the table in Question 6.

CHAPTER 8

Do the results support the idea that there is greater variation in education among Democrats than among Republicans?　　　　　　　Yes　　No

8. Now you will set up a table to present the frequency distribution for a variable in the format that you might use in a report. First, obtain the results for the variable SCHL VOUCH.

> Data File: **NES 04**
> Task: **Univariate**
> ➤ Primary Variable: **76) SCH VCHR**
> ➤ View: **Pie**

Before filling in the table below, print these results and attach the page to your assignment. (**Note:** If you have been instructed not to use the printer, just skip this task.)

Following the guidelines discussed earlier in this chapter for presentation of a frequency distribution for a report, set up the following table to present the frequency distribution for this variable. Part of the table has already been set up for you. If you would rather construct this table using the proper format in Microsoft Word, you may do so and attach your table to this exercise.

TABLE

Totals

Source:

Question:

9. Let's examine some variables from the GLOBAL file.

> ➤ Data File: **GLOBAL**
> ➤ Task: **Univariate**
> ➤ Primary Variable: **28) BIRTHRATE**
> ➤ View: **Statistics (Summary)**

In the appropriate row of the following table, write the mean and standard deviation for 28) BIRTHRATE. Then repeat this analysis for two other variables, 360) PUB EDUCAT and 138) GDPCAP PPP, and write the means and standard deviations for those two variables in the appropriate rows of the following table.

	MEAN	STANDARD DEVIATION
28) BIRTHRATE	_____	_____
360) PUB EDUCAT	_____	_____
138) GDPCAP PPP	_____	_____

Which of these three variables has the highest variation? (Circle one.)

28) BIRTHRATE   360) PUB EDUCAT   138) GDPCAP PPP

10. Now we will use the MAPPING task to look at three individual nations for variable 360) PUB EDUCAT (the percentage of the gross domestic product [GDP] spent on public education).

> Data File: **GLOBAL**
> ➤ Task: **Mapping**
> ➤ Primary Variable: **360) PUB EDUCAT**
> ➤ View: **List: Alpha**

Write the percentage (of the GDP spent on public education) for the three nations listed in the following table. Rounded off, the mean for this variable is 4.3%. For each of the three nations in the table, compute the deviation from the mean and write it in the appropriate place in the table.

	PERCENTAGE OF GDP SPENT ON PUBLIC EDUCATION	DEVIATION FROM THE MEAN
COSTA RICA	_____%	_____
CHILE	_____%	_____
CAMBODIA	_____%	_____

Which of these nations is most typical in terms of the percentage of the GDP spent on public education? (Circle one.)

> Costa Rica   Chile   Cambodia

Which of these nations is least typical in terms of the percentage of the GDP spent on public education? (Circle one.)

> Costa Rica   Chile   Cambodia

11. Now we will examine the typicality of cases using Z-scores.

Data File:	**GLOBAL**
➤ Task:	**Univariate**
➤ Primary Variable:	**22) URBAN %02**
➤ View:	**Statistics (Summary)**

The percentage of the nation's population living in urban areas is presented in the left column labeled *Range*. Thus, for the first entry, the value 8.2–8.9 represents a nation in which 8.2% of the population lives in urban areas. In the Frequency column, we see that there was one nation that was 8.2% urban. The % column indicates that this one nation represents .6% of the number of nations included. Note that there are 171 cases included in this table and that there is 1 nation that has missing data for this variable.

Moving over to the last column (Z-Score), we see that this nation (with 8.2% of its population living in urban areas) has a Z-score of –2.009. This means that this nation is 2.009 standard deviations below the mean in terms of urbanism.

Is this nation that is 8.2% urban fairly average or very unusual in comparison with urbanism in other nations? (Circle one.)

> Fairly average   Very unusual

If a nation is 20.2% urban, what is its Z-score?   Z-score = _____

If a nation is 54.5% urban, what is its Z-score?   Z-score = _____

Are the nations that are 54.5% urban fairly average or very unusual in comparison with urbanism in other nations? (Circle one.)

> Fairly average   Very unusual

If a nation is 89% urban, what is its Z-score?   Z-score = _____

How many nations were 89% urban?   _____

How many nations had a Z-score of 0.099?   _____

That's all for this lesson.

CHAPTER 9

How to Read a Cross-tabulation

Tasks: Cross-tabulation, Collapse Variables
Data Files: GSS, HOUSE, NES 04

INTRODUCTION

A **cross-tabulation** (also called a **contingency table**) cross-tabulates two nominal and/or ordinal variables by one another to determine whether a relationship exists between them.

We use cross-tabulation to examine relationships for variables that are set up in categories. Thus, to test hypotheses that involve nominal and/or ordinal variables only, we must use cross-tabulation (or contingency) tables. Therefore, this chapter will

- illustrate further how to read the contents of a cross-tabulation

- demonstrate how to present the results of a cross-tabulation in a report

- explain how and why to collapse a variable for a cross-tabulation

You have already been exposed to several cross-tabulations and should know how to read certain aspects of such tables. In this chapter, we will elaborate on reading cross-tabulations and recognizing patterns in them.

INTERPRETING THE PARTS OF A CROSS-TABULATION

To demonstrate how to read a cross-tabulation, we will start with one that cross-tabulates two variables from the GSS file. The dependent (row) variable is WELFARE $2, which concerns the respondents' views on whether too little, too much, or about the right amount is being spent on assistance to the poor. The independent (column) variable is political party preference (PARTY).

➤ Data File: **GSS**
➤ Task: **Cross-tabulation**
➤ Row Variable: **89) WELFARE $2**
➤ Column Variable: **62) PARTY**
➤ View: **Tables**
➤ Display: **Column %**

WELFARE $2   by   PARTY
Cramer's V: 0.193**

		PARTY				
		DEMOCRAT	INDEPEND.	REPUBLICAN	Missing	TOTAL
WELFARE $2	TOO LITTLE	513	234	272	15	1019
		81.3%	75.5%	54.3%		70.7%
	RIGHT	92	58	157	7	307
		14.6%	18.7%	31.3%		21.3%
	TOO MUCH	26	18	72	8	116
		4.1%	5.8%	14.4%		8.0%
	Missing	1332	687	958	61	3038
	TOTAL	631	310	501	91	1442
		100.0%	100.0%	100.0%		

To explain the parts of this table, we will create it again, one part at a time. (We will exclude the information in the table on missing cases.)

Category Labels

We usually place the labels for the categories of the independent variable across the top of the table, and the labels for the categories of the dependent variable on the left side of the table. In some situations, this arrangement is reversed. For example, if there were 15 categories in the independent variable, it would be extremely difficult to get that many categories across the top of the table. If it can be done, however, the independent variable is almost always placed across the top.

So, for this example, let's put in the labels (*Democrat, Independent,* and *Republican*) for the categories of the independent variable across the top. The labels (*Too little, Right amount,* and *Too much*) for the dependent variable (support for spending on assistance to the poor) go down the left side. (See Table 9.1.)

Table 9.1 Category Label Positions for the Independent Variable and the Dependent Variable

	Democrat	Independent	Republican
Too little			
Right amount			
Too much			

Cell Frequencies

The category formed by the intersection of a column and a row is called a *cell*. Thus, the intersection of *Democrat* and *Too little* in Table 9.1 is a cell. The number of cases in a cell is the *cell frequency*—this is the first number presented in each of the cells. It tells us how many cases there are in that particular category.

For example, in this situation, how many Democrats responded "too little" to the question about spending on assistance to the poor? We see from the MicroCase table that there are 513 cases in this cell. That is, 513 Democrats said that too little was being spent on the poor. Let's now fill in the rest of the cell frequencies in Table 9.2.

Table 9.2 Cell Frequencies for the Relationship between Attitude toward Spending on the Poor Cross-tabulated by Political Party Preference

	Democrat	Independent	Republican
Too little	513	234	272
Right amount	92	58	157
Too much	26	18	72

Let's use the underlined cell frequency as another example. That category is formed by the intersection of *Republican* and *Too much*. It means that 72 of the Republicans said that too much was being spent on assistance to the poor.

Totals

When you have a cross-tabulation on the computer screen, it includes the column totals (the total number of cases for each category of the independent variable) and row totals (the total number of cases for each category of the dependent variable). In Table 9.3, we will add the row totals on the right side and the column totals along the bottom.

Table 9.3 Cell Frequencies, Column Totals, and Row Totals for the Relationship between Attitude toward Spending on the Poor and Political Party Preference

	Democrat	Independent	Republican	Totals
Too little	513	234	272	1,019
Right amount	92	58	157	307
Too much	26	18	72	116
Totals	631	310	501	1,442

We see from the *row totals* that 1,019 people said that too little was spent on the poor, 307 said the right amount was being spent, and 116 said that too much was spent. Let's take one of these row totals to see how it is derived. There are 1,019 people who said that too little was being spent on the poor; that includes the 513 Democrats who said "too little," the 234 Independents who said "too little," and the 272 Republicans who said "too little." (See the cell frequencies for the *Too little* row: 513 + 234 + 272 = 1,019.)

We see from the *column totals* that among the respondents in this table, there are 631 Democrats, 310 Independents, and 501 Republicans. Let's take one of those column totals to see how it is derived. The column total for Democrats is 631, which consists of 513 who said "too little," 92 who said "right amount," and 26 who said "too much" (513 + 92 + 26 = 631).

How many people were included in this table? The figure at the bottom right of Table 9.3 is 1,442. That is the *grand total*, the total number of people in this particular table. If you added all the cell frequencies in this table, the sum would be 1,442. There were other people in the sample, but only about half the sample was asked this particular question about spending on the poor. Further, some people did not answer this question and/or the party identification question. Only the nonmissing cases are included in the table.

Column Percentages

The MicroCase program allows you to select three different types of percentages: column percentages, row percentages, and total percentages. We will describe all three percentages, but it is important to note that we ordinarily use only column percentages. We want to compare the percentages of cases for each category of the independent variable for a particular category of the dependent variable. Here, for example, do the percentages of Democrats, Independents, and Republicans differ from one another in terms of saying that too little was being spent on the poor? Thus, we use column percentages to determine whether there is a relationship between the dependent variable and the independent variable.

The exception to using column percentages is the situation in which we have placed the independent variable along the side of the table rather than across the top. We customarily place the independent variable across the top, but sometimes there are too many categories in the independent variable and we don't have enough room on the page to place it across the top. In such a situation, we put the independent variable along the side and use row percentages rather than column percentages.

1. We compute a *column percentage* by dividing the cell frequency by the column total.

   Example: In Table 9.3, the cell frequency for Independents who said that too little was spent on the poor is 234. The column total tells us that there are 310 Independents in this table. Therefore, the column percentage for the *Independent / Too little* cell is computed by dividing 234 by 310 and converting the result to a percentage. In this example, 75.5% of the Independents said that too little was spent on the poor.

2. We compute a *row percentage* by dividing the cell frequency by the row total.

   Example: There were 234 Independents who said that too little was spent on the poor. All together, 1,019 people said that too little was spent on the poor. We divide 234 by 1,019 and convert the result to a percentage. Here, 23.0% of those who said that too little was spent on the poor are Independents.

3. We compute a *total percentage* by dividing the cell frequency by the grand total.

   Example: There were 234 Independents who said that too little was spent on the poor. All together, there were 1,442 people in this table. We divide 234 by 1,442 and convert the result to a percentage. Thus, 16.2% of the people included in this table are Independents who think that too little is spent on the poor.

Usually, when we report the results of a cross-tabulation, we use the column percentages and exclude other types of percentages. The goal is to relate the independent variable to the dependent variable by showing what percentages of each category of the independent variable have a certain value of the dependent variable. Therefore, we will fill in only the column percentages in Table 9.4.

Table 9.4 Column Percentages, Cell Frequencies, Column Totals, and Row Totals for the Relationship between Attitude toward Spending on the Poor and Political Party Preference

	Democrat	Independent	Republican	Totals
Too little	513	234	272	1,019
	81.3%	75.5%	54.3%	70.7%
Right amount	92	58	157	307
	14.6%	18.7%	31.3%	21.3%
Too much	26	18	72	116
	4.1%	5.8%	14.4%	8.0%
Totals	631	310	501	1,442
	100.0%	100.0%	100.0%	

Let's take the 14.4% figure in the *Republican/Too much* cell in Table 9.4. That means that 14.4% of the Republicans said that too much was being spent on assistance to the poor.

Notice also that percentages have been inserted below the row totals. Those percentages are percentages of the grand total. For example, the first of those percentages is 70.7%, which is in the *Too little* row. That means that 70.7% of all the respondents in the table said that too little was spent on assistance to the poor.

Also, note that percentages have been placed underneath each of the column totals. When you sum the column percentages for a column, they will always add up to 100%, plus or minus about one-tenth of one percent for rounding error.

HOW TO PRESENT CROSS-TABULATION RESULTS IN A REPORT

We present a table in a report differently than it is presented in the computer results. Table 9.5 presents the table for the example we have been using; we will examine this format one part at a time. Let's look at the table setup in terms of the following steps.

1. Label the table.

The table needs a label so that you can reference it easily. Table labels can simply be Table 1, Table 2, and so on. Let's label this table *Table 9.5* to indicate that it is the fifth table in Chapter 9.

Table 9.5 Support for Spending on Assistance to the Poor by Political Party Preference

	Democrat	Independent	Republican	Totals
Too little	81.3%	75.5%	54.3%	70.7%
	(513)	(234)	(272)	(1,019)
Right amount	14.6%	18.7%	31.3%	21.3%
	(92)	(58)	(157)	(307)
Too much	4.1%	5.8%	14.4%	8.0%
	(26)	(18)	(72)	(116)
Totals	100.0%	100.0%	100.0%	100.0%
	(631)	(310)	(501)	(1,442)

Source: 2006 National Opinion Research Center (NORC) General Social Survey (GSS).

Question: *We are faced with many problems in this country, none of which can be solved easily or inexpensively. I'm going to name some of these problems, and for each one I'd like you to tell me whether you think we're spending too much money on it, too little money, or about the right amount: assistance to the poor.*

2. Give the table a title.

The table needs a descriptive title that indicates its content. For a cross-tabulation, the basic format of the table gives the information: [*Dependent Variable*] by [*Independent Variable*]. Therefore, the title for the table is *Support for Spending on Assistance to the Poor by Political Party Preference.*

3. Provide category labels.

Place the category labels for the independent variable across the top and the category labels for the dependent variables down the left side. Do not abbreviate these labels unless it is absolutely necessary.

4. Include column percentages and cell frequencies.

In presenting a table in a report, we usually use a format unlike that of the computer-generated cross-tabulation. We first present the column percentage and then present the cell frequency. In examining relationships between variables, or in simply describing one variable, we usually can make more sense of the percentages than of the frequencies. Thus, we give the percentages greater emphasis.

In this particular situation, the column percentage is presented first and the cell frequency is presented in parentheses below it. There are several variations on this arrangement. For example, the cell frequency might be presented in parentheses on the same line as the column percentage in the following manner: 81.3% (513).

5. Include the column totals and the row totals.

The column totals are presented along the bottom and the row totals are presented on the left side. (The row totals are sometimes omitted.)

6. Provide the source and other information if needed.

The source of the data usually is indicated, especially if more than one source of data is used in a report. There might also be other information that should be included. For example, if survey data are being used, it usually is necessary to include the wording of the questions involved, especially if a question is not a standard one that is fairly well known.

LOOKING FOR PATTERNS IN THE RESULTS

Are the cases distributed in such a way that cases in particular categories of the independent variable tend to be in particular categories of the dependent variable? That is another way of asking whether variation in the dependent variable is related to variation in the independent variable. *To examine the results of a cross-tabulation for patterns, compare the column percentages horizontally.*

For each row of a cross-tabulation, compare the column percentages horizontally. If there is no relationship between the dependent variable and the independent variable, the column percentages will be very similar as you read across. However, if there is a relationship, there will be some sort of pattern in the column percentages. One or more of the column percentages may differ substantially from the others, or there may be a steady increase or decrease in the magnitude of the column percentages as you read across the row.

For our present example, look at the column percentages for the first row (the *Too little* category). The first percentage (for Democrats) is 81.3%, and the second percentage (for Independents) is 75.5%. Thus, there is a little difference between Democrats and Independents in terms of the percentages who say that too little is being spent on assistance to the poor. Further, look at the third percentage in this row and you see that only 54.3% of the Republicans said that too little was being spent on the poor. Thus, as you read the column percentages across the row, they decline from 81.3% to 75.5% to 54.3%.

So, the pattern is that Democrats are the most supportive of spending on the poor, Independents are in the middle, and Republicans are the least supportive of spending on assistance to the poor. Therefore, there is a pattern here. Variation in the dependent variable (support for spending on assistance to the poor) is related to variation in the independent variable (political party preference). Putting this another way, political party preference helps to explain attitudes toward spending on assistance to the poor.

COLLAPSING A VARIABLE

Collapsing a variable means reducing the number of categories or values of a variable to a smaller number by combining categories or values.

Sometimes, especially when analyzing data in a cross-tabulation, we need to reduce the number of categories of a nominal or ordinal variable or collapse the values of an interval or ratio variable into a set of categories. Let's take a look at the why and how of this process.

Collapsing Nominal and Ordinal Variables

In some situations, a nominal or ordinal scale variable has too many categories to be practical for use in a cross-tabulation. For example, suppose you had an independent variable that indicated the denominational preferences of Protestants and you wanted to cross-tabulate it with political party preference. Let's say there were 30 different denominations in this variable. It would not be practical to set up a cross-tabulation with this denomination variable, because there would be 30 categories across the top of the table.

In that situation, we would collapse the variable. The denominations would need to be combined (meaningfully) into a smaller set of categories that could be used in a cross-tabulation. You will see how collapsing is done—and do some yourself—in the worksheet section of this chapter. The MicroCase method of collapsing variables makes it easy to do.

Let's take another example. The question concerning liberalism/conservatism used in the NORC GSS survey is as follows: *I'm going to show you a seven-point scale on which the political views that people might hold are arranged from extremely liberal to extremely conservative. Where would you place yourself on this scale?* Respondents select one of seven categories: extremely liberal, liberal, slightly liberal, moderate, slightly conservative, conservative, and extremely conservative.

It is useful to have seven categories for liberalism/conservatism identifications, but in some situations it is a problem to have so many categories. Thus, in your GSS file, the number of categories has been reduced to three. All three liberal categories were collapsed into one *Liberal* category, all three conservative categories were collapsed into one *Conservative* category, and the *Moderate* category was left unchanged.

Remember that when you collapse categories, it is important to do it meaningfully. The collapsed categories need to be justifiable categories, even though they are broader than the original ones.

Collapsing an Interval or Ratio Variable

Usually, we do not collapse an interval or ratio variable. By doing so, we reduce it to an ordinal variable and thus lose the precision of the original level of measurement and the ability to use higher-level statistical techniques. Even so, there are times when we need to collapse an interval or ratio variable, because we need to use it in a cross-tabulation.

Research Methods in Political Science

For example, in the NES file, variable 8) AGE is in years. It would not be practical to use age in this format in a cross-tabulation. Age can vary in this sample from 18 to 97. In order for it to be usable in cross-tabulation, there is a collapsed version of age in the data file—variable 11) AGE CATEGR. The collapsed age variable is set up as follows: 18 to 29, 30 to 44, 45 to 65, and 65 and up. The original age in years is ratio, but this collapsed variable is ordinal.

TERMS INTRODUCED IN THIS CHAPTER

Cross-tabulation (contingency table)	Collapsing a variable
Column totals	Column percent
Row totals	Row percent

FOR FURTHER READING

For further discussion of collapsing a variable, see pages 45–48 in William Fox, *Social Statistics Using MicroCase,* 4th ed. (Belmont, CA: Wadsworth, 2003).

For further discussion of cross-tabulation, see the first section in Chapter 4 of Victoria L. Mantzopoulos, *Statistics for the Social Sciences* (Englewood Cliffs, NJ: Prentice-Hall, 1995).

For an example of research that makes extensive use of cross-tabulations, see Barbara Norrander, "The Independence Gap and the Gender Gap," *Public Opinion Quarterly* 61 (Fall 1997): 464–476.

For some good examples of cross-tabulations that are straightforward and readable, browse through William H. Flanigan and Nancy H. Zingale, *Political Behavior of the American Electorate,* 9th ed. (Washington, DC: CQ Press, 1998).

For some more good examples of the use of cross-tabulation in a very readable context, see Chapter 3 of Michael A. Milburn, *Persuasion and Politics: The Social Psychology of Public Opinion* (Pacific Grove, CA: Brooks/Cole, 1991).

worksheet

NAME: _____

COURSE: _____

DATE: _____

1. Let's begin by examining a relationship from the HOUSE file. Variable 58) TAX CUTS is a vote to extend tax cuts, including capital gains through 2010 (HR 4297). Let's call this concept support for tax cuts. We might hypothesize that Republican representatives would favor this bill more than would Democratic representatives.

> ➤ Data File: **HOUSE**
> ➤ Task: **Cross-tabulation**
> ➤ Row Variable: **58) TAX CUTS**
> ➤ Column Variable: **11) PARTY**
> ➤ View: **Tables**
> ➤ Display: **Frequency**

We want to determine whether there is a relationship between the dependent variable (support for tax cuts) and the independent variable (party affiliation). First, however, let's read some parts of the table.

Altogether, how many representatives (a *row total*) voted yes on this bill?   _____

How many Democratic representatives voted yes (a *cell frequency*) on this bill?   _____

How many Republican representatives voted yes (a *cell frequency*) on this bill?   _____

Altogether, how many Democratic representatives (a *column total*) voted on this bill?   _____

Altogether, how many Republican representatives (a *column total*) voted on this bill?   _____

How many representatives (a *grand total*) voted on this bill?   _____

2. Look at the column percentages for this table.

Data File: **HOUSE**
Task: **Cross-tabulation**
Row Variable: **58) TAX CUTS**
Column Variable: **11) PARTY**
View: **Tables**
➤ Display: **Column %**

What percentage of the representatives voted yes on this bill?   _____%

What percentage of the Democratic representatives voted yes on this bill?   _____%

What percentage of the Republican representatives voted yes on this bill?   _____%

To determine whether there is a relationship between the dependent variable and the independent variable, compare the column percentages horizontally. Because there are only two rows here, we can see whether there is a relationship just by examining the column percentages for either of the two rows. Compare the column percentages for the Yes row for the two categories of the independent variable, party affiliation. If the two percentages are similar, there is no relationship between support for tax cuts and party affiliation. If the two percentages are very different, there is a relationship—and the independent variable helps to explain the dependent variable.

Look at the two choices below and circle the letter of the choice that represents your conclusion.

a. There is a relationship between voting for tax cuts and political party affiliation. The independent variable (political party affiliation) helps to explain the dependent variable (vote on this tax bill). If we know a representative's political party affiliation, this helps us to predict how the representative voted on this bill.

b. There is no relationship between voting for the Jobs and Growth Reconciliation Act and political party affiliation. The independent variable (political party affiliation) does not help to explain the dependent variable (vote on this tax bill). If we know a representative's political party affiliation, this does not help us to predict how the representative voted on this bill.

3. Before leaving this table, let's examine the other types of percentages that are available in a cross-tabulation. Begin with row percentages.

Data File: **HOUSE**
Task: **Cross-tabulation**
Row Variable: **58) TAX CUTS**
Column Variable: **11) PARTY**
View: **Tables**
➤ Display: **Row %**

What percentage of those who voted no on this bill were Democrats?   _____%

What percentage of those who voted yes on this bill were Republicans?   _____%

worksheet

Now look at the total percentages.

> Data File: **HOUSE**
> Task: **Cross-tabulation**
> Row Variable: **58) TAX CUTS**
> Column Variable: **11) PARTY**
> View: **Tables**
> ➤ Display: **Total %**

What percentage of all representatives included in this table are Democrats
who voted no on this bill? _____%

What percentage of all representatives included in this table are Republicans
who voted yes on this bill? _____%

Before leaving this table, take a brief look at the summary statistics that accompany a cross-tabulation.

> Data File: **HOUSE**
> Task: **Cross-tabulation**
> Row Variable: **58) TAX CUTS**
> Column Variable: **11) PARTY**
> ➤ View: **Statistics (Summary)**

Just look over these statistics quickly—they will be explained in the next chapter, where you
will see how these statistics are used to test the null hypothesis and to determine how well
the independent variable explains the dependent variable.

4. Next look at the relationship between the number of terms served and whether the representative
is a lawyer. We might hypothesize that lawyers will have longer service in Congress than non-
lawyers because the legal profession is more convenient for the pursuit of a political career than
are most occupations.

> Data File: **HOUSE**
> Task: **Cross-tabulation**
> ➤ Row Variable: **13) #TERMS2**
> ➤ Column Variable: **10) LAWYER?**
> ➤ View: **Tables**
> ➤ Display: **Column %**

Examine the column percentages horizontally. Look at the two choices below and circle the
letter of the choice that represents your conclusion.

a. There is a relationship between the number of terms served and whether the
representative is a lawyer. The independent variable (whether the representative
is a lawyer) helps to explain the dependent variable (number of terms served).
If we know whether the representative is a lawyer, this helps us to predict the
representative's length of service (number of terms served).

b. There is no relationship between the number of terms served and whether the representative is a lawyer. The independent variable (whether the representative is a lawyer) does not help to explain the dependent variable (number of terms served). If we know whether the representative is a lawyer, this does not help us to predict the representative's length of service (number of terms served).

Before leaving this cross-tabulation, note that the dependent variable (terms of service) has been collapsed to make this variable usable in a cross-tabulation. The collapsed variable has only three categories (1 term, 2–4 terms, 5 or more terms). If we had not collapsed this variable, we would have a cross-tabulation with too many cells and too few cases in the cells—the number of terms served ranges from 1 (newly elected representatives) to 24 terms for Representative Dingell from Michigan. Thus, if we used the uncollapsed number of terms, we would have a table with two columns (lawyer, non-lawyer) and 24 rows. The resulting table would be difficult to interpret.

5. Using the NES data file from the 2004 election, let's further demonstrate the problem that can occur when we want to use cross-tabulation to analyze relationships between variables that have too many categories.

> ➤ Data File: **NES 04**
> ➤ Task: **Cross-tabulation**
> ➤ Row Variable: **5) PARTY**
> ➤ Column Variable: **528) LIBCON7**
> ➤ View: **Tables**
> ➤ Display: **Column %**

The column variable has seven categories, and the table has so many cells that it is difficult to determine whether there is any pattern in the results. Now look at these same two variables in collapsed form.

> Data File: **NES 04**
> Task: **Cross-tabulation**
> Row Variable: **5) PARTY**
> ➤ Column Variable: **391) LIBCON3**
> ➤ View: **Tables**
> ➤ Display: **Column %**

Write the column percentages in the following table.

	LIBERAL	MODERATE	CONSERVATIVE
DEMOCRAT	_____%	_____%	_____%
INDEPENDENT	_____%	_____%	_____%
REPUBLICAN	_____%	_____%	_____%

Compare the column percentages horizontally. Is there a pattern here?   Yes   No

If you answered yes, then describe the pattern. That is, in what ways are the political party identifications of people connected to their ideological identifications? If you answered no, then indicate why you think there was no pattern.

_____

_____

_____

_____

6. Variable 499) WHO_GOVDIF consists of responses to the statement "Some people say it makes a difference who's in power. Others say that it doesn't make a difference who's in power." This is one item that, along with several others, is used to measure the concept of political efficacy, a feeling that one can have an effect in the political system. Belief that who's in power makes a difference indicates higher political efficacy, while belief that it makes no difference indicates lower efficacy.

Let's hypothesize that there is a positive relationship between political efficacy and a person's level of political knowledge.

>| | |
>|---:|:---|
>| Data File: | **NES 04** |
>| Task: | **Cross-tabulation** |
>| ➤ Row Variable: | **499) WHO_GOVDIF** |
>| ➤ Column Variable: | **527) POLITKNOW** |
>| ➤ View: | **Tables** |
>| ➤ Display: | **Column %** |

Examine the column percentages. Were the results in accord with the hypothesis we formulated? (Circle one.) Yes No

Using results from this relationship between political efficacy and political knowledge, set up in the following space a cross-tabulation in the format that would be used for a table in a final report. Use Table 9.5 as a model. Part of the table formatting has been done to give you a framework. If you would rather construct this table in a word processing program, please do so and attach your printed table to this worksheet.

Table A:

Source:

Questions:

7. Let's return to the NES data collected after the 2004 Congressional elections. We'll hypothesize that there is a positive relationship between caring about U.S. House of Representatives elections and education level. We can check this as follows:

Data File:	**NES 04**
Task:	**Cross-tabulation**
➤ Row Variable:	**127) CARE HOUSE**
➤ Column Variable:	**4) EDUCATION**
➤ View:	**Tables**
➤ Display:	**Column %**

Each of these variables has four categories, and this produces a table with 16 cells. This is not bad, but we could make the table more comprehensible by temporarily collapsing some of the categories.

Let's begin by collapsing the Not at all and the Not very categories into one category. Click on the label Not at all and then click on the label Not very. Note that both of these rows are now highlighted. Then click the [Collapse] button on the left side of the screen. In the box that appears, type a label for the new collapsed category that consists of both the Not at all category and the Not very category. Let's label this new collapsed category Low/none. So, type **Low/none** and click [OK].

Now collapse the other two categories into one category. Click on the label Prtty much and then click on the label Very much. Both of these rows are now highlighted. Then click the [Collapse] button on the left side of the screen. In the box that appears, type a label for the new collapsed category that consists of both the Prtty much category and the Very much category. Let's label this new collapsed category Mod/high. So, type **Mod/high** and click [OK].

This makes the table easier to read, and we could just stop here and interpret the results. However, to further demonstrate the temporary collapsing process so that you can use it on your own, let's also collapse two of the education categories into one. Click on the No H.S. DG label in the table and then click on the H.S. DEGR label. Then click the [Collapse] button, type **HS or less** for the label for this new collapsed category, and click [OK].

We now have a table with 6 cells, whereas the original table had 16 cells. The new table is easier to comprehend than the original table. Write the column percentages in the following table.

	HS OR LESS	SOME COLL.	COLL. GRAD
MOD/HIGH	_____%	_____%	_____%
LOW/NONE	_____%	_____%	_____%

We hypothesized that there would be a positive relationship between caring about U.S. House of Representatives elections and education level. Compare the column percentages horizontally. Are these results in accord with the hypothesis?   Yes   No

Note that this collapsing is temporary. Return to the listing of variables for cross-tabulation. The variables CARE HOUSE and EDUCATION are still selected. Simply click [OK] to return to the cross-tabulation results. Are these two variables still in their collapsed form?   Yes   No

8. Student MicroCase allows you to permanently collapse a variable (at least for some of the data files included). Actually, what you do is to create a new variable that is a collapsed version of the original variable.

We will now go through this process of permanently collapsing a variable.

Open the GSS file and note that this file contains the uncollapsed variable 887) EDUCATION (highest grade completed) and the collapsed variable 5) EDCAT (1) NO HS GRAD, 2) HS GRAD, 3) COLL EDUC). We will again collapse the education variable, but this time we will create a different set of categories and code them as follows:

1 = 12th grade or less

2 = 1–4 years of college

3 = more than 4 years of college

From the DATA MANAGEMENT menu, select the COLLAPSE VARIABLE task. From the variable list, select 887) EDUCATION as the variable to be collapsed and then click [OK]. Note that a bar graph across the top shows the frequency distribution for this uncollapsed education variable.

In the middle of the screen below the bar graph is a series of buttons that are used to provide labels for the new collapsed categories of the variable that we are going to create. At this point, each of these buttons is labeled (no label) to indicate that we have not yet assigned a label to the category.

On the right side of these buttons, there are other buttons with colors and numbers. For example, the first one has a blue rectangle on it and the number 0. This means that if we use 0 as a code for one of the new collapsed categories, this category will be represented on the new bar graph with the color blue.

However, we are not going to use the number 0 as a code. We're using the codes 1 (for 12th grade or less), 2 (for 1–4 years of college), and 3 (for more than 4 years of college). So, to start, go to the column of buttons in the middle and click on the second button down—the one to the left of the label 1 with the green rectangle. **Note:** Click on the part of the button that says (no label).

Notice that the phrase (no label) has been replaced with a blank space and the blinking cursor is in this blank space. You are now ready to type in a label for this first category. So, type **12 or less.**

Next we are going to select the bars from the bar graph that represent 12th grade or less, and these cases will be placed into this new collapsed category. In this particular situation, we need to be a little cautious because there are such a small number of cases that have 5 years or less, the bars for these cases barely show up on the screen—and we need to make sure to include them in the collapsing.

To do that, place the mouse cursor in the lower left area of the bar graph (even though no bars show up there), hold down on the left mouse button, drag the cursor to the right until you have included all bars up through the one that stands for 12th grade—the bars will turn green, the color of this first category. As you move the cursor over a bar, note that the Value area (just beneath the left side of the bar graph) changes to reflect the number of years of school. Also note that the Freq. column indicates the number of cases having each number of years of school and that this number is also converted into a percentage. When you have reached the 12 years bar (the highest bar), release the mouse button.

At this point, you should have a new bar graph started in the lower right area of the screen. Note the green horizontal bar—it should have the number 1985 after it. This means that there are 1985 people in this sample who have 12th grade or less. If this number is not 1985, then there is a mistake somewhere. If you accidentally omitted a particular bar, you can now include it by clicking on it. If you accidentally included a bar that should not be included (e.g., you went too far and included those with 1 year of college), then you can deselect the bar at this point by clicking on it.

worksheet

On the left side of the lower part of the screen, you will find the phrase Collapsed into Category 1: 0–12. That means that all cases having 0 to 12 years of school have been placed into this new collapsed category. Below that, the screen reads Original Missing: 0 cases. That means that 0 cases were missing for this education variable. Then the screen reads Unassigned: 2525 (converted to Missing Data). This simply means that there are 2525 cases that have not yet been assigned to a category and that those cases are treated as missing data until they are assigned.

Now let's set up the second category, 1–4 years of college. Click the third button in the lower center (the button below the 12 or less category button). In the blank space, type **1–4 coll.** Then, click on the bars representing 1, 2, 3, and 4 years of college. When you put the cursor on a bar, look at the number below the term Value on the left side of the screen to confirm your selection.

At this point, look at the second bar (the red bar) added to the horizontal bar graph. There should be 1949 cases in this category. The collapsing statement on the left should read Collapsed into Category 2: 13–16. That means that all cases with 1 to 4 years of college have been placed into this collapsed category. Again, if you have accidentally included or excluded any particular category of cases, you can click on the appropriate bar to exclude or include those cases.

Now let's set up the third category, more than 4 years of college. Click the fourth button in the lower center (the button below 1–4 coll) and type **>4 coll.** Click on the remaining gray bar (representing 5 or more years of school) in the bar graph. This last category has 565 cases in it, and all cases in the original variable now have been assigned to one of the three categories of the new collapsed variable.

Click [Finish] in the upper left area of the screen. The screen that appears asks for a name for the new collapsed variable, and it suggests the name EDUCATION2. However, that is not a particularly useful name. So, put the cursor in the Name box, delete the name EDUCATION2, and type **EDUC-3** (which stands for education in three categories) as a name for this new variable.

Note that you could alter the variable description for this new variable, but the variable description provided by the program is adequate. Look at the other information on this screen. At this point, if you discovered an error in the category labels, you could correct the error. When you have finished looking at the information on the screen, click [OK]. A message will tell you that a new variable has been created. Click [OK] again and the program returns to the main menu.

This new variable (EDUC-3) has been added to the end of the GSS data file, and it will be available for you to use the same as any other variable in the data file.

9. Look at the univariate statistics for this new collapsed variable.

> Data File: **GSS**
> ➤ Task: **Univariate**
> ➤ Primary Variable: **888) EDUC-3**
> ➤ View: **Pie**

Print these results and attach them to your assignment. (**Note:** If you have been instructed not to use the printer, just skip this task.)

10. When you collapse a variable, check it, if possible, against the original uncollapsed variable to make sure that you have not made any errors. Let's see how that is done.

Data File:	**GSS**
➤ Task:	**Cross-tabulation**
➤ Row Variable:	**887) EDUCATION**
➤ Column Variable:	**888) EDUC-3**
➤ View:	**Tables**
➤ Display:	**Row %**

Begin checking by reading down the column 12 or less. As you go down the rows, every row percentage through row 12 (which represents 0 through 12th grade) should be 100%. That is, all the cases for these rows should be included in the new collapsed category 12 or less.

Then, for rows 13 through 16, the row percentages should all be 100% in the middle column that represents the category 1–4 coll. Lastly, row 17 should be 100% in the third column that represents the category 4 coll.

If these results are not correct, then an error has been made in the collapsing. The best way to correct the error is to repeat the collapsing process and make sure to avoid the error this time. Then check your results again to be sure that the second time did not produce any new error.

That's all for this lesson.

Tests of Statistical Significance and Measures of Association

Tasks: Cross-tabulation
Data Files: NES 04, GSS, HOUSE

INTRODUCTION

This chapter discusses the basic process of testing hypotheses and evaluating the relationships between variables. We will focus on two topics:

• Tests of statistical significance—tests to determine whether a relationship found in a probability sample can be said to exist in the population from which the sample was selected

• Measures of association—measures that show the strength of the relationship between variables

Let's back up and review a bit concerning the research process. In the beginning stage of research, we select some aspect of political reality that we want to explain. For example, there is *variation* among people in terms of support for democratic principles. What accounts for that variation? Based on a review of the research and on our own thinking, we develop a theoretical explanation to account for variation in the aspects of political reality we are investigating. (For instance, we develop a theory to explain *why* different people have different levels of support for democratic principles.)

We then develop a research design, a plan for the way we will conduct our research to test the theory. We develop specific *hypotheses* from the theory; the tests of these hypotheses will help us to evaluate the theory. The hypotheses must be testable, they must indicate specific types of relationships between variables, and they must be derived from the theory in such a way that testing the hypotheses helps us to evaluate the overall theory. For example, one of the specific hypotheses we develop might be *There is a positive relationship between support for democratic principles and education.*

The research design also includes the *conceptual* (or *nominal*) and *operational* definitions for the basic concepts used in the research: What do we *mean* by these *concepts,* and how do we *measure* them? It specifies how and where the *data* will be collected. It also includes a plan for the *statistical analysis* of the data: What statistical techniques will we use in this analysis?

After the research design is developed, we execute it: We collect the data and prepare it for analysis. Then the analysis begins. *We try to explain the dependent variable by showing that there is a pattern between the variation in the dependent variable and the variation in the independent variable.*

We use *tests of statistical significance* and *measures of association* in this process of evaluating relationships between variables. Tests of statistical significance help us to decide whether there is any relationship at all between variables; if there is one, measures of association tell us how strong it is.

TESTS OF STATISTICAL SIGNIFICANCE

Definition and Use of Significance Tests

A *test of statistical significance* determines whether a relationship between variables in a probability sample can be generalized to the population from which the sample was selected.

Tests of statistical significance are based on probability theory. *A test of statistical significance must be used for analysis only when the data are from a probability sample.* It is not appropriate to use a test of statistical significance to analyze relationships for haphazard or quota samples.

It is also unnecessary to use a test of statistical significance when you are using the entire population rather than a sample. For example, the data included in the GSS and NES files are based on probability samples, but the data in the STATES, GLOBAL, and HOUSE files are not based on samples at all. We do not have a sample of states; we have the entire population of all 50 states. We do not have a sample of the U.S. representatives in the 108th Congress; we have the entire population of 435 representatives in the 109th Congress. Similarly, the GLOBAL file contains all nations that have a population of 200,000 or more.

On the other hand, although it is not necessary to use a test of statistical significance for the whole population, researchers sometimes do this anyway to help assess the importance of the results, especially when the total number of cases in the population is fairly small—which is the case for both the STATES file and the GLOBAL file.

Let's take an example to show what a test of statistical significance tells us. Let's say you want to test the following hypothesis using the GSS data: *Women are more likely to support gun-control laws than are men.* For the dependent variable, let's use 108) GUN LAW?, which indicates support for requiring a permit to buy a gun.

➤ Data File: **GSS**
➤ Task: **Cross-tabulation**
➤ Row Variable: **108) GUN LAW?**
➤ Column Variable: **1) SEX**
➤ View: **Tables**
➤ Display: **Column %**

GUN LAW? by SEX
Cramer's V: 0.173**

GUN LAW?	SEX: MALE	FEMALE	TOTAL
FAVOR	610	958	1568
	71.9%	85.9%	79.9%
OPPOSE	238	157	395
	28.1%	14.1%	20.1%
Missing	1155	1392	2547
TOTAL	848	1115	1963
	100.0%	100.0%	

Is there a relationship between the dependent variable support for gun-control laws *and the independent variable* gender? We compare the percentages horizontally and see that there is a pattern. Females are more likely to support gun-control laws than are males—85.9% of females favored the gun law compared with 71.9% of males.

There is a difference of 14 percentage points between males and females *in this sample.* However, it is possible that this difference in the sample occurred because of *sampling error*—error that occurred because we are using a sample rather than the entire population. Putting it differently, that relationship might have occurred in the sample (even if it doesn't exist in the population) because of *chance*—in the same way that a fair person flipping a fair coin might get six heads in a row simply by chance.

Thus, we cannot simply assume that a relationship found in a probability sample also applies to the population from which the sample was selected. That is why we need a test of statistical significance. Based on probability theory, a test of statistical significance will allow us to decide whether the relationship observed in the sample actually exists in the population.

Statistical Significance and Decisions

If we find a relationship in a sample, we use a test of statistical significance to make a decision about this relationship in the population. We usually make one of two decisions:

1. There is a real relationship between these variables in the population from which the sample was selected. We call this a *statistically significant relationship.*
2. There is *no* relationship between these variables in the population. The relationship is *not statistically significant.* Any relationship we found between these variables in the sample occurred simply by *chance*—because of sampling error.

Note that we are also testing the *null hypothesis* here. The null hypothesis states that there is no relationship between the variables.

- If we find a statistically significant relationship, we *reject* the null hypothesis. We are deciding that there is a relationship between the two variables.
- If we decide that the relationship is not statistically significant, we have decided that there is no relationship between the variables. In this situation, we might say that we accept the null hypothesis. Strictly speaking, however, it is more accurate to say that we *fail to reject* the null hypothesis.

Significance Level

A *significance level* tells us the probability that a relationship found in a probability sample occurred simply by chance (sampling error) and does not really exist in the population.

There are different kinds of significance tests, depending on the levels of measurement of the variables involved. For any significance test, however, the crucial piece of information we need is the significance level, which is often symbolized by the letter P (for "probability"). It tells us the probability that any relationship between variables in a sample occurred by chance.

We can state this in different terms: *The significance level tells us the probability that there is no real relationship between the two variables in the population from which the sample was selected.* Let's take two examples of different significance levels and show how they would be interpreted.

.01—A significance level of .01 for a relationship in a sample means there is only 1 chance out of 100 that the relationship does not exist in the population from which the sample was selected.

.05—A significance level of .05 means there are 5 chances out of 100 that the relationship found in the sample does not exist in the population from which the sample was selected.

By custom, we use the .05 level as the cutoff point to decide whether a relationship is statistically significant.

- If the significance level is *greater than .05,* we decide that the relationship is not statistically significant—that there is no real relationship between the two variables in the population from which the sample was selected.

- If the significance level is *.05 or less,* we decide that the relationship is statistically significant—that there is a real relationship between the two variables in the population from which the sample was selected.

As we have indicated before, there are various kinds of tests of statistical significance, depending primarily on the levels of measurement of the variables involved. If one variable is nominal and the other is either nominal or ordinal, we use a test of statistical significance called *chi-square*. If both variables are ordinal, we use a different test of statistical significance; if both variables are interval or ratio, we use another test.

In the preceding example, support for gun-control laws is ordinal and gender is nominal. Therefore, we would use the chi-square test of statistical significance. In this particular example, the significance level from the chi-square test is .000. (In the worksheet section of this chapter, you will see how to obtain these statistics in MicroCase.) That means that there is less than 1 chance out of 1,000 that the relationship in the sample between support for gun-control laws and gender could have occurred just by chance. That is, there is less than 1 chance out of 1,000 that this relationship does not really exist in the population. Therefore, we say that there is a *statistically significant* relationship between support for gun-control laws and gender.

Figure 10.1 Evaluation of a Relationship from a Probability Sample

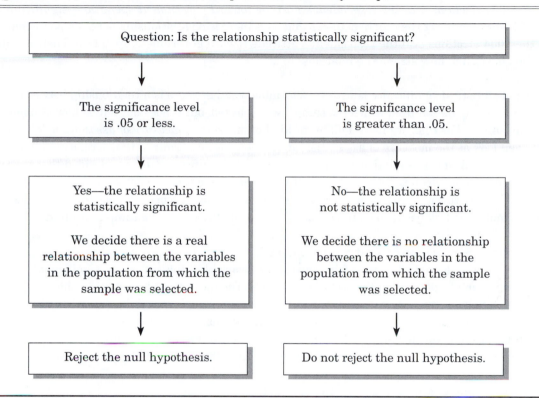

We have now decided that there is a real relationship (a statistically significant relationship) between support for gun-control laws and gender in the population from which the sample was selected. Therefore, we *reject* the null hypothesis that there is no relationship between support for gun-control laws and gender. This result would support the theory we were investigating.

In evaluating a relationship in a sample, the first question we need to ask is whether the relationship is statistically significant. To give an overall perspective on the process so far, Figure 10.1 presents a flow chart for the evaluation of a relationship from a probability sample.

Let's take another example. Using the NES data file, for the relationship between voting participation in the 2004 (NES 04) elections (VOTED?) and the respondent's attitude toward government spending (GOVT SPEND), the significance level is indicated as Prob. = .025. (**Note:** Both variables are ordinal, so we would use ordinal statistics.) That means that there are only 25 chances out of 1,000 that this relationship (between voting participation in the 2004 elections and the respondent's attitude toward government spending) occurred just because of sampling error and doesn't really exist in the population from which the sample was selected. We can be very confident (975 chances out of 1,000) that there is a real relationship between those two variables in the population from which the sample was selected. Although it is possible that we could be wrong (25 chances out of 1,000), we are deciding that this relationship really exists in the population. It didn't just occur because we were using a sample rather than the total population.

So, we conclude: *There is a statistically significant relationship between participation on the day of the 2004 elections and the respondent's attitude toward government spending—significant at the .05 level.* We reject the null hypothesis that says there is no relationship between participation in the 2004 elections and the respondent's attitude toward government spending. Then we turn to the question of how strong the relationship is.

A test of statistical significance is used to determine whether there is a relationship between variables in the population from which the sample was selected, but it does not tell us how *strong* that relationship is. For that, we need a different kind of measure: a *measure of association*. We might not even look at the measure of association at all if we have determined that a relationship is statistically significant. If a relationship is not statistically significant, we have decided that there is *no* relationship between the variables, and it would not make sense to ask how strong a "nonrelationship" is. However, there is a qualification to this, and before discussing measures of association, let's examine the link between statistical significance and the size of the sample involved.

Statistical Significance and Sample Size

Given a certain degree of relationship between two variables, the statistical significance of that relationship might depend on the size of the sample. The more cases in a sample, the more likely that a relationship will be statistically significant. If the sample size is large, we should be confident that a relationship in a sample exists in the population, because we have more cases on which to base our conclusion. On the other hand, when we are dealing with a small sample, we will be less confident that we can generalize results from the sample to the population.

In a large sample, a very weak relationship between two variables might be statistically significant. For an example of an extremely large sample size, there is the National Survey of Religious Identification, 1989–90, which contains more than 100,000 cases. With a sample that large, even the tiniest relationship between two variables will be statistically significant.

In a small sample, however, a strong relationship between two variables might not be statistically significant. What should we do about such a relationship? If we are using a small sample, then we should consider examining that relationship again with a larger sample.

MEASURES OF ASSOCIATION

A *measure of association* is a measure of the degree of relationship between two variables.

A test of statistical significance helps to determine whether a relationship between variables actually *exists;* a measure of association tells us *how strong* that relationship is. Relationships between variables can be anywhere from extremely weak to perfect, so we need to measure just how strong the relationship is.

Costner's P-R-E Criterion

As with significance tests, we must select the right measure of association on the basis of the measurement levels of the variables involved. Given a particular level of measurement, however, there are still many different measures of association from which to choose.

Herbert Costner developed a way to sort out measures of association that he considered to be most useful: the *P-R-E criterion*. P-R-E stands for *proportional reduction in error*. In explaining this P-R-E criterion, we will further demonstrate the idea of a measure of association and discuss the ways in which some researchers sort out different measures of association. However, not all of the measures of association that we will discuss are P-R-E measures.

The distinctive feature of measures of association that meet the P-R-E criterion is that they can be interpreted in a certain way. The ***P-R-E interpretation*** *of such measures of association is the proportion by which we can reduce the number of errors in predicting the dependent variable by knowing the relationship between the dependent variable and the independent variable.*

Let's use an example to demonstrate the P-R-E criterion. Based on the HOUSE file, the graphic below presents a cross-tabulation (with the cell frequencies, column totals, and row totals) between the political party affiliations of representatives and how they voted on a bill to authorize military tribunals and ban torture.

➤ Data File: **HOUSE**
➤ Task: **Cross-tabulation**
➤ Row Variable: **11) PARTY**
➤ Column Variable: **64) TRIBUNALS**
➤ View: **Tables**
➤ Display: **Frequency**

PARTY   by   TRIBUNALS
Cramer's V: 0.805**

		TRIBUNALS			
		NO	YES	Missing	TOTAL
PARTY	Democrat	162	35	8	197
	Republican	7	215	7	222
	Missing	1	0	0	1
	TOTAL	169	250	15	419

Predicting Without *Knowledge of the Independent Variable*

As you can see, there is a very strong relationship between political party preference and one's vote on the tribunals. Suppose, however, that you had no knowledge of that relationship. Instead, let's say that you knew only that of the 419 representatives who voted on this bill, 169 voted against it and 250 voted for it. Your job is to predict the dependent variable (vote on this bill) on the basis of this information without knowledge of the independent variable (political party affiliation).

That is, you need to predict how each of the 419 representatives voted, without knowing anything about them except that 169 voted against the bill and 250 voted for the bill. How would you do that? You would have no choice except to guess.

In that situation, how many errors would you make in your predictions? That, of course, would depend on your guessing strategy and on how lucky you were. However, there is one way to determine exactly how many errors you would make by just guessing. Further, there is no other strategy you could use that would be sure to increase your prediction success. The strategy is this: Because more people voted for the bill, simply predict that all of them voted for the bill. That way, you would make *169 errors* (those who voted against the bill). There is no better guessing strategy than that. So, let's use 169 as the estimate of the number of errors you would make in predicting the dependent variable *without knowledge of the independent variable.*

Predicting With *Knowledge of the Independent Variable*

Now suppose you have knowledge of the relationship between the dependent and independent variables. You have all the information in the previous table, you know each representative's political party affiliation, and you want to predict how each individual representative voted. Thus, you are trying to predict a person's vote on the bill by knowing that person's political party affiliation.

What guessing strategy would you use now? Because the great majority of the Democrats voted against the bill, let's predict that each Democrat voted against the bill. We will make 35 errors, because 35 Democrats voted for the bill.

Because all but 7 of the Republicans voted for the bill, let's predict that each Republican voted for the bill. We will make 7 errors here, because 7 Republicans voted against the bill.

How many total errors do we make *with* knowledge of the independent variable? We make 35 errors for the Democrats and 7 errors for the Republicans—a total of 42 errors with knowledge of the independent variable.

Proportional Reduction in Errors

In this particular example, we started out by making 169 errors in predicting the dependent variable *without* knowledge of the independent variable. *With* knowledge of the independent variable, we reduced the number of errors to 42. By what proportion have we reduced the number of errors in predicting the dependent variable by knowing the independent variable? We can compute this with the following formula:

$$\frac{\text{(errors without knowledge)} - \text{(errors with knowledge)}}{\text{(errors without knowledge)}} = \frac{(169 - 42)}{169} = .75$$

Thus, by knowing the independent variable *political party affiliation,* we can reduce the number of errors in predicting voting on this bill by .75 (or 75%). That is, we make 75% fewer errors this way than we did when we were simply guessing without knowledge of the political party affiliation of the representatives and without knowledge of the connection between political party affiliation and voting on this bill. This is a very strong relationship.

When we use a P-R-E measure of association, we can interpret the results in several ways, but ultimately they all mean basically the same thing. A P-R-E measure of association tells us

- the *degree of relationship* between the dependent variable and the independent variable

- how well we can *predict* the dependent variable by knowing the independent variable

- how well the independent variable *explains* the dependent variable

All three interpretations basically mean the same thing: We are explaining the dependent variable by relating variation in it to variation in the independent variable.

Nominal Measures of Association

MicroCase has three commonly used measures of association for the situation in which one variable is nominal and the other is either nominal or ordinal: *lambda, Cramer's V,* and the *contingency coefficient.* For purposes of this book, we will just use lambda and Cramer's V.

Lambda

The preceding example (political party affiliation and voting on the tribunals bill) demonstrated the basic idea underlying the P-R-E criterion: the proportion by which we can reduce the number of errors in predicting the dependent variable by knowing the independent variable. However, the example also demonstrated the computation of a particular P-R-E measure of association: lambda. In this example, lambda = .75. (Lambda has a possible range of 0 to 1.0.)

- When lambda = 0, there is *no relationship at all* between two variables: Knowing the independent variable would not help us to reduce the number of errors in predicting the dependent variable at all.

- If lambda = 1.0, there is a *perfect relationship* between the dependent variable and the independent variable: If we know the independent variable, we can predict the dependent variable with 100% success.

Although lambda has the advantage of being a P-R-E measure, it sometimes underestimates the relationship between the dependent variable and the independent variable. Therefore, in this situation, one of the other measures of association may provide a more meaningful estimate of the degree of relationship between the dependent and independent variables.

Lambda underestimates the relationships between two variables when one or both of the variables is highly *skewed.* For our purposes here, a variable is skewed when there are great numbers of cases in some categories but only small numbers of cases in other categories. For example, race is a skewed variable in the United States—the great majority of people are white. On the other hand, gender is not skewed—roughly half of the population is male and roughly half is female. Another skewed variable is the attitude toward capital punishment—the great majority of people favor capital punishment.

If either variable in a cross-tabulation is highly skewed, then lambda will usually underestimate the degree of relationship between the two variables. If *both* variables are skewed, this will probably make the problem even worse—as you will see in the worksheet section when you examine the relationship between race and support for capital punishment.

Another limitation of lambda is that it will always be 0 when the modal value of the dependent variable is the same across all categories of the independent variable. What does that mean? It means that one particular row of the dependent variable has more cases in it for each category of the independent variable than does any other row—for example, if we were looking at the relationship between support for requiring a police permit to buy a gun and political party preference.

➤ Data File: **GSS**
    ➤ Task: **Cross-tabulation**
➤ Row Variable: **108) GUN LAW?**
➤ Column Variable: **62) PARTY**
    ➤ View: **Column %**

GUN LAW?   by   PARTY
Cramer's V: 0.139**

		PARTY				
		DEMOCRAT	INDEPEND.	REPUBLICAN	Missing	TOTAL
GUN LAW?	FAVOR	721	327	489	31	1537
		86.0%	79.2%	73.5%		80.2%
	OPPOSE	117	86	176	16	379
		14.0%	20.8%	26.5%		19.8%
	Missing	1125	584	794	44	2547
	TOTAL	838	413	665	91	1916
		100.0%	100.0%	100.0%		

In this analysis we find that a majority of Democrats are in the *Favor* row, a majority of Independents are in the *Favor* row, and a majority of Republicans are in the *Favor* row. Thus, the modal value of the dependent variable is the same (*Favor*) for all categories of the independent variable (political party preference). Because of the way in which lambda is computed, it will always come out close to zero in such circumstances even when there is a relationship between the two variables involved. You can see the value of lambda when we switch to the Statistics view.

Data File: **GSS**
    Task: **Cross-tabulation**
Row Variable: **108) GUN LAW?**
Column Variable: **62) PARTY**
    ➤ View: **Statistics (Summary)**

GUN LAW?   by   PARTY

Nominal Statistics

Chi-Square: 36.895   (DF =   2; Prob. = 0.000)
V: 0.139   C: 0.137
Lambda: 0.055   Lambda: 0.000   Lambda: 0.040
(DV=62)   (DV=108)

Ordinal Statistics

Gamma: 0.284   Tau-b: 0.131   Tau-c: 0.119
s.error   0.047   s.error   0.022   s.error   0.020

Dyx: 0.092   Dxy: 0.187
s.error   0.015   s.error   0.031

Prob. =   0.000

In this example, Republicans (73.5%) are less likely than Democrats (86.0%) and Independents (79.2%) to favor a gun permit, and the relationship is statistically significant (Prob. = .000), but lambda is close to zero.

Researchers may choose among the different nominal measures of association on the basis of the particular variables involved and the ways in which these variables are distributed. The decision might be based on which measure of association seems to provide the best representation of the relationship between the variables. Sometimes it makes a difference in the conclusions which nominal measure of association is used; sometimes it makes little difference.

Cramer's V

Cramer's V is not a P-R-E measure except in limited circumstances, but it is a measure of the degree of relationship between the dependent variable and the independent variable. Cramer's V uses a possible range of 0 to 1.0 to indicate the strength of the relationship between the dependent variable and the independent variable. When Cramer's V is 0, it means there is no relationship at all between the variables. When Cramer's V is 1.0, this means there is a perfect relationship between the two variables.

For the worksheet section of this chapter, we will use both Cramer's V and lambda. You will see that Cramer's V is useful in situations in which lambda underestimates the degree of relationship.

Ordinal Measures of Association

MicroCase provides three major measures of association for ordinal scale variables: *gamma, Kendall's tau,* and *Somers' D.* Before discussing those measures individually, let's note four points that apply to all three measures.

1. All three are P-R-E measures—thus, we interpret each one as the proportion by which we can reduce the number of errors in predicting the dependent variable by knowing the independent variable.

2. In terms of magnitude, each has a possible range of 0 to 1.0. As with nominal measures of association, when an ordinal measure of association is 0, there is no relationship at all between the dependent variable and the independent variable. Conversely, when the measure of association is 1.0, there is a perfect relationship between the two variables.

3. Unlike nominal measures of association, ordinal measures of association have *direction.* A hypothesis for a relationship between two ordinal variables specifies a certain direction (positive or negative) for the relationship, so ordinal measures of association have positive or negative direction. Please note, however, that the *direction* of a relationship has nothing to do with its *strength.* A measure of association of, say, −.60 is exactly as strong as a measure of +.60.

4. MicroCase computes one significance level, which applies to all three of these measures.

Let's use an example to demonstrate. In the NES 04 file, Kendall's tau for the relationship between support for legal abortion (ABORTION) and frequency of praying (PRAY) is −.287 and the significance level is .000. How would we interpret those results? Let's look at three aspects of those results.

- **Statistical Significance.** *There is a statistically significant relationship between support for legal abortions and frequency of praying, significant at the .000 level.* Thus, there is less than 1 chance out of 1,000 that the relationship in the sample occurred because of sampling error. We can have a great deal of confidence that this relationship, found in the sample, also exists in the population from which the sample was selected.

- **Direction of the Relationship.** This is a *negative* relationship—the more frequently people pray, the less willing they are to allow a legal abortion.

- **P-R-E Interpretation.** By knowing the independent variable (frequency of praying), we can reduce by 28.7% the number of errors in predicting the dependent variable (support for legal abortions). Thus, we have a substantial relationship between the dependent variable and the independent variable.

Because the three ordinal measures of association have all of this in common, what difference does it make which we use? Because all three are P-R-E measures of association, we might expect that they would all produce the same result. However, because of differences in their assumptions and calculations, it is best to say that they provide different *estimates* of the proportional reduction in error. They do not produce exactly the same results. Your conclusion about the degree of relationship between the dependent variable and the independent variable might differ somewhat depending on which measure of association you used.

Both Kendall's tau and Somers' D are conservative estimates of the degree of relationship between the dependent variable and the independent variable. They produce results that are very similar. By contrast, because of the way it is computed, gamma always provides the highest estimate of the proportional reduction in error. Gamma sometimes exaggerates the degree of relationship between the dependent variable and the independent variable. For the purposes of this book, we will use Kendall's tau. Keep in mind, however, that other ordinal measures of association, such as Somers' D and gamma, are similar to Kendall's tau in purpose and interpretation.

In political research, Kendall's tau is one of the most commonly used measures of association for ordinal variables. Thus, if you are not sure which ordinal measure of association to use, it usually is a good idea to use Kendall's tau. MicroCase has two versions of Kendall's tau: *tau-b* and *tau-c*. Which should you use?

- Use Kendall's tau-b if the table is *square*. A square table is one in which the number of categories in the dependent variable is the same as the number in the independent variable. For example, let's say we cross-tabulated interest in politics (*High, Medium,* or *Low*) by age category (Under 30, 30 to 50, or Over 50). In this example, there would be three categories in each variable, so we would use tau-b.

- Use Kendall's tau-c if the table is not square. For example, let's say we cross-tabulated support for gun-control legislation (*Favor* or *Oppose*) by political interest (*High, Medium,* or *Low*). In this example, there are two categories in one variable (support for gun-control legislation) and three categories in the other (political interest), so we would use tau-c.

One caution should be kept in mind when looking at the direction of a relationship: Because of the way in which variables are coded (the way in which numbers are assigned to the categories of the variable), the direction of a relationship might not be as it first appears. Let's take an example. In the GSS file, Kendall's tau-b for the relationship between FAM INCOME and

EDUCATION is .364 and the relationship is statistically significant at the .000 level. That relationship between family income and education is positive, as would be expected, and there is no problem there.

For both of the variables, the higher numbers represent higher degrees of the variable. FAM INCOME is coded 1 for less than $35,000; 2 for 35k–69.9k; and so on. Thus, the higher a person's family income, the higher the code assigned to the person for this variable. Similarly, EDCAT is coded 1 for under 12 years of school, 2 for 12 years of school, 3 for 1–3 years of college, and 4 for 4 or more years of college. Thus, the higher a person's education, the higher the code assigned to the person for this variable.

A problem of interpretation would arise, however, if one of the variables had been coded so that the higher codes represent lower degrees of the variable. In this situation, Kendall's tau would be negative—even though the actual relationship between family income and education was still the same. Suppose we coded education as follows: 1 = 4 or more years of college; 2 = 1–3 years of college; 3 = 12 years of school; and 4 = under 12 years of school. In this case, the higher codes would represent less education and the lower codes would represent more education. Further, if we coded education that way and examined the relationship between education and family income, Kendall's tau would show a negative relationship simply because of the way education was coded. Thus, when you examine the direction of a relationship, first look at the ways in which the two variables are coded.

Measure of Association for Interval or Ratio Variables

When both variables are either interval or ratio, we use the *Pearson correlation coefficient,* which is designated by the letter *r.* We will briefly describe this measure of association here and return to it in Chapter 13, on correlation and regression.

A Pearson correlation coefficient (r) measures the degree of relationship between two metric (interval or ratio) variables. It also shows the direction (positive or negative) of the relationship. In terms of magnitude, r varies from 0 to 1.0 in the same way as the other measures of association we have discussed. When r = 0, there is no relationship between the dependent variable and the independent variable; when the magnitude of r = 1.0 (r is either +1.0 or –1.0), there is a perfect relationship.

Pearson's correlation is accompanied by a test of statistical significance. We use the significance level to determine whether the relationship is statistically significant. If it is, we use the Pearson correlation coefficient to measure the degree of the relationship.

Guidelines

How strong should a relationship between variables be before we consider it to be important? There is no commonly accepted standard. Table 10.1 presents some rough guidelines. Use these guidelines loosely for the absolute value (the magnitude, whether the value is positive or negative) of either nominal or ordinal measures of association. We will have different guidelines later for Pearson's correlation coefficient. Remember that some measures of association tend to overestimate relationships and others tend to underestimate them; keep that in mind when applying these guidelines.

Table 10.1 Rough Guidelines for Interpreting the Strength of a Nominal or Ordinal Measure of Association

If the absolute value of a nominal or ordinal measure of association is	Then, as a rough guideline, let's say the relationship is
Under .1	Very weak—perhaps too weak to be of any importance
Between .10 and .19	Weak
Between .20 and .29	Moderate
.30 or above	Strong

In case you have become a little confused about all the measures of association, Table 10.2 presents a quick guide for some of the basics covered here. Keep in mind, too, that these measures of association will become clearer as you use them in the worksheet section.

Table 10.2 Brief Information for Selected Measures of Association

Levels of Measurement	Measure of Association	Is It a P-R-E Measure?	Comments
Two nominal variables *or*	Lambda *or*	Yes	In some situations, lambda underestimates the degree of relationship.
One nominal variable and one ordinal variable	Cramer's V	No	Among non–P-R-E measures, this one is very good. Use it if lambda underestimates the relationship.
Two ordinal variables variables	Kendall's tau	Yes	This is a very commonly used ordinal measure of association. Use it if you are not sure which ordinal measure to use. Use tau-b for square tables (same number of categories in each variable); otherwise, use tau-c.
Two interval or ratio variables	Pearson correlation coefficient (r)	Yes	Pearson's r will be covered more fully in Chapter 13, on correlation and regression.

Research Methods in Political Science

More Examples

Let's run through three more examples of relationships using the GSS data file—one example that uses nominal statistics and two that use ordinal statistics.

Example 1: Support for Social Welfare by Race

Based upon what we know from our analysis of the GSS (FAM INCOME by RACE), African Americans generally have had worse economic situations than have white Americans, so let's hypothesize that African Americans will be more likely to support social welfare programs than will white Americans. For this particular analysis, we will use the belief that it should be the government's responsibility to reduce income differences between the rich and the poor (EQUAL-IZE $) as an indicator of support for social welfare. The column percentages are presented below.

➤ Data File: **GSS**
➤ Task: **Cross-tabulation**
➤ Row Variable: **90) EQUALIZE $**
➤ Column Variable: **38) RACE**
➤ View: **Tables**
➤ Display: **Column %**

EQUALIZE $ by RACE
Cramer's V: .105**

		RACE			
		WHITE	BLACK	Missing	TOTAL
E Q U A L I Z E $	SHOULD 1-3	644	147	131	791
		45.1%	54.2%		46.6%
	MODERATE 4	280	65	65	345
		19.6%	24.0%		20.3%
	SHDN'T.5-7	503	59	62	562
		35.2%	21.8%		33.1%
	Missing	1857	363	334	2554
	TOTAL	1427	271	592	1698
		100.0%	100.0%		

When we compare the column percentages horizontally, we see that African Americans are more likely than white Americans to say that it should be the government's responsibility to reduce income differences between the rich and the poor. Now we need to test this for statistical significance.

Data File: **GSS**
Task: **Cross-tabulation**
Row Variable: **90) EQUALIZE $**
Column Variable: **38) RACE**
➤ View: **Statistics (Summary)**

EQUALIZE $ by RACE

Nominal Statistics

Chi-Square: 18.694 (DF = 2; Prob. = 0.000)					
V:	0.105	C:	0.104		
Lambda:	0.000	Lambda:	0.000	Lambda:	0.000
(DV=38)		(DV=90)			

Ordinal Statistics

Gamma:	-0.211	Tau-b:	-0.087	Tau-c:	-0.071
s.error	0.053	s.error	0.022	s.error	0.018
Dyx:	-0.133	Dxy:	-0.056		
s.error	0.034	s.error	0.014		
Prob. =	0.000				

Support for social welfare is an ordinal variable, but race is nominal, so we will need nominal statistics. Looking at the Statistics view, we see that the significance level (from the chi-square test) is indicated as Prob. = .000. Thus, there is less than 1 chance out of 1,000 that this relationship could have occurred just by chance if it didn't exist in the population (U.S. adults) from which the sample was selected. Because this is less than .050, we can be confident that there is a real relationship between those two variables. So, we term this a statistically significant relationship, and we reject the null hypothesis that there is no relationship between support for social welfare and race.

Now we need a measure of association to tell us the strength of this relationship. Lambda = .000. In addition, if we look back at the table, this can be explained by the fact that the mode for both categories of the independent variable is the same: A plurality of both whites and blacks believe that the government should do something to equalize incomes. You will remember that when the modes of all categories of a nominal variable are the same, the value of lambda is 0. The variable *race* is skewed and because of the way in which lambda is computed, it underestimates the degree of relationship. In this situation, Cramer's V is .105, and this is a better reflection of the degree of relationship between the two variables.

Example 2: Environmental Regulation by Family Income Level

Now let's hypothesize a positive relationship between the opinion that government should do more to protect the environment and family income level. The column percentages for the cross-tabulation of the opinion that America is doing enough to protect the world environment (GRN LAWS) and family income (FAM INCOME) are given below.

Data File: **GSS**
Task: **Cross-tabulation**
➤ Row Variable: **328) GRNLAWS**
➤ Column Variable: **57) FAM.INCOME**
➤ View: **Tables**
➤ Display: **Column %**

GRNLAWS   by   FAM.INCOME
Cramer's V: 0.028**

		FAM.INCOME				
		$1K-$14999	$15K-24999	25K & UP	Missing	TOTAL
GRNLAWS	SHOULD	183	168	856	196	1207
		94.3%	95.5%	93.6%		93.9%
	SHOULD NOT	11	8	59	16	78
		5.7%	4.5%	6.4%		6.1%
	Missing	446	334	1808	425	3013
	TOTAL	194	176	915	637	1285
		100.0%	100.0%	100.0%		

If you compare the column percentages horizontally, you see that there is some variation in these percentages but that there is no real pattern. The variations in the percentages might have occurred just by chance through sampling error. So, we need to check the significance level.

Data File: **GSS**
Task: **Cross-tabulation**
Row Variable: **328) GRNLAWS**
Column Variable: **57) FAM.INCOME**
➤ View: **Statistics (Summary)**

GRNLAWS   by   FAM.INCOME

Nominal Statistics
_____

Chi-Square: 1.001   (DF =   2; Prob. = 0.606)
V: 0.028   C: 0.028
Lambda: 0.000   Lambda: 0.000   Lambda: 0.000
(DV=57)   (DV=328)

Ordinal Statistics
_____

Gamma: 0.101   Tau-b: 0.022   Tau-c: 0.010
s.error   0.121   s.error   0.026   s.error   0.012

Dyx: 0.011   Dxy: 0.043
s.error   0.013   s.error   0.052

Prob. =   0.406

Here we have two ordinal variables, so we need ordinal statistics. The significance level is listed as Prob. = .406. This means that there are 406 chances out of 1,000 that this relationship could have occurred just by chance. Putting it differently, there are 406 chances out of 1,000 that there is no relationship between these two variables in the population (U.S. adults) from which the GSS sample was selected.

Because .406 is much greater than our .05 cutoff point, we need to conclude that there is not a statistically significant relationship between the two variables. Thus, we do not reject the null hypothesis that there is no relationship between the opinion that America is doing enough for the world environment and family income level.

Because we have decided that there is no relationship between the two variables, we really don't need to go any further. There is nothing in the table to suggest that there might be an important relationship here that needs further investigation, such as a larger sample.

Even so, let's take a look at the measure of association to satisfy curiosity. Let's use Kendall's tau. We don't have the same number of categories in both variables: Family income level has four categories and the environmental protection variable has two. Because we don't have the same number of categories in both variables, we will need Kendall's tau-c. In this situation, Kendall's tau-c is −.010. This means that (if the relationship were statistically significant) we could reduce errors in predicting the dependent variable (environmental protection) by 1.0% by knowing the independent variable (family income level).

Even if that relationship were statistically significant, it would not be strong enough to be theoretically important. That is, family income level does not go far in helping to explain the opinion that the government is doing enough to protect the environment.

Example 3: Environmental Spending by Level of Education

Let's examine another variable that might be related to the opinion that the government should do more to protect the environment—the level of education (EDCAT). Let's hypothesize a positive relationship.

Data File: **GSS**
Task: **Cross-tabulation**
Row Variable: **310) SP.ENVIRON**
➤ Column Variable: **34) EDCAT**
➤ View: **Tables**
➤ Display: **Column %**

SP.ENVIRON by EDCAT
Cramer's V: 0.081**

| | EDCAT | | | | |
		NO HS GRAD	HS GRAD	COLL EDUC	Missing	TOTAL
SP.ENVIRON	MORE	132	214	455	1	801
		48.7%	48.2%	59.5%		54.1%
	SAME	95	166	227	4	488
		35.1%	37.4%	29.7%		33.0%
	LESS	44	64	83	2	191
		16.2%	14.4%	10.8%		12.9%
	Missing	510	760	1749	4	3023
	TOTAL	271	444	765	11	1480
		100.0%	100.0%	100.0%		

As we compare the column percentages horizontally, we see a definite pattern. The higher the level of education, the more likely an individual is to believe that the government should spend more to protect the environment. We need to determine next whether the relationship is statistically significant. Because both variables are ordinal, we need ordinal statistics.

➤ View: **Statistics (Summary)**

The significance level (Prob. = .000) indicates that there is less than 1 chance out of 1,000 that this relationship could have occurred just by chance alone if there were not a relationship between the variables in the population from which the sample was selected. Because the significance level is below .05, we say that this relationship is statistically significant. Thus, we reject the null hypothesis that there is no relationship between the opinion that America is doing enough for the world environment and an individual's education level.

Next, we need a measure of association to determine how strong the relationship is. Let's use Kendall's tau again. Because we do not have the same number of categories in both variables, we need Kendall's tau-c. Here Kendall's tau-c = -.088, indicating a weak degree of relationship between the two variables. The P-R-E (Proportional Reduction in Error) interpretation is: By knowing the independent variable (education level), we can reduce the number of errors in predicting the dependent variable (the opinion on environmental spending) by 8.8%.

TERMS INTRODUCED IN THIS CHAPTER

Test of statistical significance   Measure of association
Significance level   P-R-E interpretation

FOR FURTHER READING

For further information on tests of statistical significance and measures of association, see Chapters 5 and 6 of William Fox, *Social Statistics Using MicroCase,* 4th ed. (Belmont, CA: Wadsworth, 2003).

For another good source, see Chapters 9, 10, and 18 of Susan Ann Kay, *Introduction to the Analysis of Political Data* (Englewood Cliffs, NJ: Prentice-Hall, 1991).

A good introduction to these topics is given in Chapters 4 through 7 of Leonard Champney, *Introduction to Quantitative Political Science* (New York: HarperCollins, 1995).

For a research example, see Paul D. Senese, "Between Dispute and War: The Effect of Joint Democracy on Interstate Conflict Escalation," *Journal of Politics* 59 (February 1997): 1–27.

For some other research examples, browse through the readings presented in Marcus E. Ethridge, *The Political Research Experience: Readings and Analysis,* 2nd ed. (Guilford, CT: Dushkin, 1994).

worksheet

CHAPTER **10**

NAME:

COURSE:

DATE:

Workbook exercises and software are copyrighted. Copying is prohibited by law.

1. People's views on government spending depend somewhat on their own incomes. People who have more income have less need of economic assistance programs from the government. Also, those with more income are more likely to feel that they are paying for the assistance programs. On the other hand, people with less income have a greater need of economic assistance programs from the government. Let's state the hypothesis and null hypothesis as follows:

Hypothesis: There is a negative relationship between support for spending to help the poor and income level.

Null hypothesis: There is no relationship between support for spending to help the poor and income level.

Let's test this hypothesis using variables from the GSS data file. (**Note:** As you select the variables for the statistical analysis in these exercises, please be sure to read the variable descriptions.)

> ➤ Data File: **GSS**
> ➤ Task: **Cross-tabulation**
> ➤ Row Variable: **233) HELP POOR?**
> ➤ Column Variable: **57) FAM.INCOME**
> ➤ View: **Tables**
> ➤ Display: **Column %**

Briefly describe the pattern in the results displayed in this table.

_____

_____

_____

_____

Now obtain the significance level and measure of association.

> Data File: **GSS**
> Task: **Cross-tabulation**
> Row Variable: **233) HELP POOR?**
> Column Variable: **57) FAM INCOME**
> ➤ View: **Statistics (Summary)**

Chapter 10   Worksheet   199

worksheet

Because both of these variables are ordinal, we need ordinal statistics. Write the significance level.   Prob. = _____

Is this relationship statistically significant?   Yes   No

Do we reject the null hypothesis?   Yes   No

Write the value of Kendall's tau-c (use tau-c because the dependent variable does not have the same number of categories as the independent variable).   Kendall's tau-c = _____

With regard to the strength of the relationship, there is a moderately weak relationship between support for spending to help the poor and family income. We might have expected that relationship to be stronger. That is one piece of evidence to support the idea that economic self-interest is not the only factor that determines people's views on government spending issues.

With regard to the direction of the relationship, there is a positive relationship. We hypothesized a negative relationship. Were we wrong? Actually, the relationship is the kind of relationship that we hypothesized—it just doesn't appear so because of the way the dependent variable is coded. There is a problem here that must be kept in mind whenever you examine the direction of a relationship. Let's examine both the independent variable and the dependent variable to see what caused the sign of Kendall's tau to be positive when we expected a negative relationship.

Look at the variable description for 57) FAM.INCOME. Note that this variable is coded in such a way that the higher the number, the greater the family income. The code 1 stands for the lowest income category (<$15,000) and the code 3 stands for the highest income category ($25K & up). That is fine—the higher code represents the higher degree of the concept, and vice versa.

Now look at the variable description for 233) HELP POOR?. If we conceptualize this variable as support for spending to help the poor, then the lowest code (1) represents the highest support (government should help) and the highest code (3) represents the lowest support (people should help themselves).

Thus, the dependent variable is coded in the opposite fashion from what we might expect. For variables that have direction (ordinal, interval, and ratio), we usually want higher numbers to represent higher degrees of the concept and lower numbers to represent lower degrees of the concept. When the coding is not set up that way, it causes the problem we just encountered— the direction of the relationship does not conveniently reflect the reality of the relationship.

We can do one of two things about this problem: First, we can recode the variable so that this problem will not occur at all. Second, we can simply reverse the signs of the results and make a note that we have reversed the signs because of the coding problem. In this situation, for example, despite the fact that Kendall's tau is positive, there actually is a negative relationship between the two concepts: People with more family income have less support for spending to help the poor.

2. We will now examine a relationship that demonstrates that lambda sometimes underestimates the degree of relationship and that Cramer's V can be more useful in such situations. Look at the relationship between support for capital punishment and race. Given that a disproportionate number of African Americans have been subject to the death penalty, we will hypothesize that African Americans are more opposed to capital punishment than are white Americans.

worksheet

Data File: **GSS**
Task: **Cross-tabulation**
➤ Row Variable: **107) EXECUTE?**
➤ Column Variable: **38) RACE**
➤ View: **Tables**
➤ Display: **Column %**

Is there a pattern in those results? Do African Americans oppose capital punishment more than do white Americans? (Circle one.)   Yes   No

Now look at the significance level and measure of association.

Data File: **GSS**
Task: **Cross-tabulation**
Row Variable: **107) EXECUTE?**
Column Variable: **38) RACE**
➤ View: **Statistics (Summary)**

Because race is a nominal variable, we need to use nominal statistics. Based on the chi-square test of statistical significance, what is the significance level here?   Prob. = _____

Is this relationship statistically significant?   Yes   No

The null hypothesis is that there is no relationship between support for capital punishment and race. Do we reject the null hypothesis?   Yes   No

Because we need nominal statistics here, we will use lambda as a measure of association to tell us how strong the relationship is between attitude toward the death penalty and race. (**Note:** There are three lambda measures. Because we have always been using the row variable as the dependent variable, we will need the middle lambda, in which the row variable—Variable 107 in this situation—is specified as the dependent variable by the letters DV. Therefore, for all the analysis in this book, whenever you need to use lambda, use the middle lambda.)

Next, write in the value of lambda and the value of Cramer's V for this relationship.

Lambda = _____   Cramer's V = _____

In this situation, if we had used lambda, we would have concluded that the independent variable (race) did not help to explain the dependent variable (support for capital punishment), even though we saw that there was a substantial difference in the column percentages for whites and African Americans. However, if we use Cramer's V, we see that there is a strong relationship. Thus, in this situation, lambda understates the relationship between the two variables. Therefore, for this relationship, we would be better off using Cramer's V than lambda.

Using Cramer's V, the relationship is still not as strong as you might expect on the basis of looking at the column percentages. The reason is that both variables have skewed distributions: The great majority of the respondents are white, and the great majority of the respondents favor capital punishment. Because of the ways in which these two variables are distributed in the United States, lambda does not help to explain the relationship between race and capital punishment attitudes in the United States.

3. Do men and women differ on the issue of abortion? Let's hypothesize: Men are more likely to support allowing an abortion than are women. For our purposes, we will use variable ABORT POOR (attitude toward an abortion in the situation in which the family has a very low income and cannot afford any more children) to operationally define the concept of support for allowing an abortion.

Keep in mind, however, that a fuller testing of this hypothesis would require fuller measurement of the concept of support for allowing an abortion. Note that the GSS data file contains seven questions asking about abortion in various situations and that it also contains a composite index (a combined measure) based on six of these questions combined. After this exercise, you might want to examine the relationship between responses to these other abortion questions (or the composite index) and gender. For now, however, let's stick with the single question ABORT NO$.

Data File:	**GSS**
Task:	**Cross-tabulation**
➤ Row Variable:	**188) ABORT NO$**
➤ Column Variable:	**1) SEX**
➤ View:	**Tables**
➤ Display:	**Column %**

Compare the column percentages horizontally. Is there a pattern? That is, do males and females differ substantially in their responses to this question about allowing an abortion? (Circle one.)   Yes   No

Look at the significance level and the measure of association.

Data File:	**GSS**
Task:	**Cross-tabulation**
Row Variable:	**188) ABORT NO$**
Column Variable:	**1) SEX**
➤ View:	**Statistics (Summary)**

Because gender is a nominal variable, we need to use nominal statistics. Based on the chi-square test of statistical significance, what is the significance level here?   Prob. = _____

Is this relationship statistically significant?   Yes   No

The null hypothesis is: There is no relationship between support for allowing an abortion and gender. Do we reject the null hypothesis?   Yes   No

4. What kind of relationship is there between support for allowing an abortion and view of the Bible? Variable 127) BIBLE asks people which of three views about the Bible is closest to their own view: 1 = The Bible is the actual word of God and is to be taken literally . . . ; 2 = The Bible is the inspired word of God but not everything in it should be taken literally . . . ; 3 = The Bible is an ancient book of fables, . . . recorded by men.

Because of the way in which the variable is coded, let's conceptualize variable 127) BIBLE as biblical liberalism. Thus, those who selected option 1 (actual word of God) have the lowest biblical liberalism, those who selected option 2 (inspired word of God) are in the middle, and those who selected option 3 (ancient book of fables) have the highest biblical liberalism.

Based on our thoughts about how people's views of the Bible are related to their views on a variety of social issues, including abortion, we can formulate the following hypothesis and null hypothesis:

Hypothesis: There is a positive relationship between support for allowing an abortion and biblical liberalism.

Null hypothesis: There is no relationship between support for allowing an abortion and biblical liberalism.

Let's test the hypothesis.

Data File:	**GSS**
Task:	**Cross-tabulation**
Row Variable:	**188) ABORT NO$**
➤ Column Variable:	**127) BIBLE**
➤ View:	**Tables**
➤ Display:	**Column %**

Is it more appropriate here to use nominal or ordinal statistics? (**Hint:** Note that the hypothesis here has direction.) (Circle one.)

Nominal statistics   Ordinal statistics

Present the significance level for this relationship.   Prob. = _____

Is this relationship statistically significant?   Yes   No

Do we reject the null hypothesis?   Yes   No

Now generate the results of the analysis of association. Print this page and attach it to the exercise.

Which measure of association would be most appropriate here? (Circle one.)

a. Lambda

b. Cramer's V

c. Kendall's tau-b

d. Kendall's tau-c

Present the value of the measure of association you selected above.   _____

Is this relationship positive or negative? (Circle one.)

     Positive   Negative

Are the results in accord with the hypothesis?   Yes   No

Give a P-R-E interpretation of these results.

_____

_____

_____

_____

5. Is there any relationship between political distrust and how much people think elections cause government to pay attention to them? If people believe that elections cause the government to pay attention to what they think, then they will probably have lower political distrust. Thus, we hypothesize a negative relationship between political distrust and the belief that elections cause government to pay attention to the people. Let's test this hypothesis using variables from the NES file.

> ➤ Data File: **NES 04**
> ➤ Task: **Cross-tabulation**
> ➤ Row Variable: **94) TRUST GOV**
> ➤ Column Variable: **100) ELECT ATTN**
> ➤ View: **Tables**
> ➤ Display: **Column %**

Compare the column percentages horizontally. Remember that if the column percentages are pretty much the same as you read across the row, then there is no pattern—the dependent variable and the independent variable are not related. However, if one or more of the column percentages varies substantially from the others (or if there is a steadily increasing or decreasing pattern), then there is a relationship.

In this situation, is there a relationship between political distrust and the
belief that elections cause government to pay attention to the people?   Yes   No

If you answered yes above, briefly describe the kind of relationship that
exists between political distrust and the belief that elections cause
government to pay attention to the people.

_____

_____

_____

worksheet

These results are based on a probability sample, and any relationship in these results might have occurred just by chance. So, we need to check the significance level next.

Data File: **NES 04**
Task: **Cross-tabulation**
Row Variable: **94) TRUST GOV**
Column Variable: **100) ELECT ATTN**
➤ View: **Statistics (Summary)**

Important reminder: The computer presents both nominal statistics (top part of the screen) and ordinal statistics (bottom part of the screen) each time you obtain a cross-tabulation, regardless of the level of measurement involved. The computer cannot determine the level of measurement of the variables or decide whether nominal or ordinal statistics are most appropriate. Thus, it is up to us to select the appropriate statistics to use on the basis of the levels of measurement of the variables involved.

Both variables are ordinal, so we will use ordinal statistics. The significance level for ordinal variables is presented on the last line of the statistics. Write in the significance level.   Prob. = _____

Is this relationship statistically significant?   Yes   No

If we say that there is a statistically significant relationship between trust in government and the belief that elections cause government to pay attention to the people, what would that mean? That is, what decision are we making concerning these results based on a sample?

_____

_____

_____

_____

The null hypothesis in this situation is that there is no relationship between trust in government and the belief that elections cause the government to pay attention to the people. Based on these results, should we reject the null hypothesis?   Yes   No

Now let's look at the strength and direction of the relationship. Because both variables are ordinal, we will use Kendall's tau. Specifically, because both variables do not have the same number of categories, we will use Kendall's tau-c. Write in the value of this measure of association.   Kendall's tau-c = _____

Is this relationship positive or negative?

        Positive   Negative

worksheet

Thus, people who feel confident that elections make the government pay attention to them are more likely to have (circle one)

Higher government trust   Lower government trust

Give a P-R-E interpretation of Kendall's tau in this situation.

_____

_____

_____

_____

6. Let's examine the extent to which political party identification explains voting preferences in the 2004 presidential election. We can set up the hypothesis and the null hypothesis as follows:

Hypothesis: Democrats preferred Kerry, Republicans preferred Bush, and Independents preferred Nader.

Null hypothesis: There is no relationship between political party identification and 2004 presidential voting preference.

➤ Data File: **NES 04**
   ➤ Task: **Cross-tabulation**
➤ Row Variable: **242) WHO_VOTE?**
➤ Column Variable: **5) PARTY**
      ➤ View: **Tables**
   ➤ Display: **Column %**

Do the results mostly support the hypothesized pattern?   Yes   No

For which of the following groups are the results least in accord with the hypothesized pattern? (Circle one.)

Democrats   Independents   Republicans

Look at the significance level and measure of association.

         Data File: **NES 04**
            Task: **Cross-tabulation**
     Row Variable: **242) WHO_VOTE?**
  Column Variable: **5) PARTY**
         ➤ View: **Statistics (Summary)**

Because both variables are nominal, we need nominal statistics here. The significance level for nominal variables is presented on the chi-square line. The name of the test of statistical significance is chi-square, but all we need from this test is the significance level. Write in the significance level in the space provided.

Prob. = _____

Is this relationship between party identification and 2004 presidential voting preference statistically significant?

Yes   No

The null hypothesis here is that there is no relationship between political identification and 2004 presidential voting preference. Do we reject the null hypothesis?

Yes   No

Write the value of lambda.

Lambda = _____

According to lambda, by what percentage have we reduced the number of errors in predicting the dependent variable (2004 presidential voting preference) by knowing the independent variable (political party identification)?

_____%

On the basis of those results, what would you conclude about the extent to which political party identification is related to voting preferences in the 2004 presidential election?

_____

_____

_____

That's all for this lesson.

CHAPTER

11

Bivariate Analysis Using ANOVA

Tasks: Scatterplot, Univariate, ANOVA
Data Files: GLOBAL, STATES, NES 04

INTRODUCTION

ANOVA, or **Analysis of Variance,** allows the researcher to examine the relationship between variables where the independent variable is nominal or ordinal, and the independent variable is interval or ratio.

This chapter will explain

• how and when to conduct bivariate analysis

• how to compare mean scores, standard deviations

• how to interpret and evaluate eta-squared results in analysis

• that one needs to be attentive to the types of variables used in analysis before selecting a particular statistical method for use in analysis

Cross-tabulation is the best approach to analyzing the relationship between two variables when they are ordinal or nominal with just a few categories. When the independent variable is nominal or ordinal and the dependent variable is interval or ratio, a crosstab would have far too many columns or rows to make analysis practical. This chapter will demonstrate and explain a method that researchers use when they are trying to understand the relationship between these two different types of variables.

Let's examine the relationship between political participation and the type of nation-state using the GLOBAL file. Our hypothesis will be that "conventional forms of political participation are higher in developed democracies than in those that are less developed." One of the most conventional forms of participation is voter turnout, but this is a ratio variable. What we want to do is look at the relationship between the percentage of the population that turns out to vote at an election and a nominal variable that measures the level of political and economic development of a nation. You may want to take a look at the variable description for 135) WORLDS.7 before you conduct this analysis so that you can understand this variable. Conduct the following analysis and then I'll explain why the results aren't very useful to us.

➤ Data File: **GLOBAL**
➤ Task: **Scatterplot**
➤ Dependent Variable: **330) %TURNOUT**
➤ Independent Variable: **135) WORLDS.7**
➤ View: **Reg. Line**

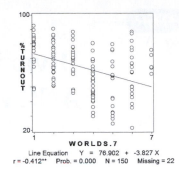

Line Equation   Y = 76.902 + -3.827 X
r = -0.412**   Prob. = 0.000   N = 150   Missing = 22

Carefully examine the regression line and think about how you might summarize the relationship between these two variables. In scatterplot analysis (or any type of correlation analysis), you want to be able to say that as the values for one variable increase, the values for the other variable increase (a positive correlation) or decrease (a negative correlation). However, in order to make such an interpretation, the category values for both variables must have some type of natural or intrinsic meaning. That is, a category of 2 (Communist/Postcommunist) must have more of whatever the variable is measuring than a category coded 1 (Liberal Democracy). A category of 3 (New Industrializing Country) must have more of that something than a category coded 2 (Communist/Postcommunist), and so forth. But as you examine the WORLDS.7 variable, you quickly notice that the categories 1 through 7 do not have an intrinsic order. It is a nominal variable. For example, it wouldn't make any sense to say that as the type of state *increases,* the voter turnout *decreases.* Nor would it make any sense to say that a liberal democratic state is less of a state than a newly industrialized country (NIC). With the WORLDS.7 variable, the values 1 through 7 are used strictly to represent different groupings of countries. The category numbers have no other meaning. Hence, this variable cannot be meaningfully used in correlation or scatterplot analysis.

You might be thinking, "Why don't we use the CROSS-TABULATION task?" Good question. The WORLDS.7 variable can be used in cross-tabulations. The problem is with the other variable, %TURNOUT. The voter turnout variable is a decimal variable that has over 100 different category values ranging from 4.0% to 98.0%. Cross-tabulations work best when both variables have pre-determined or grouped categories (e.g., First World, Second World, Third World; or Yes, No). If you try to create a cross-tabulation using WORLDS.7 and %TURNOUT, your table will have 3 columns and about 100 rows! Such a table would be useless. (In fact, MicroCase and most other statistics programs won't even let you create a table that has more than 100 categories or uses a variable with decimal digits.)

So, what do you do when one variable has a limited set of categories (e.g., WORLDS.7) and the other variable has a wide range of values that go from low to high? If the independent variable (i.e., the variable causing the effect in the other variable) is the one that has a limited set of categories, you can use the ANALYSIS OF VARIANCE task. Return to the main menu and select ANOVA (the acronym for ANalysis Of VAriance).

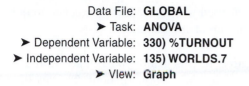

Data File: **GLOBAL**
➤ Task: **ANOVA**
➤ Dependent Variable: **330) %TURNOUT**
➤ Independent Variable: **135) WORLDS.7**
➤ VIew: **Graph**

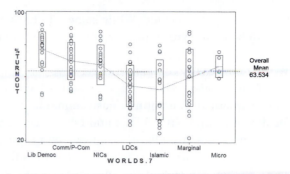

The graph that is presented is called a box and whisker plot. What does this graph tell us? To begin with, just like a scatterplot, each nation is represented by one of the dots on the graph. The location of a nation on the graph is based on the percentage of voter turnout in the nation's national election (the vertical axis) and its category in the seven worlds classification (the horizontal axis). First the dot is placed horizontally according to its category. You will notice that on the bottom of the graph, each category in the seven worlds classification is represented. For example, the country of Italy would be placed in the Liberal Democracy category. Then Italy is placed vertically according to its voter turnout in the last election (approximately 92.5%), which is scaled on the left-hand side of the graph. You can click on the dot at the very top of the dots in the Liberal Democracy category to see Italy.

You will also notice that there is a green dotted line drawn across the entire graph. This line indicates the mean of the dependent variable for all categories. In this case, we see that the mean voter turnout for all countries in this analysis is 63.5%.

Now you may wonder about the red lines that are drawn from the middle of one purple box to another. These lines point to the mean voter turnout for each group of countries. The line from the Liberal Democracies to the Communist/Postcommunist countries helps you to see that mean voter turnout is higher in Liberal Democracies than it is in Communist/Postcommunist countries. You can also see that voter turnout in both of these types of countries is actually higher than the overall mean.

When you read a box and whisker plot, focus on the mean (i.e., the average voter turnout) for each category of the independent variable (WORLDS.7). The location of the mean is shown with a flat line in the center of each rectangle. Your task, then, is to compare the mean for one category against the means for the other categories. It's fairly easy to see whether a mean for one category is higher or lower than a mean for another category because there is a line that connects each of these mean points. The flatter the lines between the means, the less difference there is between the categories. For example, there is a very substantial difference in average voter turnout between NICs and Islamic countries, but very little difference between Islamic countries and Less Developed Countries (LDCs).

The purple rectangle shown for each category of the independent variable (WORLDS.7) indicates plus or minus one standard deviation about the mean. You will remember from Chapter 8 that plus or minus one standard deviation is the boundary in which about 68% of countries in that category are located. While some countries will be located outside of this range, the majority will be found within plus or minus one standard deviation of the mean.

We can now easily compare different types of nation-states. In this graph you can see that Liberal Democracies, NICs, and Microstates have the highest levels of voter turnout. The average voter turnout in Communist/Postcommunist systems is slightly lower than it is in the Liberal Democracies and NICs. LDCs and Islamic countries have the lowest levels of voter turnout and Marginal states are slightly higher. The graph provides a very good visual representation of these relationships, but researchers need results that are more precise than what the graphic can offer. You can look at the average turnout values themselves in the form of a table that compares the means and standard deviations for each group.

Data File: **GLOBAL**

Task: **ANOVA**

Dependent Variable: **330)%TURNOUT**

Independent Variable: **135) WORLDS.7**

➤ View: **Means**

Means, Standard Deviations and Number of Cases of Dependent Var: %TURNOUT by Categories of Independent Var: WORLDS.7
Difference of means across groups is statistically significant (Prob. = 0.000)

	N	Mean	Std.Dev.
Lib Democ	24	77.054	11.187
Comm/P-Com	28	69.882	11.780
NICs	21	67.552	12.488
LDCs	34	54.291	12.990
Islamic	18	52.039	18.756
Marginal	20	59.475	17.976
Micro	5	66.680	6.895

If you are continuing from the previous example, select the [Means] button.

This table shows the actual average level of voter turnout within each category of the independent variable (WORLDS.7). As we can see, Liberal Democratic systems have the highest average level of voter turnout (77.1%). Communist/Postcommunist states have lower average turnout (69.9%), and NICs are slightly below them (67.6%). LDCs (54.3%) and Islamic states (52.0%) also have very similar voter turnout rates. Interestingly enough, Marginal states (states in the midst of civil wars) have much higher voter turnout rates (59.5%). Microstates (66.7%), with very small populations, tend to have turnout rates similar to those in NICs.

The ANOVA task is pretty easy to use. The initial graphic provides a clear picture of whether the pattern supports your initial hypothesis. If it does, then go to the screen with the means to view the actual numbers behind the table. There is one more issue: statistical significance. How do you know if the differences between the means are due to chance or if you can consider the results statistically significant? Simple. As in our earlier analyses, there is a probability value shown directly above the table containing the means. If the difference is statistically significant, there is a sentence that states that the "difference of means across groups is statistically significant." This can be verified by examining the probability value. If it is less than .05, we can feel confident that the differences between the means are not random findings. If the value is over .05, there is a chance that our findings are due to randomness. In this case, since the probability value is 0.000, we know that these results are statistically significant. If the significance is greater than .05, then we cannot say that there is a relationship between the two variables in our analysis.

The last question that we need to ask ourselves about this relationship is the strength of relationship between the two variables. You will remember from Chapter 10 that we used lambda and Cramer's V for the analysis of relationships between nominal variables and Kendall's tau and Somers' D for analysis of ordinal data. For a relationship where the dependent variable is ratio or interval and the independent variable is nominal or ordinal, we use a measure of association called eta-squared. To understand this statistic it is important to review the concept of variance.

Eta-squared is a P-R-E measure that represents the amount of reduction in the total variance that has occurred as a result of dividing the cases into groups based on the independent variable.

Imagine that you work on the House Transportation Committee and have been given the task of trying to understand factors that might influence the pattern of single-driver commuting to and from work. From the transportation policy point of view, some of the representatives on the committee believe that this is not an efficient form of transportation, but individual decisions about getting to and from work are dependent upon a host of very complicated factors. Your job is to begin to understand some of these factors.

You start by conducting a simple univariate analysis of the variable that measures the percentage of commuters who drive only themselves to work in the United States in the year 2004: 633) SNGL DRIVE.

➤ Data File: **STATES**
➤ Task: **Univariate**
➤ Primary Variable: **633) SNGL DRIVE**
➤ View: **Summary**

SNGL DRIVE -- Percent of Commuters Who Drive to Work Alone: 2004

Categories generated by truncating last digit.   Median is estimated.
Mean: 78.748   Std.Dev.:   5.143   N: 50
Median: 80.400   Variance: 26.452   Missing: 0

Range	Freq.	%	Cum.%	Z-Score
56.30 - 56.39	1	2.0	2.0	-4.365
68.40 - 68.49	1	2.0	4.0	-2.012
68.80 - 68.89	1	2.0	6.0	-1.934
73.50 - 73.59	1	2.0	8.0	-1.020
73.80 - 73.89	2	4.0	12.0	-0.962
74.30 - 74.39	1	2.0	14.0	-0.865
74.80 - 74.89	1	2.0	16.0	-0.768
74.90 - 74.99	1	2.0	18.0	-0.748
75.30 - 75.39	1	2.0	20.0	-0.670
75.40 - 75.49	1	2.0	22.0	-0.651

From this analysis you see that 78.7% of those who work outside the home in the United States commute to work by themselves. You also notice that the variance for this average is 26.5 and the standard deviation is 5.1. (If you don't remember how the variance and standard deviation are calculated or what these statistics mean, you may want to refer to Chapter 8).

Now that you have examined univariate statistics, you suspect that this average may vary by region. In the West, people may need to travel longer distances to work through less densely populated areas where there is no public transportation. In the East, people are congregated around large metropolitan areas with public transportation. What you would like to know is whether or not you can reduce the variance in the dependent variable (SNGL DRIVE) as a result of dividing cases into groups based on an independent variable (REGION). Let's compare the means of the four regions to see whether or not this reduces the variance in single-driving commuters:

Data File: **STATES**
➤ Task: **ANOVA**
➤ Dependent Variable: **633) SNGL DRIVE**
➤ Independent Variable: **1744) REGION**
➤ View: **Means**

Means, Standard Deviations and Number of Cases of Dependent Var: SNGL DRIVE by Categories of Independent Var: REGION
Difference of means across groups is statistically significant (Prob. = 0.000)

	N	Mean	Std.Dev.
WEST	13	74.854	3.296
SOUTH	16	81.644	2.539
MIDWEST	12	80.775	2.972
NORTHEAST	9	76.522	8.267

If you remember that the 78.7% of all Americans who work outside the home in the United States commute to work by themselves, you will be able to compare the mean for each region to the overall mean. The logic here is the same as in CROSS-TABULATION. In a cross-tabulation analysis you compare across the categories of the independent variable, and in the comparison of means you do the same thing. You will notice that the mean doesn't change all that much from region to region, but it drops a little in the West (74.9%) and Northeast (76.5%), and is a little higher in the South (81.6%) and Midwest (80.8%).

Tables like this that display the mean almost always give a statistic that helps the reader to understand the variation about the mean. The standard approach is to calculate the standard deviation. You will remember that the standard deviation for the variable 633) SNGL DRIVE was 5.1. From the means table we can compare this standard deviation to the standard deviation for each group of the independent variable. You will notice that by grouping the dependent variable by region we have reduced the variation in three of the four categories of the independent variable. The standard deviation is much lower in the West, South, and Midwest than the overall standard deviation. But the standard deviation is also much higher in the Northeast than it is in the other regions of the country. Based upon a preliminary look at the means and standard deviation, we can conclude that (1) the means do appear to vary from region to region, and (2) variation seems to be reduced within each category of the independent variable (except the Northeast).

As you look at this table, you can see that the means change for each group and that the variance is lower for the West, South, and Midwest and that it is very high for the Northeast. We can see these differences, but we still need to assess whether or not these differences are significant, and the strength of relationship between the dependent and independent variables.

The strength of relationship is assessed using a statistic called eta-squared. Eta-squared is a lot like lambda in that it is a P-R-E measure. We can see the value of eta-squared if we select the ANOVA view.

Research Methods in Political Science

Data File:	**STATES**
Task:	**ANOVA**
Dependent Variable:	**633) SNGL DRIVE**
Independent Variable:	**1744) REGION**
➤ View:	**ANOVA**

Analysis Of Variance
Dependent Variable: SNGL DRIVE
Independent Variable: REGION
N: 50   Missing: 0

ETA Square = 0.328

TEST FOR NON-LINEARITY:
R Square = 0.017   F = 10.647   Prob. = 0.000

Source	Sum of Squares	DF	Mean Square	F	Prob.
Between	425.195	3	141.732	7.486	0.000
Within	870.950	46	18.934		
TOTAL	1296.144	49			

Eta-squared represents the amount of reduction in the total variance that has occurred as a result of dividing the cases into groups based on the independent variable. It is a proportion, so it is always on the same scale as other correlation coefficients: 0 = no relationship between the independent and dependent variables; 1.0 = a perfect relationship between the independent and dependent variables. In this analysis, eta-squared will tell us whether or not we can better understand the variance in single-driver commuters by dividing the analysis of the United States into regions. To understand eta-squared, we need to know a few more things about variance.

The variance in single-driver commuters in the United States is called the total variance. If we were to guess the percentage of single-passenger commuters for each state without knowing anything about which region that state is a part of, the best we could do is to guess the overall mean for all states. We would make errors, of course, and the total variance is a measure of the maximum value of the errors that we would make if we guessed the mean for each state. From the table you can see that the total variance for this analysis is 1296.144.

But what if we know the region of each state? Then we could improve our guess of the percentage of single-passenger commuters by guessing the mean percentage of single-passenger commuters for that state's region. We might actually increase our errors for some states, but if SNGL DRIVE and REGION are related, then on average our guesses would reduce errors. Of course, there would still be errors but these errors are errors measured by the within-group variance. The within-group variance is the variance that occurs within each category of the independent variable (REGION); as you can see from the table, the within-group variance is 870.950.

We have reduced our errors in guessing the percentage of those who drive alone to work in a state by using our knowledge of that state's region. But how much have we reduced our errors? We have reduced errors by the difference between the total variance and the within-group variance, which is the between-groups variance.

Total variance – Within-group variance = Between-groups variance

In our example this would be

1296.14 – 870.95 = 425.19

The between-groups variance is the measure of the amount of errors that we have reduced in our guessing of the dependent variable using our knowledge of the independent variable. Now that we know the total variance and the unexplained variance, we can understand the formula for eta-squared, which is

$$E^2 = \frac{\text{Between-groups variance}}{\text{Total variance}}$$

In our example this would be

$$E^2 = \frac{425.19}{1296.14} = .328$$

Eta-squared is a measure of association. It describes how strongly the dependent variable is related to the independent variable. So, E^2 is a proportional reduction in error measure of association since it describes the proportion by which errors in guessing the dependent variable scores are reduced by knowledge of the independent variable. A P-R-E interpretation of the result listed above would be that we reduce errors in estimating the percentage of those who drive alone to work in a state by 32.8% when we know the independent variable. E^2 is like lambda in this respect although, of course, it is based on a different "guessing rule." E^2 gauges error reduction if we guess the mean dependent variable score for each category of the independent variable rather than guessing the total mean.

Another way to express the same thing is to say that E^2 is the proportion of variation in the dependent variable that is explained by the independent variable. With $E^2 = .328$ we say that region explains 32.8% of the variation in the percentage of people who drive to work alone. Finally, because the independent variable is often nominal, E^2 is not expressed in terms of an integer. Thus, we cannot attribute direction (positive or negative) to the relationship.

In the worksheet section that follows, we will work with a few more examples using ANOVA.

TERMS INTRODUCED IN THIS CHAPTER

Analysis of Variance (ANOVA)   Eta-squared

FOR FURTHER READING

For further information on ANOVA, see Chapter 9 of William Fox, *Social Statistics Using Micro-Case*, 4th ed. (Belmont, CA: Wadsworth, 2003).

Also, for a readable introductory discussion of ANOVA, see pages 363–369 of Janet Buttolph Johnson, Richard A. Joslyn, and H. T. Reynolds, *Political Science Research Methods*, 4th ed. (Washington, DC: CQ Press, 2001).

worksheet

NAME: _____

COURSE: _____

DATE: _____

1. Let's continue with our study of transportation policy in the STATES data file. So far, we under-stand patterns of single-driver commuting only by region. How is region associated with other forms of transportation use?

> Data File: **STATES**
> Task: **ANOVA**
> Dependent Variable: **634) CARPOOL%**
> Column Variable: **1744) REGION**
> View: **Summary**

What is the overall mean percentage of the population that uses a carpool to get to work?   _____

Data File: **STATES**
Task: **ANOVA**
Dependent Variable: **634) CARPOOL%**
Column Variable: **1744) REGION**
> View: **Means**

Now write down the mean and standard deviation for each category of the independent variable.

REGION	MEAN	STD. DEV.
WEST	_____	_____
SOUTH	_____	_____
MIDWEST	_____	_____
NORTHEAST	_____	_____

What is the probability that this result is the result of random factors?   Prob. = _____

Is the result significant?   Yes   No

worksheet

CHAPTER **11**

Data File: **STATES**
Task: **ANOVA**
Dependent Variable: **634) CARPOOL%**
Column Variable: **1744) REGION**
➤ View: **ANOVA**

What is the value of eta-squared? $E^2 =$ _____

Which of the following best describes the relationship between region and patterns of carpooling? (Circle one.)

    a. There is a strong, significant relationship between the percentage of the population who uses a carpool to get to work and the region that the population is from.

    b. The farther that people go out West, the more likely they are to carpool than if they stay in the Northeast.

    c. There is a weak, but significant, relationship between the percentage of the population who uses a carpool to get to work and the region that the population is from.

    d. There is no relationship between carpooling patterns and region.

2. Now let's take a look at the NES 04 data file. In this file there are a number of interesting variables called "thermometers." These thermometer questions ask respondents to indicate how they feel toward different political candidates or groups in society. Respondents rate their feelings on an interval scale from 0 = Cold, 50 = Neutral, to 100 = Warm. Warm is a very positive feeling toward the candidate or group, whereas cold is a very negative feeling. First, let's take a look at the thermometer of attitude toward President Bush.

➤ Data File: **NES 04**
➤ Task: **Univariate**
➤ Primary Variable: **529) BUSH_THERM**
➤ View: **Summary**

What is the mean?   Mean = _____

What is the standard deviation?   Standard Deviation = _____

Now let's see whether or not one's party affiliation is associated with attitudes toward President Bush.

Data File: **NES 04**
➤ Task: **ANOVA**
➤ Dependent Variable: **529) BUSH_THERM**
➤ Independent Variable: **5) PARTY**
➤ View: **Summary**

218   *Research Methods in Political Science*

worksheet

In the space below, respond to the validity of the following hypothesis. Be sure to support your answer with evidence from the analysis (including means and probability statistics).

There is no relationship between an individual's attitude toward President Bush and that individual's party affiliation.

_____

_____

_____

_____

Now let's take a look at the relationship between attitudes toward Bush and the respondent's race.

Data File:	**NES 04**
Task:	**ANOVA**
Dependent Variable:	**529) BUSH_THERM**
➤ Independent Variable:	**2) RACE**
➤ View:	**Summary**

In the space below, respond to the validity of the following hypothesis. Be sure to support your answer with evidence from the analysis (including means and probability statistics).

There is no relationship between an individual's attitude toward President Bush and that individual's race.

_____

_____

_____

_____

Which racial group is most likely to have positive attitudes toward President Bush? _____

Which racial group is the least likely to have positive attitudes toward President Bush? _____

We can say that the greater the variation (expressed in terms of a standard deviation) there is on a thermometer score, the lower the consensus there is for that group.

Of all the racial groups in this analysis, which one has the greatest consensus about their feelings toward President Bush? _____

Which group has the least consensus (most variation) in their feelings toward President Bush? _____

In the space provided below, please describe the evidence that you used to answer the previous four questions.

_____

_____

_____

_____

3. We can use ANOVA for the analysis of data on members of the House of Representatives too. Let's try to understand the factors that are related to campaign spending. Consider the following hypotheses:

Hyp$_1$: There is no relationship between net campaign expenditures and the incumbency status of a member of the House of Representatives.

Hyp$_2$: There is no relationship between net campaign expenditures and the party affiliation of a member of the House of Representatives.

Hyp$_3$: There is no relationship between net campaign expenditures and the number of terms served by a member.

Using the HOUSE data file, net campaign expenditures is operationalized by using the variable 33) TOT EXPEN. Select the best independent variables and discuss the validity of the aforementioned hypotheses. **Also, print all of the evidence that supports your analysis for the third hypothesis**.

	IND. VARIABLE NAME	DEP. VARIABLE
HYPOTHESIS 1:	_____	33) TOT EXPEN

Is the first hypothesis valid? Please discuss the evidence upon which you base your conclusion.

_____

_____

_____

	IND. VARIABLE NAME	DEP. VARIABLE
HYPOTHESIS 2:	_____	33) TOT EXPEN

Is the second hypothesis valid? Please discuss the evidence upon which you base your conclusion.

_____

_____

_____

	IND. VARIABLE NAME	DEP. VARIABLE
HYPOTHESIS 3:	13) #TERMS2	33) TOT EXPEN

Is the third hypothesis valid? Please discuss the evidence upon which you base your conclusion.

_____

_____

_____

4. Now let's examine one more phenomenon in the GLOBAL file. Transparency International uses a rating system from 0 to 10 to evaluate the corruption levels of nation-states. For the variable 309) INDX:CORPT, this scale rating of 0 equals a highly corrupt state and 10 equals a state that is relatively free of corruption. The variable 311) FREEDOM is an ordinal variable that combines the assessment of political rights and civil liberties. The categories for the FREEDOM variable are 1) Free, 2) Part Free, and 3) Not Free. Is there a relationship between political freedom and corruption? Let's find out.

Assess the following hypothesis and support your conclusion with evidence:

There is no relationship between the level of corruption in a country and the level of political freedom in a country.

_____

_____

_____

_____

5. Imagine that you are working for the U.S. Department of Commerce and given the task of preparing a presentation for Fortune 500 executives on "Global Foreign Investments That Avoid Corruption." You have organized the world into seven groups of countries along the lines of the variable 135) WORLDS.7 to prepare for your presentation. The executives assume that Liberal Democracies are a safe bet, but where else should they put their investment dollars? Which group of countries is the least likely to entangle these companies in corrupt practices? Which group of countries is the most likely to entangle these companies in corrupt practices? How confident can you be in your results? Conduct your analysis, and present the results of your findings in the space below.

Cross-tabulation and Statistics: Controlling for a Third Variable

Tasks: Cross-tabulation
Data Files: GSS, GSS 04, HOUSE, NES 04

INTRODUCTION

This chapter will explain and demonstrate the process of controlling for a third variable (an *antecedent variable* or an *intervening variable*) when you are using a cross-tabulation to examine the relationship between a dependent variable and an independent variable. Whenever we examine a relationship between a dependent variable and an independent variable, we need to consider other variables that we think might have some effect on the relationship. Before looking at the process by which we control for a third variable (either antecedent or intervening) while examining the relationship between the dependent and independent variables, let's review the definitions of these different types of variables:

A *dependent variable* is a variable whose variation is to be explained in a study.

An *independent variable* is a variable that is used to explain a dependent variable.

An *intervening variable* is one that occurs between the independent variable and the dependent variable and affects the relationship between them.

An *antecedent variable* is one that occurs before both the independent variable and the dependent variable.

This chapter will explain the process for controlling a nominal or ordinal variable when you are using a cross-tabulation to examine the relationship between a dependent variable and an independent variable. In the next chapter, you will see how to control for a nominal or ordinal variable while using Pearson correlation to examine relationships between metric (interval or ratio) variables.

CONTROLLING FOR A THIRD VARIABLE:
THE BASIC PROCEDURE

The *control variable* allows us to hold constant a third variable in an analysis. A control variable may or may not turn out to be an antecedent or intervening variable—we won't know that until after we have tested whether it actually has an effect on the relationship between the dependent variable and the independent variable.

When we are using a cross-tabulation to examine the relationship between a dependent variable and an independent variable, the basic procedure used to control for a nominal or ordinal control variable is this:

- Create a cross-tabulation showing the relationship between the dependent variable and the independent variable *before* you control for the control variable.

- For each category of the control variable, get a separate cross-tabulation showing the relationship between the dependent variable and the independent variable.

- Compare the relationships in the different tables. There are basically two kinds of situations in which the control variable makes a difference in the relationship between the dependent variable and the independent variable.

    1. The relationships in the different tables (one table for each category of the control variable) are different from the relationship you originally found before controlling for the control variable.

    2. The relationships in the different tables are substantially different from each other.

- If the relationships in the different tables are basically the same as each other and basically the same as the relationship in the original table (before controlling for anything), then the control variable is not really an antecedent or intervening variable—it does not affect the relationship between the dependent variable and the independent variable.

MicroCase makes it easy to control for a variable when analyzing relationships between variables in a cross-tabulation. After opening a file and selecting the CROSS-TABULATION task, you select the dependent variable and the independent variable as usual. Then you select the control variable and click [OK]. For each category of the control variable, there will be a table showing the relationship between the dependent variable and the independent variable. You move from one table to the next by clicking on the right arrow below the Control box on the left side of the screen.

EXAMPLE: PARTY IDENTIFICATION AND IDEOLOGICAL IDENTIFICATION

Education as a Control Variable

In the United States, there is a relationship between political party identification and ideological (liberal/conservative) self-classification. Liberals tend to be Democrats and conservatives tend to be Republicans. However, this relationship is not perfect by any means—there are conservative Democrats and liberal Republicans. Based on the GSS 04 data file, the following table shows this relationship. To simplify our example, we will exclude independents and moderates in this analysis.

Once you have created the table, remove the Independent and Moderate categories from the analysis in order to simplify this example. To remove the Independent category, click on the word INDEPEND. The row for this category should be highlighted. Now click on the [Collapse] button. You should see the Collapse Categories window. Select "Convert to Missing Data (Drop)" and click [OK]. The Independents are now dropped from the analysis and the column percentages are recalculated. Now do the same with the Moderate column. Once your table looks like the one pictured above, continue with the analysis.

➤ Data File: **GSS 04**
➤ Task: **Cross-tabulation**
➤ Row Variable: **65) PARTY**
➤ Column Variable: **66) POL. VIEW**
➤ View: **Tables**
➤ Display: **Column %**

PARTY   by   POL. VIEW
Cramer's V: 0.545**

| | | POL. VIEW | | | | |
		LIBERAL	MODERATE	CONSERV.	Missing	TOTAL
PARTY	DEMOCRAT	239	226	123	652	588
		76.4%	46.3%	25.2%		45.6%
	INDEPEND.	29	112	56	274	197
		9.3%	23.0%	11.5%		15.3%
	REPUBLICAN	45	150	309	556	504
		14.4%	30.7%	63.3%		39.1%
	Missing	6	9	5	21	41
	TOTAL	313	488	488	1503	1289
		100.0%	100.0%	100.0%		

Cramer's V for the relationship between party identification and ideological identification is .545. Thus, the relationship is very strong, but it is far from perfect.

What other variables might affect this relationship between party identification and ideological identification? One possibility is education: The relationship between party identification and ideological identification might vary by education level. People with more education probably have greater knowledge about political and social issues. Therefore, we might expect that people with higher levels of education would be more consistent in their political attitudes. Thus, the link between political party identification and ideological identification would be stronger among those with higher levels of education. Conversely, we would expect the link to be weaker among those with less education.

So, we will examine the relationship between party identification and ideological identification for different levels of education.

Data File: **GSS 04**
Task: **Cross-tabulation**
Row Variable: **65) PARTY**
Column Variable: **66) POL. VIEW**
➤ Control Variable: **34) EDUCATION**
➤ View: **Tables**
➤ Display: **Column %**

PARTY   by   POL. VIEW
Controls: EDUCATION: NO HS GRAD
Cramer's V: 0.160**

| | | POL. VIEW | | | | |
		LIBERAL	MODERATE	CONSERV.	Missing	TOTAL
PARTY	DEMOCRAT	20	35	19	101	74
		55.6%	44.3%	31.1%		42.0%
	INDEPEND.	5	25	18	61	48
		13.9%	31.6%	29.5%		27.3%
	REPUBLICAN	11	19	24	53	54
		30.6%	24.1%	39.3%		30.7%
	Missing	1	2	0	2	5
	TOTAL	36	79	61	217	176
		100.0%	100.0%	100.0%		

The tables in this analysis present the results for three education levels. Look at the first table for a moment. In this table, we are examining the relationship between the dependent variable (party identification) and the independent variable (political ideology), but only among those who did not complete high school. In the next table we are examining the relationship between party identification and political ideology again, but only among those who are college educated. Finally, the last table again describes the relationship between party identification and political ideology, but only among those with 4 or more years of higher education. This is the method by which we control for education level to determine whether it affects the relationship between party identification and political ideology.

There are two methods that can be used to compare the results for these different tables to determine whether the control variable affects the relationship between the dependent variable and the independent variable. First, we can compare the percentages in the rows of the different tables. Second, we can compare the measures of association for each of the tables. Both of those methods should be used to determine the effects of the control variable.

Comparing Rows in the Different Tables
We can compare the same row of results for the different tables. Are the results similar or different for the different tables? In that example, the four tables represent the three different values of the control variable (here, levels of education). If the results are basically the same from one value of the control variable to another (and basically the same as the results in the original table before controlling for anything), then the control variable has no effect on the relationship between the dependent variable and the independent variable. On the other hand, if the results for one or more of the tables are substantially different from the other results, then the control variable affects the relationship between the dependent variable and the independent variable.

Let's just compare the *Democrats* rows for all three tables and the original table (before controlling for anything). The percentages of liberals and conservatives who are Democrats for each of the four education levels are as follows:

	Liberals	Conservatives
NO HS Graduate	64.5%	44.2%
HS Graduate	80.0%	36.1%
College Educated	88.6%	23.6%
Original results before controlling	84.2%	28.5%

Is there a difference from one table to another? Yes, there is an important pattern of differences: The gap between liberals and conservatives—in terms of the percentage who identify as Democrats—increases with education level.

- Among those who did not complete high school, more liberals than conservatives are Democrats, but the gap is only 20.3 percentage points (64.5% of liberals are Democrats, compared with 44.2% of conservatives).

- Among those who completed high school, the gap increases to 43.9 percentage points (80.0% of liberals are Democrats, compared with 36.1% of conservatives).

- Among those with college education, the gap widens still farther, to 65.0 percentage points.

There is a clear pattern here. The link between party identification (dependent variable) and ideological identification (independent variable) varies by education level (control variable). The higher a person's education level, the stronger the link between party identification and ideological identification.

Note, however, that the change from one education level to another was more pronounced among those who identified themselves as conservatives. The percentage of liberals who are Democrats does not vary as greatly from one education level to another. However, the percentage of conservatives who are Democrats decreases steadily as education level increases.

Comparing Measures of Association for Each Table

We can use the measure of association (Cramer's V, in this situation) to show the degree of relationship between the two variables for each of the different tables. If the measure of association is basically the same from one value of the control variable to another, and if it is basically the same as it was in the original (before controlling) table, then the control variable has no important effect on the relationship between the dependent variable and the independent variable. On the other hand, if the measure of association for one or more of the tables is substantially different from the others, then the control variable does affect the relationship between the dependent variable and the independent variable.

In this example, the preceding tables demonstrate that the relationship between party identification and ideological identification definitely varies by education level. The relationships between party identification and ideological identification are statistically significant (Prob. = .000) at all four levels of education, but the strength of the relationship varies substantially among the four levels of education.

- Among those who did not complete high school, there is a moderately strong relationship between ideological identification and party identification: Cramer's V = .201, but the result is not significant.

- Among those who completed high school, there is a slightly stronger relationship: Cramer's V = .428.

- Among those with college education, the relationship is extremely strong: Cramer's V is .632. Thus, among those with college education, there is a very high degree of consistency between party identification and ideological identification.

PARTY AFFILIATION AS A CONTROL VARIABLE

Sometimes we find a relationship between variables that doesn't seem to have any logic. In that situation, it might be that the two variables are related because both are linked to some other variable.

For the HOUSE file, the following table shows the relationship between a bill to cut taxes and a bill to allow limited stem cell research.

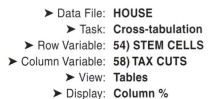

➤ Data File: **HOUSE**
➤ Task: **Cross-tabulation**
➤ Row Variable: **54) STEM CELLS**
➤ Column Variable: **58) TAX CUTS**
➤ View: **Tables**
➤ Display: **Column %**

STEM CELLS   by   TAX CUTS
Cramer's V: 0.702**

		TAX CUTS			
		NO	YES	Missing	TOTAL
STEM CELLS	NO	10	183	0	193
		5.4%	75.9%		45.4%
	YES	174	58	6	232
		94.6%	24.1%		54.6%
	Missing	1	3	0	4
	TOTAL	184	241	6	425
		100.0%	100.0%		

Those results show an extremely strong relationship (Cramer's V = .702**). An examination of the column percentages shows that 94.6% of the representatives who voted *no* on the tax cuts bill voted *yes* on the stem cell bill. Further, 75.9% who voted *yes* on the tax cut bill also voted *no* on the stem cell bill. Why is there such a strong relationship between views on these two bills that seem so unconnected in terms of content? One possibility is that the Democratic Party and the Republican Party have staked out opposite positions on both of these bills. Let's control for the party affiliation of representatives.

Data File: **HOUSE**
Task: **Cross-tabulation**
Row Variable: **54) STEM CELLS**
Column Variable: **50) TAX CUTS**
➤ Control Variable: **11) PARTY**
➤ View: **Tables**
➤ Display: **Column %**

STEM CELLS by TAX CUTS
Controls: PARTY: Democrat
Cramer's V: 0.342**

		TAX CUTS			
		NO	YES	Missing	TOTAL
STEM CELLS	NO	10	7	0	17
		5.5%	38.9%		8.5%
	YES	171	11	5	182
		94.5%	61.1%		91.5%
	Missing	1	0	0	1
	TOTAL	181	18	5	199
		100.0%	100.0%		

For Democratic representatives the first table represents the relationship between support for the stem cell bill by support for tax cuts. The second table does the same thing for Republican representatives. Having done this analysis, we see that most of the Democrats voted *no* on the tax cuts bill regardless of how they voted on the stem cell bill. Almost all of the Republicans voted *yes* on the tax bill regardless of how they voted on the stem cell bill.

Unlike the extremely strong relationship in the original table (.702 before controlling), there is a relatively weaker relationship between the two variables (support for tax cuts and support for stem cell research. Thus, the control variable (party affiliation) is extremely important in this situation. It greatly affected the relationship between the dependent variable (support for stem cell research) and the independent variable (support for tax cuts).

EXAMPLE OF NO IMPORTANT EFFECT

The next example shows a situation in which the control variable has no important effect on the relationship between the dependent variable and the independent variable. There is a negative relationship between support for spending on defense and age. Older people support defense spending more than do younger people. However, gender can sometimes affect relationships among variables. In the analysis of the relationship between support for defense spending and age, gender might also affect this relationship. So, let's use gender as a control variable.

Using the GSS data file, we will operationally define support for defense spending with variable 72) DEFENSE $—spending on military, armaments, and defense.

	Data File:	**GSS**
➤	Task:	**Cross-tabulation**
➤	Row Variable:	**72) DEFENSE $**
➤	Column Variable:	**32) AGE**
➤	View:	**Tables**
➤	Display:	**Column %**

DEFENSE $ by   AGE
Cramer's V: 0.103**

			AGE			
		<30	**30-49**	**50 AND UP**	**Missing**	**TOTAL**
D E F E N S E $	TOO LITTLE	40	144	195	0	379
		17.4%	23.4%	32.8%		26.3%
	RIGHT	77	200	196	2	473
		33.5%	32.5%	33.0%		32.8%
	TOO MUCH	113	272	203	0	588
		49.1%	44.2%	34.2%		40.8%
	Missing	536	1242	1274	16	3068
	TOTAL	230	616	594	18	1440
		100.0%	100.0%	100.0%		

The previous table shows that there is a modest negative relationship between support for defense spending and age. Kendall's tau-c is −.123 and the relationship is statistically significant at the .05 level.

Data File:	**GSS**
Task:	**Cross-tabulation**
Row Variable:	**72) DEFENSE $**
Column Variable:	**32) AGE**
➤ Control Variable:	**1) SEX**
➤ View:	**Tables**
➤ Display:	**Column %**

DEFENSE $ by   AGE
Controls: SEX: MALE
Cramer's V: 0.103**

			AGE			
		<30	**30-49**	**50 AND UP**	**Missing**	**TOTAL**
D E F E N S E $	TOO LITTLE	19	66	87	0	172
		19.0%	24.2%	33.9%		27.3%
	RIGHT	31	82	81	1	194
		31.0%	30.0%	31.5%		30.8%
	TOO MUCH	50	125	89	0	264
		50.0%	45.8%	34.6%		41.9%
	Missing	251	559	553	9	1372
	TOTAL	100	273	257	10	630
		100.0%	100.0%	100.0%		

Both tables show that the results for males and females are similar to each other and to the original results before controlling. Although there are some differences in the results between males and females, those differences are minor. In fact, if the strength of relationship does not change +/− .10, then we can say that the control variable had no effect. Remember that Kendall's tau-c is −.123 and the significance level is .000 for the original table. Tau-c is −.124 and the significance is .000 in the table with males only. Tau-c is −.122 and the significance is .000 in the table with females only. Because the control variable does not change the original tau-c value by more than +/−.10, the control variable, gender, has no important effect on the relationship between support for defense spending and age.

EXAMPLE: POLITICS, RELIGION, AND RACE

In the United States, some political attitudes and religious attitudes are related to one another. However, the links between politics and religion can vary by race. White Americans and African Americans have different historical backgrounds, including somewhat different roles for religion and churches in shaping their political orientations. For example, African American churches have often been the center of political activity in African American communities. Using the GSS data file, let's look at the influence on 2004 presidential voting choice of the

REBORN variable ("Would you call yourself a born-again Christian—that is, have you personally had a conversion experience related to Jesus Christ?").

➤ Data File: **GSS**
➤ Task: **Cross-tabulation**
➤ Row Variable: **541) WHO IN 04?**
➤ Column Variable: **237) REBORN**
➤ View: **Tables**
➤ Display: **Column %**

WHO IN 04?　by　REBORN
Cramer's V: 0.118**

		REBORN			
		YES	NO	Missing	TOTAL
WHO IN 04?	KERRY	310	617	507	927
		41.5%	52.4%		48.2%
	BUSH	429	536	481	965
		57.4%	45.5%		50.2%
	NADER	8	24	15	32
		1.1%	2.0%		1.7%
	Missing	357	685	541	1583
	TOTAL	747	1177	1544	1924
		100.0%	100.0%		

The table shows that there is a modest relationship (Cramer's V = .118, and it is statistically significant at the .000 level). By comparing the column percentages horizontally, we can see that those who said they were born again were less likely to vote for Kerry than were those who said they were not born again. On the other hand, those who said they were born again were more likely to vote for Bush than were those who said they were not born again. There is not really any pattern concerning the born-again status and voting for Nader.

Now let's use race as a control variable to see whether it affects this relationship. Because our goal here is to compare white and African Americans, we will use 38) RACE, which includes respondents in those two racial categories and excludes the other three categories (Asian, Native American, and Hispanic) used in the GSS survey.

Data File: **GSS**
Task: **Cross-tabulation**
Row Variable: **541) WHO IN 04?**
Column Variable: **237) REBORN**
➤ Control Variable: **38) RACE**
➤ View: **Table: (RACE:WHITE)**
➤ Display: **Column %**

WHO IN 04?　by　REBORN
Controls:　RACE: WHITE
Cramer's V: 0.222**

		REBORN			
		YES	NO	Missing	TOTAL
WHO IN 04?	KERRY	133	478	341	611
		25.1%	47.5%		39.8%
	BUSH	388	507	444	895
		73.3%	50.4%		58.3%
	NADER	8	21	10	29
		1.5%	2.1%		1.9%
	Missing	207	421	326	954
	TOTAL	529	1006	1121	1535
		100.0%	100.0%		

Data File:	**GSS**
Task:	**Cross-tabulation**
Row Variable:	**541) WHO IN 04?**
Column Variable:	**237) REBORN**
➤ Control Variable:	**38) RACE**
➤ View:	**Table: (RACE:BLACK)**
➤ Display:	**Column %**

WHO IN 04?   by   REBORN
Controls: RACE: BLACK
Cramer's V: 0.068**

		REBORN			
		YES	NO	Missing	TOTAL
WHO IN 04?	KERRY	156	81	130	237
		90.2%	94.2%		91.5%
	BUSH	17	5	14	22
		9.8%	5.8%		8.5%
	NADER	0	0	2	0
		0.0%	0.0%		0.0%
	Missing	84	74	71	229
	TOTAL	173	86	217	259
		100.0%	100.0%		

The first table presents the results for white Americans, and the second table presents the results for African Americans. As you can see, the control variable (race) does affect the relationship between the dependent variable (2004 presidential voting choice) and the independent variable (answers to the born-again question). Among white respondents, the relationship is stronger than it was in the table without the control. Cramer's V for the relationship is .222 for white respondents—compared with .118 for both white and African American respondents combined (in the original table). Among whites, 47.5% of those who said that they had not been born again voted for Kerry, compared to 25.1% of those who said that they had been born again. 73.3% of those who said that they had been born again voted for Bush compared to 50.4% of those who had not been born again.

On the other hand, among African Americans there is no relationship between 2004 presidential voting choice and born-again responses. African Americans voted overwhelmingly for Kerry regardless of their responses to the born-again question. Thus, these results show that analysis of relationships between political orientations and religious orientations need to take race into account because these relationships can vary by race.

THE NUMBER-OF-CASES PROBLEM

When we examine the relationship between a dependent variable and an independent variable in a cross-tabulation while controlling for a control variable, a serious problem sometimes occurs: We might not have enough cases within categories of a control variable to do meaningful analysis.

Let's take an example. If we cross-tabulate political party identification by family income in the NES 04 data file, we find that there is a weak relationship (Cramer's V = .121 and the significance level is .000). Suppose, however, that we expect this relationship to vary by race and we want to do separate analyses for whites and African Americans. For white respondents, there is no problem when we analyze the relationship between party identification and family income. However, there are only 180 African American respondents in the NES 04 data file. Further, there were only 145 African American respondents who answered both the political party question and the family income question.

Thus, when we cross-tabulate political party preference by family income for African American respondents only, we end up with a table that has very few cases for analysis. For example, for African American respondents, there are only 27 cases in the more-than-$75,000 income category. When the number of cases in a cross-tabulation is small, it is very difficult to find reliable patterns that can be generalized to the population from which the sample was selected. Further, the smaller the number of cases involved in the analysis, the more difficult it is to obtain statistically significant relationships. In this particular example, the program gives us a warning that there is a "potential significance problem."

The number-of-cases problem becomes even more likely and more extreme when we try to control for two variables at once. For example, suppose you wanted to examine the relationship between support for spending on the poor and frequency of praying, and you expected that any connection between these two variables might be affected by both the race and the gender of respondents. Thus, to do a full analysis, you would want to control for each of those variables separately and then also control for them both at the same time. To control for the variables at the same time, you would create four tables showing the relationship between support for spending on the poor and frequency of praying: a table for African American males, a table for African American females, a table for white males, and a table for white females.

What can we do about the number-of-cases problem? In many situations, we might not be able to do much about the problem. Sometimes, however, we can do one or more things to reduce the problem. We will briefly describe two of these procedures.

- Collapse the categories of the variable into very broad categories. For example, in this situation we might collapse family income into two categories (lower 50% and upper 50%) rather than the four categories now being used. That would increase the number of cases in each (collapsed) category.

- If the data are available, pool (combine) several different data files if possible. For example, instead of using just the NES data file for 2004, we might combine it with NES data for other years. Similarly, we could combine GSS data files for several different years. That process would provide a much larger number of cases for analysis.

The number-of-cases problem will be demonstrated further in the worksheet section.

TERMS INTRODUCED IN THIS CHAPTER

Control variable   Number-of-cases problem

FOR FURTHER READING

For further information on controlling variables, see Chapter 10 of William Fox, *Social Statistics Using MicroCase,* 4th ed. (Belmont, CA: Wadsworth, 2003).

Also, for a readable introductory discussion of controlling, see pages 129–144 of Leonard Champney, *Introduction to Quantitative Political Science* (New York: HarperCollins, 1995).

For some actual research examples, browse through the readings presented in Marcus E. Ethridge, *The Political Research Experience: Readings and Analysis,* 2nd ed. (Guilford, CT: Dushkin, 1994).

worksheet

NAME: _____

COURSE: _____

DATE: _____

1. Using the GSS data file, let's examine the relationship between conservatism on economic issues and degree of conservative (as opposed to liberal or moderate) self-classification. To operationally define conservatism on economic issues, we will use the variable 233) HELP POOR?

We would expect that people who take a conservative position on the issue of whether the government should improve living standards would be more likely to classify themselves as conservatives. Conversely, those who take a liberal view on that issue would be more likely to classify themselves as liberals. Moderates would be in the middle.

Thus, we hypothesize: There is a positive relationship between conservatism on economic issues and degree of conservative self-classification. The null hypothesis is: There is no relationship between conservatism on economic issues and degree of conservative self-classification. Let's test the null hypothesis.

> ➤ Data File: **GSS**
> ➤ Task: **Cross-tabulation**
> ➤ Row Variable: **63) POL. VIEW**
> ➤ Column Variable: **233) HELP POOR?**
> ➤ View: **Tables**
> ➤ Display: **Column %**

The HELP SELF response is the position that indicates the most conservative response to the HELP POOR? question. Examine the column percentages horizontally in the Conservative row in the cross-tabulation. On the basis of these results, are people who took the more conservative view on helping the poor more likely to classify themselves as conservatives, and vice versa? (Circle one.)   Yes   No

Obtain the significance level and Kendall's tau-b, and write them in the spaces provided.

> Data File: **GSS**
> Task: **Cross-tabulation**
> Row Variable: **63) POL. VIEW**
> Column Variable: **233) HELP POOR?**
> ➤ View: **Statistics (Summary)**

Prob. = _____

Kendall's tau-b = _____

Is this relationship statistically significant?   Yes   No

worksheet

Do you reject the null hypothesis?   Yes   No

2. There are other variables that might affect the relationship between conservative self-classification and conservatism on economic issues. Let's examine the effects of education on this relationship.

Data File:	**GSS**
Task:	**Cross-tabulation**
Row Variable:	**63) POL.VIEW**
Column Variable:	**233) HELP POOR?**
➤ Control Variable:	**34) EDCAT**
➤ View:	**Tables**
➤ Display:	**Column %**

This analysis produces three tables—one table for each category of the control variable, education. For this analysis, we will just compare the measures of association. Browse through the four tables, obtain Kendall's tau-b and the significance level for each table, and write these statistics in the following table. To get you started, the first set of results (for those who have less than a high school education) has been provided.

Relationships Between Conservative Self-Classification and Conservatism on Economic Issues by Education Category

EDUCATION CATEGORY	KENDALL'S TAU-B	PROB.
NO HS GRAD	.007	.901
HS GRAD	_____	_____
COLL EDUC	_____	_____

Examine these results and the original results you obtained before controlling for education. Does the control variable, education, affect the relationship between conservative self-identification and conservatism on economic issues?   Yes   No

If you answered *yes* above, describe how the relationship between conservative self-identification and conservatism on economic issues varies by education level. If you answered *no*, explain why you think education had no impact on the relationship between conservative self-identification and conservatism on economic issues.

_____

_____

_____

3. Next, let's examine the relationship between voting choices in the 2004 presidential election and the religious fundamentalism/liberalism of the respondent's religious tradition. Based on the respondent's general religious preference and (among Protestants) her or his denominational preferences, variable 116) R.FUND/LIB classifies the religious tradition of respondents as fun-

damentalist, moderate, or liberal. Let's conceptualize this variable as liberalism of the respondent's religious tradition.

> Data File: **GSS**
> Task: **Cross-tabulation**
> ➤ Row Variable: **541) WHO IN 04?**
> ➤ Column Variable: **116) R.FUND/LIB**
> ➤ View: **Tables**
> ➤ Display: **Column %**

Note: Before performing the analysis in the guide above, it would be a good idea to click on [Clear All] to make sure that the control variable used previously has been cleared.

Compare the column percentages horizontally. Note that Nader received more votes from religious liberals than any other group. Since the group of Nader voters is so small, let's exclude the Nader category to focus more on the Gore and Bush voters.

> Data File: **GSS**
> Task: **Cross-tabulation**
> Row Variable: **541) WHO IN 04?**
> Column Variable: **116) R.FUND/LIB**
> ➤ Subset Variable: **541) WHO IN 04?**
> ➤ Subset Categories: **Include: 1) Kerry**
> **2) Bush**
> ➤ View: **Tables**
> ➤ Display: **Column %**

The option for selecting a subset variable is located on the same screen you use to select other variables. For this example, select 541) WHO IN 04? as a subset variable. A window will appear that shows you the categories of the subset variable. Select 1) Kerry and 2) Bush as your subset categories. Next choose the [Include] option. Then click [OK] and continue as usual. With this particular subset selected, the results will be limited to those who voted for Kerry or Bush. The subset selection continues until you exit the task, delete all subset variables, or clear all variables.

Write the column percentages in the following table.

	FUNDAMENTALIST	MODERATE	LIBERAL
KERRY	_____%	_____%	_____%
BUSH	_____%	_____%	_____%

Which religious tradition shows the lowest support for the Democratic candidate, Kerry? (Circle one.)

Fundamentalists   Moderates   Liberals

Which religious tradition shows the highest support for the Republican candidate, Bush? (Circle one.)

Fundamentalists   Moderates   Liberals

Let's check the significance level and measure of association. We'll use Cramer's V for the measure of association.

Data File:	**GSS**
Task:	**Cross-tabulation**
Row Variable:	**541) WHO IN 04?**
Column Variable:	**116) R.FUND/LIB**
Subset Variable:	**541) WHO IN 04?**
Subset Categories:	**Include: 1) Kerry**
	2) Bush
➤ View:	**Statistics (Summary)**

Write in the significance level for this relationship.

Prob. = _____

Write in Cramer's V for this relationship.

Cramer's V = _____

Is this relationship statistically significant?   Yes   No

Do you reject the null hypothesis that there is no relationship between 2004 presidential voting choice and the liberalism of the respondent's religious tradition?   Yes   No

4. In the preceding analysis, we found a very weak relationship between 2004 presidential voting choice and liberalism of the respondent's religious tradition. However, there are other variables that might affect that relationship. White Americans and African Americans are different from each other in terms of how certain religious orientations relate to political views. Thus, let's use race as a control variable here to see whether it affects the relationship between 2004 presidential voting choice and liberalism of the respondent's religious tradition.

Data File:	**GSS**
Task:	**Cross-tabulation**
Row Variable:	**541) WHO IN 04?**
Column Variable:	**116) R.FUND/LIB**
Subset Variable:	**541) WHO IN 04?**
Subset Categories:	**Include: 1) Kerry**
	2) Bush
➤ Control Variable:	**38) RACE**
➤ View:	**Tables**
➤ Display:	**Column %**

worksheet

The option for selecting a control variable is located on the same screen you use to select other variables. For this example, select 38) RACE as a control variable and then click [OK] to continue as usual. Separate tables showing the relationship between the dependent variable and the independent variable will be presented for white Americans and African Americans.

The first table shows the relationship between 541) WHO IN 04? and 116) R.FUND/LIB for white Americans. Write the column percentages in the following table, which is labeled Control Category: White. Also, check the summary statistics and write in the significance level and Cramer's V.

Control Category: White

	FUNDAMENTALIST	MODERATE	LIBERAL
KERRY	_____%	_____%	_____%
BUSH	_____%	_____%	_____%

Prob. = _____

Cramer's V = _____

Among white Americans, is the relationship (between 2004 presidential voting choice and liberalism of the respondent's religious tradition) statistically significant?   Yes   No

Now move to the next table and write the column percentages in the table that is labeled Control Category: African American. Again, write in the significance level and Cramer's V.

Control Category: African American

	FUNDAMENTALIST	MODERATE	LIBERAL
KERRY	_____%	_____%	_____%
BUSH	_____%	_____%	_____%

Prob. = _____

Cramer's V = _____

Among African Americans, is the relationship (between 2004 presidential voting choice and liberalism of the respondent's religious tradition) statistically significant?   Yes   No

5. There are two ways that we can compare the results when controlling. First, we can compare the percentages in the tables to see whether the basic patterns are the same. Second, we can compare the measures of association for the tables to see whether they are basically the same or basically different. We will use both methods here. First, we will compare the percentages.

worksheet

To compare the percentages in the tables, it is often helpful to compare a particular row from each table. Here, let's compare the Kerry row from all tables, including the original table before we controlled for anything. In the following table, write in the percentages from the Kerry row from each of the preceding tables. To provide a starting point, the percentages from the original table (before controlling) have been provided.

	FUNDAMENTALIST	MODERATE	LIBERAL
ORIGINAL TABLE	44.8%	46.9%	56.9%
WHITE AMERICANS	_____%	_____%	_____%
AFRICAN AMERICANS	_____%	_____%	_____%

Compare the results that you just wrote in this table for whites and African Americans. Are the patterns in those percentages basically the same as or basically different from each other? (Circle one.)

Basically the same   Basically different

Among white Americans, which group was least likely to vote for Kerry? (Circle one.)

Fundamentalists   Moderates   Liberals

Among African Americans, which group was least likely to vote for Kerry? (Circle one.)

Fundamentalists   Moderates   Liberals

Given these results, which of the following statements is most accurate?

a. There is no important difference between white Americans and African Americans in terms of the relationship between 2004 presidential voting choice and liberalism of the respondent's religious tradition.

b. The relationship (between 2004 presidential voting choice and liberalism of the respondent's religious tradition) follows the same basic pattern among white Americans and African Americans, but it is a stronger relationship among white Americans.

c. Among white Americans, the more liberal the religious tradition from which one comes, the more likely one is to vote for Kerry; however, African Americans voted overwhelmingly for Kerry regardless of religious tradition. Further, among African Americans, to the extent that there was any difference among the three religious traditions, it was the opposite of the pattern among white Americans.

On the basis of that comparison of percentages, does race affect the relationship between 2004 presidential voting choice and liberalism of the respondent's religious tradition?   Yes   No

worksheet

6. Now let's do the comparison by using the measures of association. In the following table, we have provided Cramer's V and the significance level for the original table (before controlling). Go back to the table for whites and the table for African Americans and, in the following table, write the Cramer's V and the significance level for each.

Relationships Between Presidential Voting Choice and Liberalism of Respondent's Religious Tradition by Race

	CRAMER'S V	SIGNIFICANCE LEVEL
ORIGINAL TABLE	.080	.000
WHITE AMERICANS	_____	_____
AFRICAN AMERICANS	_____	_____

If the measures of association are basically the same for all of the tables, then the control variable (race) has no effect on the relationship between 2004 presidential voting choice and liberalism of the respondent's religious tradition. If one or more of the measures of association is substantially different from the others, then the control variable does affect the relationship between the dependent variable and the independent variable. Which of the following conclusions is most justified by the results? (Circle the letter of your choice.)

a. The relationships are basically the same for all the categories of the control variable and for the original table. Thus, the control variable (race) does not affect the relationship between 2004 presidential voting choice and liberalism of the respondent's religious tradition.

b. The relationship between 2004 presidential voting choice and liberalism of the respondent's religious tradition is different for white Americans and African Americans. Specifically, among white Americans, liberalism of one's religious tradition is related to 2004 presidential voting choice; that relationship does not exist among African Americans.

7. Using the NES 04 data file, let's examine the relationship between variable 37) GOVT SPEND and variable 391) LIBCON3. The first variable can be used to operationally define the concept of support for increased governmental services, and the second variable can be conceptualized as degree of conservative self-identification.

When people identify themselves as liberals, moderates, or conservatives, some of them have a reasonably clear meaning of the labels in mind and some do not. The matter becomes more complicated when we take into consideration that some people might classify themselves as liberals, moderates, or conservatives on the basis of one type of issue whereas someone else might do it on different grounds.

Nevertheless, in this situation we would hypothesize that there is a negative relationship between degree of conservative self-identification and support for increased governmental services. Let's test the hypothesis.

➤ Data File: **NES 04**
➤ Task: **Cross-tabulation**
➤ Row Variable: **391) LIBCON3**
➤ Column Variable: **37) GOVT SPEND**
➤ View: **Tables**
➤ Display: **Column %**

Compare the column percentages horizontally. Are these results in accord
with what we hypothesized?   Yes   No

8. Now obtain the significance level and Kendall's tau-b, and write them in the spaces provided.

Data File: **NES 04**
Task: **Cross-tabulation**
Row Variable: **391) LIBCON3**
Column Variable: **37) GOVT SPEND**
➤ View: **Statistics (Summary)**

Prob. = _____

Kendall's tau-b = _____

Is the relationship between degree of conservative self-identification and
support for increased governmental services statistically significant?   Yes   No

Do you reject the null hypothesis?   Yes   No

9. The preceding results show that there is a moderate, negative relationship between degree
of conservative self-identification and support for increased governmental services. It seems
reasonable to expect that the strength of this relationship might vary depending on the level of
political information that people have. So, let's use variable 57) INFORMED? as a control variable. Interviewers ranked respondents as low, average, or high in terms of the interviewer's perception of the respondent's level of information about politics and public affairs.

Data File: **NES 04**
Task: **Cross-tabulation**
Row Variable: **391) LIBCON3**
Column Variable: **37) GOVT SPEND**
➤ Control Variable: **57) INFORMED?**
➤ View: **Tables**
➤ Display: **Column %**

This process will produce three tables showing the relationship between degree of conservative
self-identification and support for increased governmental services. The first table shows this
relationship for those whose political information is high. The second table is for those whose
political information is average, and the third table is for those whose political information is low.

To compare the percentages in these three tables, let's just look at one particular row—the Conservative row—in each table. Look at the first table and write the percentages from the Conservative row in the High political information row of the following table. The first of these percentages has been provided to help you get started—this percentage means that among those with high political information, 84.9% of those who want to reduce government spending classify themselves as conservatives.

After entering the column percentages, obtain the summary statistics for this first table and write in the value of Kendall's tau-b and the significance level.

Then go to the next table (average political information) and write the Conservative row of percentages, Kendall's tau-b, and the significance level in the appropriate places. Then do the same thing for the third table (low political information).

Percentages Classifying Themselves as Conservatives by Level of Support for Increased Governmental Services by Political Information Level

	FEWER SERVICES	BETWEEN	MORE SERVICES	KENDALL'S TAU-B	PROB.
High political information	84.9%	_____%	_____%	_____	_____
Average political information	_____%	_____%	_____%	_____	_____
Low political information	_____%	_____%	_____%	_____	_____

10. Examine the preceding results. Which of the following conclusions is most appropriate? (Circle the letter of your choice.)

   a. The level of political information of respondents has no effect on the relationship between degree of conservative self-identification and support for increased governmental services.

   b. The level of political information of respondents affects the relationship between degree of conservative self-identification and support for increased governmental services: The higher the level of political information of respondents, the stronger the relationship between degree of conservative self-identification and support for increased governmental services.

   c. The level of political information of respondents affects the relationship between degree of conservative self-identification and support for increased governmental services: The higher the level of political information of respondents, the weaker the relationship between degree of conservative self-identification and support for increased governmental services.

11. Now we will examine the problem that occurs when the use of a control variable results in tables having too few cases. We'll also see how to deal with this problem in doing analysis. Let's start by examining the relationship between degree of concern about congressional elections and income.

Data File: **NES 04**
Task: **Cross-tabulation**
➤ Row Variable: **127) CARE HOUSE**
➤ Column Variable: **3) INCOME**
➤ View: **Tables**
➤ Display: **Column %**

Note: Before performing the analysis in the guide above, it would be a good idea to click on [Clear All] to ensure that the control variable used previously has been cleared.

Examine the column percentages in this table. In this situation, it is somewhat difficult to determine whether there is any pattern. So, check the significance level.

Data File: **NES 04**
Task: **Cross-tabulation**
Row Variable: **127) CARE HOUSE**
Column Variable: **3) INCOME**
➤ View: **Statistics (Summary)**

We need ordinal statistics here. Write in the significance level for this relationship.

Prob. = _____

Is this relationship statistically significant?   Yes   No

12. The preceding relationship might be affected by a number of other variables. Let's investigate the effects of gender and race on this relationship. Thus, we have two control variables. Although we would ordinarily begin by controlling for each of these variables separately, let's jump ahead and control for both of them at once.

Data File: **NES 04**
Task: **Cross-tabulation**
Row Variable: **127) CARE HOUSE**
Column Variable: **3) INCOME**
➤ Control Variables: **1) SEX**
                             2) RACE
➤ View: **Tables**
➤ Display: **Column %**

Just quickly browse through the tables created by this analysis. Note that most of the tables have a warning about a potential significance problem. One problem here is that the race categories Hispanic, Native American, and Asian have very few cases—each of those categories contains less than 1.5% of the respondents in the sample. Thus, unfortunately, we cannot really do any meaningful analysis for those categories. So, we need to exclude those categories from this analysis. We do that by using the subset procedure.

worksheet

Data File: **NES 04**

Task: **Cross-tabulation**

Row Variable: **127) CARE HOUSE**

Column Variable: **3) INCOME**

Control Variables: **1) SEX**

2) RACE

➤ Subset Variable: **2)RACE**

➤ Subset Categories: **Include: 1) White**

2) Black

➤ View: **Tables**

➤ Display: **Column %**

> The option for selecting a subset variable is located on the same screen you use
> to select other variables. For this example, select 2) RACE as a subset variable. A
> window will appear that shows you the categories of the subset variable. Select
> 1) White and 2) Black as your subset categories. Then choose the [Include] option.
> Then click [OK] and continue as usual. With this particular subset selected, the
> results will be limited to white Americans and African Americans. The subset
> selection continues until you exit the task, delete all subset variables, or clear all
> variables.

This analysis produces six tables that show the relationship between the
dependent variable (degree of concern about congressional elections) and
the independent variable (income). The first table is for male white American
respondents, the second table is for male African American respondents,
the third is for female white Americans, and the fourth is for female African
Americans. How many of these four tables still have a warning about a
potential significance problem? (Circle one.)

None   One   Two   Three   All Four

13. We can reduce the number-of-cases problem by collapsing the categories into a smaller number of categories.

First, in any one of the four tables, click the Not at all label, and that row will be highlighted. Next, click
the *Not very* label in the table, and that row will be highlighted. Then click the [Collapse] button on the
lower left area of the screen. The program asks for a name for the new collapsed category. Place the
cursor in the New Category Label box, delete the text already in the box, and type ***Not much.*** Then
click [OK].

Now click the *Prtty much* label and the *Very much* label to highlight both of them. Then click the [Col-
lapse] button. For the new category label, type **Much** and then click [OK].

Now browse through the four tables again. How many of those four tables
still have a warning about a potential significance problem? (Circle one.)

None   One   Two   Three   All Four

In that situation, did collapsing the variables reduce the number-of-cases problem that can occur when we examine a relationship between two variables while controlling for one or more other variables?   Yes   No

Print the fourth table (showing the relationship between CARE HOUSE and INCOME for female African Americans). Attach this table to your assignment. (**Note:** If your computer is not connected to a printer, or you have been instructed not to use the printer, just skip this step.)

That's all for this lesson.

CHAPTER 13

Correlation and Regression

Tasks: Mapping, Scatterplot, Correlation, Regression
Data Files: STATES, GLOBAL, HOUSE, NES 04

INTRODUCTION

This chapter will explain the analysis to be used when both the dependent variable and the independent variable are metric (either interval or ratio). The topics are

*   correlation: measuring the degree of relationship between two variables

*   regression: expressing a dependent variable as a function of an independent variable

Once again, the emphasis is on *explanation*. We want to explain the dependent variable by relating variation in it to variation in an independent variable. Correlation tells us the *degree* and the *direction* of the relationship between two variables; regression tells us how much an independent variable affects the dependent variable. Strictly speaking, we should use correlation and regression only with *metric* (interval or ratio) variables, but we do sometimes bend the rules and use ordinal variables; there is even a restricted way to include nominal variables.

CORRELATION

In an exercise in Chapter 4, we used the MAPPING task for the STATES file to compare the violent crime rate and urbanism, the percentage of the population living in urban areas. Let's look at those two maps again.

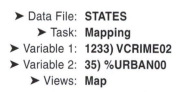

➤ Data File: **STATES**
   ➤ Task: **Mapping**
➤ Variable 1: **1233) VCRIME02**
➤ Variable 2: **35) %URBAN00**
    ➤ Views: **Map**

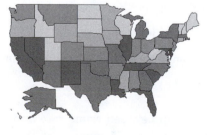

VCRIME02 -- 2002: NUMBER OF VIOLENT CRIMES PER 100,000 POPULATION (UCR)

r = 0.365**

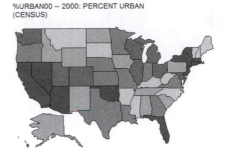

%URBAN00 -- 2000: PERCENT URBAN
(CENSUS)

Note that these maps are fairly similar. States that are darker on one map are darker on the other map; states that are lighter on one map are lighter on the other. This means that states that are more urban have higher crime rates and states that are less urban have lower crime rates. Thus, variation in the dependent variable (crime rate) is related to variation in the independent variable (urbanism).

The MAPPING task can be useful for examining relationships between variables; we can also obtain a summary measure of this relationship by looking at the correlation on the right side of the screen about halfway down.

The **_Pearson correlation coefficient (r)_** is a measure of the degree of relationship between two metric (interval or ratio) variables.

The Pearson correlation coefficient (r) shows how strong the relationship is between two variables; it also shows the direction—positive or negative—of that relationship. When r = 0, there is no relationship at all between the dependent variable and the independent variable. When the absolute value of r = 1.0 (r is either +1.0 or –1.0), there is a perfect relationship.

In interpreting the _strength_ of this correlation, let's _loosely_ use the following guidelines for the absolute value (ignoring whether the relationship is positive or negative) of r.

If r is

- under .25, the relationship is too weak to be useful

- between .25 and .34, the relationship is weak

- between .35 and .39, the relationship is moderate

- .40 or above, the relationship is strong

For the relationship between crime rate and urbanism, the correlation coefficient is .365. The two asterisks after the .365 mean that this correlation is statistically significant at the .01 level; a single asterisk would mean that the correlation is significant at the .05 level. Thus, in

Research Methods in Political Science

this example, we interpret the results as follows: There is a *statistically significant,* positive relationship between the rate of violent crime and the degree of urbanism—significant at the .01 level or better.

THE SCATTERPLOT AND THE REGRESSION LINE

A scatterplot is another way of expressing the relationship between two interval or ratio variables. It plots each case on a grid in which the dependent variable is the vertical axis and the independent variable is the horizontal axis. Below is a scatterplot for the violent crime rate (vertical axis) and urbanism (horizontal axis).

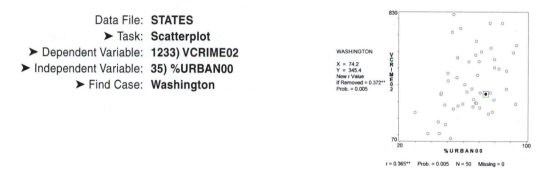

Data File: **STATES**
➤ Task: **Scatterplot**
➤ Dependent Variable: **1233) VCRIME02**
➤ Independent Variable: **35) %URBAN00**
➤ Find Case: **Washington**

Each dot—or data point—on the scatterplot represents a state's violent crime rate (the vertical distance) and the state's urbanism (the horizontal distance). For example, Washington state has a crime rate of 345.4 (violent crimes per 100,000 population) and it is 74.2% urban. Go across the horizontal axis to where you think 74 would be (for 74.2% urban), and then go up the vertical axis about halfway to where you think 345 is. You will see a data point there for Washington, indicated here with a box around it.

When we compared the maps for these two variables, we saw that there was a pattern. Similarly, we see a pattern here: States that are higher on urbanism have higher crime rates, and vice versa. Now let's place a *regression line* through the center of the data points.

Data File: **STATES**
Task: **Scatterplot**
Dependent Variable: **1233) VCRIME02**
Independent Variable: **35) %URBAN00**
➤ Find Case: **Washington**
➤ View: **Reg. Line**

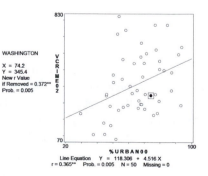

This regression line expresses the form and the direction of the relationship between the two variables. If the regression line slants upward (as it does here), the relationship is positive. If it slants downward, the relationship is negative.

The regression line can be thought of as a prediction line. If there were a perfect relationship between the two variables, then all the data points would be right on the regression line and we could perfectly predict the dependent variable by knowing the independent variable. The closer the data points are to the regression line, the stronger is the relationship between the two variables. On the other hand, if the data points are scattered about the regression line completely randomly, there is no relationship between the two variables.

Regression expresses a dependent variable as a function of an independent variable.

As indicated above, the distance between a data point and the regression line shows the amount of error involved in predicting that case on the basis of the relationship between the dependent variable and the independent variable. This distance (error) is called a *residual*. It is the difference between the actual value for a case and the predicted value—the dependent variable value that would be predicted for a case on the basis of its value on the independent variable—given the relationship that exists between the dependent variable and the independent variable. The next scatterplot shows these residuals for the example that we've been using.

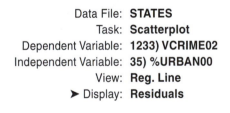

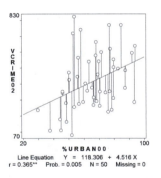

The lines from the cases to the regression line indicate the amount of error involved in predicting the values of the cases on the dependent variable by knowing the values of the independent variable.

MicroCase presents other information below the scatterplot, such as the correlation coefficient (r = .365**—it is the same value shown earlier in the MAPPING task) and the significance level (Prob. = .005). In the worksheet section of this chapter, we will examine some other features of this SCATTERPLOT task that can be useful, such as the identification of *outliers*—particular cases that have a disproportional effect on the correlation coefficient.

THE CORRELATION MATRIX

Although the comparison of maps (for ecological data) and the scatterplot are both useful in *looking* at relationships between variables, they can be inefficient, in the sense that we can examine only one relationship at a time. Given a set of variables, the CORRELATION task in MicroCase produces a correlation matrix that lists correlations for all possible pairs of variables in the set—including the correlation of a variable with itself. For example, using the STATES file, the correlation matrix below is produced when we specify variables 1233) VCRIME02, 35) %URBAN00, 830) %UNEMP 01, and 1622) %VOTED 04 as the variables to be correlated.

Data File: **STATES**
➤ Task: **Correlation**
➤ Variables: **1233) VCRIME02**
35) %URBAN00
830) %UNEMP 01
1622) %VOTED 04
➤ View: **Reg. Line**
➤ Display: **Residuals**

Correlation Coefficients
PAIRWISE deletion (1-tailed test)   Significance Levels: ** =.01, * =.05

	VCRIME02	%URBAN00	%UNEMP 01	%VOTED 04
VCRIME02	1.000 (50)	0.365 ** (50)	0.399 ** (50)	-0.355 ** (50)
%URBAN00	0.365 ** (50)	1.000 (50)	0.027 (50)	-0.041 (50)
%UNEMP 01	0.399 ** (50)	0.027 (50)	1.000 (50)	-0.207 (50)
%VOTED 04	-0.355 ** (50)	-0.041 (50)	-0.207 (50)	1.000 (50)

Note that, diagonally, the matrix presents each variable correlated with itself and, of course, that the correlation of a variable with itself is 1.0. This provides no useful information, but the program presents results for *all* possible pairs of variables that have been specified. For each pair, the program presents the correlation coefficient, the number of cases involved, and an indication of the statistical significance level. Notice that the correlation between crime rate and urbanism is .365**—the same correlation presented for this relationship when we examined it in mapping, and the same correlation presented by the scatterplot.

Note, for example, that the correlation between the crime rate and the percentage unemployed is .399**—a relatively weak degree of relationship. This correlation has two asterisks next to it, which signifies that the relationship is statistically significant at the .01 level or better.

P-R-E INTERPRETATION OF CORRELATION

The Pearson correlation coefficient is a P-R-E measure of association. However, to give it a proportional-reduction-in-error interpretation, we must square it. We also word the interpretation somewhat differently. The squared Pearson correlation coefficient, r^2, is interpreted as follows:

r^2 = the proportion of variation in the dependent variable explained by the independent variable

After squaring the Pearson correlation coefficient, we multiply it by 100 to obtain the *percentage* of variation in the dependent variable that is explained by the independent variable. In the preceding example, the Pearson correlation coefficient (r) between violent crime rate and percentage unemployed is .399. When we square .399 and multiply the result by 100, we see that the independent variable unemployment explains 15.9% of the variation in the crime rate.

As another example, the correlation coefficient between violent crime rate and urbanism is .365. We square .365 and multiply the result by 100 to obtain a percentage. Thus, the independent variable urbanism explains 13.3% of the variation in the dependent variable violent crime rate. Therefore, we have a moderate relationship between the violent crime rate and urbanism in states. If we know the degree of urbanism of a state, we can make fair predictions about its rate of violent crime.

Let's look at this P-R-E interpretation of the Pearson correlation coefficient another way, taking the scatterplot and regression line into consideration. Let's say that we are trying to explain variation in the dependent variable violent crime rates among the states by using urbanism as an independent variable. How would you go about predicting the violent crime rate for a particular state *before* you had any information about the relationship between crime rate and urbanism? For example, if you wanted to predict the violent crime rate in Washington, what would you guess? Your best guess would be the mean of the violent crime rates for the states: 413.7 violent crimes per 100,000 population.

With knowledge of the relationship between the crime rate and urbanism, however, you could make a better prediction. If you obtained a scatterplot of the relationship between these two variables, you could locate Washington's degree of urbanism (74.2) on the horizontal axis and draw a line straight up to the regression line. Then you would draw a line horizontally to the vertical axis, and that point would be the *predicted* crime rate for Washington. The stronger the relationship is between the dependent variable and the independent variable, the more useful this process would be in predicting (and thus explaining variation in) the dependent variable. The squared Pearson correlation coefficient provides a measure of how much better we can do in predicting the value of the dependent variable by knowing about the relationship between it and the independent variable.

CONTROLLING FOR OTHER VARIABLES IN CORRELATION

We see that unemployment in a state explains 15.9% of the variation in the crime rate. Does that mean that unemployment causes an increase in the crime rate? Perhaps and perhaps not. It is possible that the relationship is spurious or partly spurious—that some other variable affects *both* the crime rate and unemployment in such a way that it appears that unemployment increases the crime rate. When we look at the relationship between two variables, we need to consider possible intervening or antecedent variables that might affect the relationship and to control for the effects of these other variables. Depending on the level of measurement of the control variable, there are two ways to assess the effect of control variables when using Pearson correlation.

Controlling for Nominal or Ordinal Variables
If the control variable is nominal or ordinal, we control for it using a process similar to the one we used for controlling while using cross-tabulation. *We compute separate correlation coef-*

ficients for each category of the control variable. Then we compare the coefficients for the different categories of the control variable to see whether they are basically the same or substantially different.

If the correlations between the dependent variable and the independent variable are basically the same for different categories of the control variable, the control variable does not affect the relationship. If one or more of the correlations are substantially different from the others, the control variable does affect the relationship.

For example, if we want to examine the relationship between political participation and education while controlling for gender, we compute one correlation coefficient for males and another for females. Then we compare the two correlation coefficients to see whether they are substantially different. If they are substantially different from one another, then we know that gender affects the relationship between political participation and education. If they are not substantially different, then gender does not affect this relationship.

We also compare the original correlation coefficient (before controlling for anything) with the correlation coefficients for each category of the control variable. If the correlations for each category of the control variable are substantially the same as each other and the same as the original correlation, then the control variable has no effect. If one or more of the correlations from the categories of the control variable are substantially different from the original correlation, then the control variable does affect the relationship between the dependent variable and the independent variable.

We can control for more than one variable at a time using this process. For example, we could control for race and gender by computing separate correlations for white males, white females, black males, and black females. However, when we control for two or more variables at the same time, the number of cases for each category can be quite low, which may make the correlation coefficient less meaningful.

Controlling for Metric Variables

If the control variable is metric (interval or ratio), we use a statistical technique called *partial correlation*. This technique computes a partial correlation coefficient that shows the degree of relationship between the dependent variable and the independent variable while controlling for one or more control variables. Partial correlation allows us to control for more than one variable without the number-of-cases problem associated with controlling in cross-tabulation analysis.

We will not work with partial correlation here. The topic is beyond the scope of this book. However, in discussing multiple regression and correlation, we will touch on some ideas related to it.

MULTIPLE REGRESSION AND CORRELATION

In *multiple regression or correlation,* we use more than one independent variable to explain the dependent variable.

Let's return to the crime rate and urbanism example. Realistically, if we were trying to explain variation in crime rates among states, we would not rely on just one independent variable (urbanism). We would develop a theory that would include a *set* of independent variables. In addition to urbanism, we would use such variables as poverty, population density, drug-use rates, expenditures on law enforcement, and so on.

When we use multiple regression and correlation, we want to answer two primary questions:

1. How well does the set of independent variables explain the dependent variable?
2. What impact does a particular independent variable have on the dependent variable when we control for the effects of the other independent variables included in the set?

The first question is answered by the squared multiple correlation coefficient (R^2); the second question is answered by beta coefficients.

The Multiple Correlation Coefficient (R)

The *multiple correlation coefficient (R)* is a measure of the degree of relationship between the dependent variable and a set of independent variables taken collectively.

Like the Pearson correlation coefficient, the multiple correlation coefficient must be squared for us to give it a P-R-E interpretation. R^2 = *the proportion of variation in the dependent variable explained by the set of independent variables collectively.* Unlike the Pearson correlation coefficients, the multiple correlation coefficient has no direction. The reason is that more than one independent variable is involved and one independent variable might be positively related to the dependent variable while another independent variable might be negatively related to the dependent variable. R varies from 0 (no relationship at all) to 1.0 (a perfect relationship). The higher R is, the better we can predict the dependent variable on the basis of the set of independent variables.

For example, let's use two independent variables (urbanism and unemployment) to explain variation in crime rates among the states.

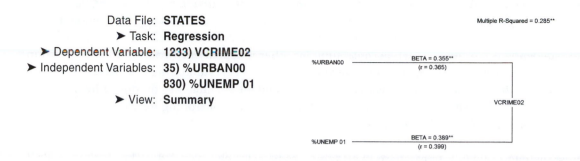

Data File: **STATES**
➤ Task: **Regression**
➤ Dependent Variable: **1233) VCRIME02**
➤ Independent Variables: **35) %URBAN00**
830) %UNEMP 01
➤ View: **Summary**

Note *Multiple R-Squared = 0.285*** in the upper right corner. This means that the two independent variables (urbanism and unemployment) together explain 28.5% of the variation in the dependent variable crime rate.

The two asterisks next to the R-squared figure of 0.285 mean that this squared multiple coefficient (R^2) is statistically significant at the .01 level of significance or better. One asterisk would mean that the squared multiple correlation coefficient was significant at the .05 level. If there is no asterisk, then the squared multiple correlation coefficient is not statistically significant.

The graphic presents a line from each independent variable (listed on the left) to the dependent variable (listed on the right). Below each line is the Pearson correlation coefficient, showing the degree of relationship between the independent variable and the dependent variable. The correlation (r) between urbanism and crime rate is (once again) .365, and the correlation between unemployment and crime rate is .399.

If we square these correlations, urbanism explains 13.3% of the variation in crime rates and unemployment explains 15.9%. If we were to add these two, we might erroneously conclude that they explain 29.2% of the variation in crime rates. Actually, however, as we saw in looking at R-squared, the two together explain 28.5% of the variation in crime rates. The reason is that the two independent variables (urbanism and unemployment) are correlated with one another, so they are both explaining some of the same variation in crime rates.

How much effect does each of these variables have on the dependent variable while we control for the effects of the other? To answer that question, we need to look at the beta coefficients.

Beta Coefficients

Beta coefficients are used to answer this question: How much effect does an independent variable have on a dependent variable while controlling for the effects of other independent variables in multiple regression?

A ***beta coefficient*** shows how many standard deviations of change in the dependent variable are produced by one standard deviation of change in a particular independent variable while controlling for the effects of all other independent variables in the regression equation.

Beta coefficients (also called *beta weights*) are *standardized partial regression coefficients*. In that term, *regression* means that the coefficient tells us how much effect the independent variable has on the dependent variable. *Partial* means that the coefficient tells us how much effect the independent variable has while controlling for other independent variables that are used in the analysis. *Standardized* means that the variables have been standardized so that we can say how many *standard deviations* of change in the dependent variable are produced by one standard deviation of change in the independent variable—while controlling for the effects of other independent variables in the analysis.

Thus, instead of having to compare apples and oranges, we can now judge the relative impact of different independent variables in terms of standard deviations of change in the dependent variable caused by one standard deviation of change in one particular independent variable while we control for the effects of the other independent variables in the analysis. Note that in the previous graphic, the beta coefficients are presented above the line for each independent variable. The beta coefficient for urbanism is .355** and the beta coefficient for unemployment is .389**. Let's interpret those results.

- A change of one standard deviation in urbanism produces .355 standard deviation of change in crime rates among the states, while controlling for the effects of unemployment.

- A change of one standard deviation in unemployment produces .389 standard deviation of change in crime rates among the states, while controlling for the effects of urbanism.

Thus, unemployment has a slightly greater effect on crime rates among the states than does urbanism. We can use the beta coefficients to measure the relative importance of independent variables—the higher the beta coefficient for an independent variable, the more important the independent variable in explaining the dependent variable while controlling for the effects of the other independent variables.

You may have noted in the regression graphic that the beta coefficient for %URBAN00 is followed by two asterisks, which signifies that the relationship is statistically significant at the .01 level or better—while controlling for the effect of the other independent variable (unemployment). The beta coefficient for unemployment also is followed by two asterisks. Thus, unemployment rate also is statistically significant at the .01 level. That means that the unemployment rates in states do affect the violent crime rates, while controlling for the effect of the other independent variable, urbanism.

Let's look at one more example. Using the HOUSE data file, let's examine the relationship between the percentage of the vote received by representatives—27) %VOTE(U)—and two independent variables: the number of terms served—12) #TERMS—and the amount of campaign expenditures—33) TOT EXPEN. We would expect that both independent variables would contribute to the margin by which a representative wins an election. Representatives who have served more terms have had longer to build support in their constituencies through providing services and meeting with people. We might expect that candidates who are able to spend more on campaigns have an advantage over those who have less to spend.

Research Methods in Political Science

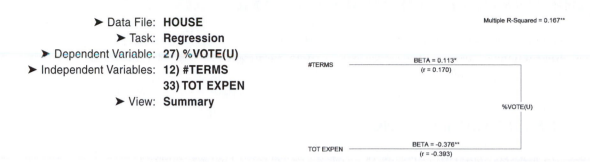

➤ Data File: **HOUSE**
➤ Task: **Regression**
➤ Dependent Variable: **27) %VOTE(U)**
➤ Independent Variables: **12) #TERMS**
33) TOT EXPEN
➤ View: **Summary**

Multiple R-Squared = 0.167**

#TERMS — BETA = 0.113*
(r = 0.170)

%VOTE(U)

TOT EXPEN — BETA = -0.376**
(r = -0.393)

Let's interpret the results. First, we look at the squared multiple correlation coefficient and we see that it is .167 and has two asterisks after it. This means that the two independent variables (number of terms served and campaign expenditures) explain 16.7% of the variation in the dependent variable (percentage of the vote received). Further, the two asterisks mean that the squared multiple correlation coefficient is statistically significant at the .01 level or better.

The beta coefficient for number of terms served is .113*. (For each standard deviation change in the independent variable number of terms served, there is an increase of .113 standard deviation in the dependent variable percentage of the vote received, while controlling for amount of campaign expenditures.) Thus, the number of terms served does have a statistically significant effect on the percentage of the vote received, while controlling for the other independent variable (campaign expenditures). Further, as expected, this beta coefficient is positive: Representatives who had served more terms received a higher percentage of the vote in their most recent election, while controlling for campaign expenditures.

The beta coefficient for campaign expenditures is −.376**. (For each standard deviation change in the independent variable amount of campaign expenditures, there is a *decrease* of .376 standard deviation in the dependent variable percentage of the vote received, while controlling for number of terms served.) The relationship is statistically significant at the .01 level. Thus, campaign expenditures do have a statistically significant effect on the percentage of the vote received, while controlling for the other independent variable (number of terms served). Further, note that this beta is substantially larger than the beta for number of terms served. Therefore, the amount of campaign expenditures is more important in explaining percentage of the vote received than is the number of terms served. Note, however, that this is a negative relationship! This is not what we predicted. Representatives who spent more money actually received a smaller percentage of the vote. Can you think of an explanation for this? (**Hint:** We might need to reverse our dependent and independent variables here.)

TERMS INTRODUCED IN THIS CHAPTER

Pearson correlation coefficient (r)
Regression
Multiple regression

Multiple correlation coefficient (R)
Beta coefficient

FOR FURTHER READING

For further information on correlation and regression, see Chapters 9 and 11 of William Fox, *Social Statistics Using MicroCase,* 4th ed. (Belmont, CA: Wadsworth, 2003).

Also see Chapters 4 and 9 of Leonard Champney, *Introduction to Quantitative Political Science* (New York: HarperCollins, 1995).

For a very readable example of examining the effects of independent variables one at a time and then putting them all together in multiple regression and correlation, see Chapter 3 of Michael A. Milburn, *Persuasion and Politics: The Social Psychology of Public Opinion* (Pacific Grove, CA: Brooks/Cole, 1995).

For an intermediate level of complexity, see the examples of correlation and regression in Chapters 12 and 13 of Marcus E. Ethridge, *The Political Research Experience: Readings and Analysis,* 2nd ed. (Guilford, CT: Dushkin, 1994).

For an interesting but more complex example of correlation and regression, see Richard R. Lau, "An Analysis of the Accuracy of 'Trial Heat' Polls During the 1992 Presidential Election," *Public Opinion Quarterly* 58 (Spring 1994): 2–20.

Another interesting but complex example of correlation and regression is Matthew Gabel, "Public Support for European Integration: An Empirical Test of Five Theories," *Journal of Politics* 60 (May 1998): 333–354.

An interesting shorter article that uses regression is Sean P. O'Brien and Donald P. Haider-Markel, "Fueling the Fire: Social and Political Correlates of Citizen Militia Activity," *Social Science Quarterly* 79 (June 1998): 456–465.

worksheet

CHAPTER
13

NAME: _____

COURSE: _____

DATE: _____

1. Let's begin by examining a relationship between civil liberties and newspaper availability in nations. There is a great deal of variation among the nations of the world in the extent to which people enjoy civil liberties, and the level of newspaper availability might help to account for that.

In the GLOBAL data file, take a close look at the variables 316) CIVIL LIBS95 and 213) NEWS/CP before evaluating the hypothesis. In particular, look at how the CIVIL LIBS95 variable is coded. A civil liberties rating of one is most free, while a rating of seven is least free. So, if the extent of newspaper availability is high in countries where there is more freedom, this would mean a high number for NEWS/CP and a low rating for CIVIL LIBS95—or a negative relationship.

Hypothesis: There is a negative relationship between the extent of civil liberties in nations and the extent of newspaper availability.

Null hypothesis: There is no relationship between the extent of civil liberties in nations and the extent of newspaper availability.

We will start by mapping these two variables.

➤ Data File: **GLOBAL**
➤ Task: **Mapping**
➤ Variable 1: **316) CIV LIBS95**
➤ Variable 2: **213) NEWS/CP**
➤ View: **Map**

Compare the two maps. If there is little or no relationship between these two variables (extent of civil liberties and extent of newspaper availability), then the two maps should be unrelated to each other. If there is a positive relationship between the two variables, then the two maps should be similar to one another (light-colored nations on one map will be light on the other map and dark-colored nations on one map will be dark on the other). If there is a negative relationship between the two variables, then the two maps will tend to be opposite of each other (light-colored nations on one map will be dark on the other map, and vice versa).

Are these two maps basically unrelated, similar to one another, or opposite of one another? (Circle one.)

Unrelated   Similar   Opposite

Look at the Pearson correlation coefficient (r) on the right side of the screen. Write this correlation coefficient in the space provided.

Pearson Correlation Coefficient (r) = _____

Chapter 13 Worksheet

259

Is this correlation coefficient statistically significant?   Yes   No

Which of the following conclusions is most appropriate? (Circle one.)

a. There is no relationship among these nations between extent of civil liberties and extent of newspaper availability. (This is the null hypothesis.)

b. There is a strong positive relationship among these nations between extent of civil liberties and extent of newspaper availability.

c. There is a strong negative relationship among these nations between extent of civil liberties and extent of newspaper availability.

2. Now let's look at this same relationship in terms of a scatterplot.

> Data File: **GLOBAL**
> ➤ Task: **Scatterplot**
> ➤ Dependent Variable: **316) CIV LIBS95**
> ➤ Independent Variable: **213) NEWS/CP**
> ➤ View: **Reg. Line**

Each data point on this scatterplot represents a nation for the dependent variable (extent of civil liberties) and for the independent variable (extent of newspaper availability). However, there might be two or more data points that share the same location on the scatterplot—two nations could have the same civil liberties score and the same newspaper availability score.

Let's look at some specific nations. One way to do that is to click on a particular data point, and the screen will present the name of the nation represented by that data point. Click on the data point that is in the bottom right corner of the screen. A box appears around this data point and information about this nation is presented to the right of the scatterplot.

Note that when you click on the data point, the program also presents the value of the dependent variable Y (extent of civil liberties) and the independent variable X (extent of newspaper availability) for this nation.

Write the name of this nation, its value for the dependent variable Y (extent of civil liberties), and its value for the independent variable X (extent of newspaper availability).

Name of Nation: _____

Civil Liberties Score: _____

Newspaper Availability Score: _____

Next click the [Find Case] option to deselect the nation you have highlighted. To find a specific nation (e.g., Canada) on the scatterplot, use the [Find: Case] procedure.

Data File:	**GLOBAL**
Task:	**Scatterplot**
Dependent Variable:	**316) CIV LIBS95**
Independent Variable:	**213) NEWS/CP**
View:	**Reg. Line**
➤ Display:	**Find Case: Canada**

Click the [Find Case] option, and the screen will list the nations. Scroll down to Canada, and click in the box to the left of the name. Then click [OK]. When finished, you can clear the selection of a particular case by clicking on [Find Case] again.

Note that a box has been drawn around the data point that represents Canada. What are the values of the dependent variable Y (extent of civil liberties) and the independent variable X (extent of newspaper availability) for Canada?

Civil Liberties Score: _____

Newspaper Availability Score: _____

Click the [Find Case] option to deselect Canada. Then click the [Find Case] option again and use this same procedure to locate Singapore. What are the values of the dependent variable Y (extent of civil liberties) and the independent variable X (extent of newspaper availability) for Singapore?

Civil Liberties Score: _____

Newspaper Availability Score: _____

3. The Pearson correlation coefficient (r), the significance level (Prob.), and the number of cases (N) are presented below the scatterplot. Write these figures here.

Pearson Correlation Coefficient (r) = _____

Prob. = _____

Number of Cases (N) = _____

Is this relationship statistically significant?   Yes   No

What percentage of the variation in the dependent variable (extent of civil liberties) is explained by the independent variable (extent of newspaper availability)? (Remember to square r and convert the resulting proportion into a percentage.)   _____%

4. Let's look at the residuals. If you have not already done so, first clear the [Find: Case] procedure.

Data File:	**GLOBAL**
Task:	**Scatterplot**
Dependent Variable:	**316) CIV LIBS95**
Independent Variable:	**213) NEWS/CP**
View:	**Reg. Line**
➤ Display:	**Residuals**

To show the residuals, select the [Residuals] option as well as the [Reg. Line] option.

The vertical line from the regression line to the data point shows the residual for a case. A residual is the difference between the actual value of the dependent variable and the predicted value—the value we would predict on the basis of the relationship between the dependent variable and the independent variable.

We want to predict the value of the dependent variable for a case on the basis of our knowledge of the independent variable and the way in which it relates to the dependent variable. Here, we want to use a nation's newspaper availability to predict the nation's civil liberties score. The residual for each case shows us how close the prediction is for the case.

Some of the lines in this scatterplot are very short. This means that the predicted value and the actual value (for extent of civil liberties) are very close to one another. Some of the lines are longer, showing a bigger difference between the actual value and the predicted value.

Let's look at two specific nations (North Korea and the United Kingdom) to see how close the predicted value is to the actual value for the extent of civil liberties.

Data File:	**GLOBAL**
Task:	**Scatterplot**
Dependent Variable:	**316) CIV LIBS95**
Independent Variable:	**213) NEWS/CP**
➤ View	**Reg. Line/Residuals**
➤ Display:	**Find Case: North Korea**

On the basis of how close North Korea's data point is to the regression line, which of the following is the more accurate conclusion? (Circle the letter of your choice.)

    a. On the basis of knowledge of North Korea's newspaper availability, we could predict fairly well its extent of civil liberties.

    b. On the basis of knowledge of North Korea's newspaper availability, we could not predict very well its extent of civil liberties.

Data File:	**GLOBAL**
Task:	**Scatterplot**
Dependent Variable:	**316) CIV LIBS95**
Independent Variable:	**213) NEWS/CP**
View:	**Reg. Line/Residuals**
➤ Display:	**Find Case: United Kingdom**

worksheet

CHAPTER 13

Click the [Find Case] option to deselect North Korea. Then click the [Find Case] option again to select the United Kingdom.

On the basis of how close the United Kingdom's data point is to the regression line, which of the following is the more accurate conclusion? (Circle the letter of your choice.)

a. On the basis of knowledge of the United Kingdom's newspaper availability, we could predict fairly well its extent of civil liberties.

b. On the basis of knowledge of the United Kingdom's newspaper availability, we could not predict very well its extent of civil liberties.

5. Let's look at the CORRELATION task. With this task, you can list variables and obtain a correlation matrix, a listing of Pearson correlation coefficients for each possible pair of variables, including the correlation of a variable with itself. We will obtain a correlation matrix for three variables here.

Data File:	**GLOBAL**
➤ Task:	**Correlation**
➤ Variables:	**314) CIV LIBS04**
	367) EDUC INDEX
	138) GDPCAP PPP

Note that you need to select all three of the variables listed.

The screen tells us that Pearson correlations marked with two asterisks (**) are significant at the .01 level or better, and those marked with one asterisk (*) are significant at the .05 level. In each cell of the correlation matrix, there are two numbers: the Pearson correlation coefficient and the number of cases on which the particular correlation coefficient is based. Note that different variables can have different numbers of missing cases, so the number of cases varies from one correlation coefficient to another.

Write the Pearson correlation coefficients in the following matrix.

	CIV LIBS04	EDUC INDEX	GDPCAP PPP
CIV LIBS04	_____	_____	_____
EDUC INDEX	_____	_____	_____
GDPCAP PPP	_____	_____	_____

The correlation of any variable with itself is 1.0 by definition, so this doesn't tell us anything. Let's look at the correlation between extent of civil liberties in nations and the education level for people in those nations. The correlation between extent of civil liberties in 2004 and education is −.473, and the two asterisks next to that correlation show that the relationship is statistically significant at the .01 level or better. Note that the correlation is negative—nations that have a higher expected education level have a lower civil liberties rating for their citizens, and vice versa. In this instance, though, it is important to remember how the civil liberties variable is coded. A civil liberties rating of one is the most free, while a rating of seven is least free. So, as

education levels increase, nations tend to have lower civil liberties ratings (more freedom). By squaring −.473 and multiplying by 100, we see that expected education level explains 22.3% of the variation in the extent of civil liberties in nations.

The correlation between education level and gross domestic product per capita is .616. If we square .616, we get .379. What percentage of variation in education is explained by gross domestic product per capita? _____%

6. An outlier is a case that is unusual in some way and has a large impact on the results. Outliers can be defined differently for different types of statistical analysis. For example, in univariate statistics, if you were computing the mean income of a group of 50 people, it would greatly affect the mean income if one of these people happened to be a billionaire.

Here, in the SCATTERPLOT task, an outlier is a case that has the most effect on the correlation coefficient. In some situations, eliminating an outlier from the analysis can substantially change the correlation coefficient. Let's look at an example from the STATES data file.

➤ Data File: **STATES**
➤ Task: **Scatterplot**
➤ Dependent Variable: **955) ED$PC02**
➤ Independent Variable: **925) SL_EXP$PC**
➤ View **Reg. Line**

Among the states, it makes sense to expect a positive relationship between the total per capita state expenditures and the per capita state educational expenditures. States that spend more money on a per capita basis will probably spend more money on education per capita. Write the Pearson correlation coefficient below.

Pearson Correlation Coefficient (r) = _____

Thus, we see that there is a strong relationship between these two variables. Let's next check for outliers.

Data File: **STATES**
Task: **Scatterplot**
Dependent Variable: **955) ED$PC02**
Independent Variable: **925) SL_EXP$PC**
View **Reg. Line**
➤ Display **Outlier**

Find the outlier by selecting the [Outlier] option. A box will appear around the dot representing the outlier case. (You can remove this case by clicking the [Remove] button, but do not do that yet.)

Note that the case that has the most effect on the correlation is in the upper right corner all by itself. Write the name of this state below.

worksheet

Below the name of the state that has been identified is the value of this state for the dependent variable and the independent variable. Then below that, the program presents the value of the correlation coefficient if we were to remove this case from the analysis. In this situation, what would be the new value of the correlation?

New r value if outlier removed = _____

Print these results and attach them to your assignment. (**Note:** If you have been instructed not to submit the printout, just skip this task.)

Compare this value of r with the original value. Which of the following best represents what would happen to the strength of the relationship if this case were removed from the analysis? (Circle the letter of your choice.)

a. It would have little effect on the relationship.

b. It would substantially decrease the relationship.

c. It would substantially increase the relationship.

Click the [Remove] button to remove the outlier, and note how the scatterplot changes as you do that. Also note that the new correlation coefficient now appears at the bottom of the screen. Now click the [Find Outlier] option again to see the new possible outlier. The new possible outlier is Wyoming. If Wyoming were removed from the analysis, what effect would that have on the strength of the relationship? (Circle the letter of your choice.)

a. It would have no effect on the relationship.

b. It would slightly decrease the relationship.

c. It would slightly increase the relationship.

7. Using the NES 04 data file, let's see how to correlate two metric (interval or ratio) variables while controlling for a nonmetric (nominal or ordinal) variable. First, let's obtain a correlation between respondents' ratings of the Democratic Party and their ratings of the Republican Party. We hypothesize that there is a negative relationship between Democratic Party ratings and Republican Party ratings. We expect that those who rate the Democratic Party high will rate the Republican Party low, and vice versa.

➤ Data File: **NES 04**
➤ Task: **Correlation**
➤ Variables: **536) DEMS_THRM**
537) REPUB_THRM

Write the Pearson correlation coefficient for the relationship between ratings of the Democratic Party and ratings of the Republican Party.

Pearson Correlation Coefficient (r) = _____

Is this relationship statistically significant?   Yes   No

Is this relationship negative as hypothesized?   Yes   No

Chapter 13 Worksheet   265

worksheet

CHAPTER **13**

We see that people who rated the Democratic Party high tended to rate the Republican Party low, and people who rated the Republican Party high tended to rate the Democratic Party low. But that is not a very strong relationship. We might expect that this relationship would vary according to whether people feel that there are important differences between the Democratic Party and the Republican Party. We would expect that the correlation between the ratings would be stronger among those who feel that there are important differences.

So, using the subset procedure, let's repeat the preceding analysis controlling for whether the respondent feels that there are important differences between the Democratic Party and the Republican Party.

> Data File: **NES 04**
> Task: **Correlation**
> Variables: **536) DEMS_THRM**
> **537) REPUB_THRM**
> ➤ Subset Variable: **426) PARTY_DIFF**
> ➤ Subset Category: **Include: 2) No**

> The option for selecting a subset variable is located on the same screen you use to select other variables. For this example, select 426) PARTY_DIFF as a subset variable. A window will appear that shows you the categories of the subset variable. Select 2) No as your subset category. Next, choose the [Include] option. Then click [OK] and continue as usual. With this particular subset selected, the results will be limited to those who did not think that there are important differences between the Democratic Party and the Republican Party. The subset selection continues until you exit the task, delete all subset variables, or clear all variables.

Among those who did not think that there are important differences between the Democratic Party and the Republican Party, what is the value of the correlation coefficient for ratings of the Democratic Party and the Republican Party?

r = _____

Is this relationship statistically significant?   Yes   No

Now let's obtain the correlation coefficient for ratings of the Democratic Party and the Republican Party among those who believe that there are important differences between the two.

> Data File: **NES 04**
> Task: **Correlation**
> Variables: **536) DEMS_THRM**
> **537) REPUB_THRM**
> Subset Variable: **426) PARTY_DIFF**
> ➤ Subset Category: **Include: 1) Yes**

> The easiest way to change the subset category from No to Yes is to first delete the subset variable, 426) PARTY_DIFF. Then reselect 426) PARTY_DIFF as the subset variable. Include 1) Yes as your subset category. Then click [OK] and continue as usual.

Research Methods in Political Science

Among those who thought that there are important differences between the Democratic Party and the Republican Party, what is the value of the correlation coefficient for ratings of the Democratic Party and the Republican Party?

r = _____

Is this relationship statistically significant?   Yes   No

Is this relationship among those who think that there are important differences between the Democratic and Republican Parties noticeably stronger than the relationship among those who do not think that there are important differences between the Democratic and Republican Parties?   Yes   No

8. Now let's turn to multiple correlation and regression. Multiple correlation and regression allows us to examine relationships between a dependent variable and two or more independent variables taken collectively. Let's start, however, with just one independent variable.

Using the GLOBAL data file again, we will hypothesize that there is a negative relationship between the extent of civil liberties in nations and the per capita gross domestic product.

> ➤ Data File: **GLOBAL**
> ➤ Task: **Regression**
> ➤ Dependent Variable: **314) CIV LIBS04**
> ➤ Independent Variable: **138) GDPCAP PPP**
> ➤ View: **Graph**

On the left side of the graph is the independent variable, per capita gross domestic product. On the right side is the dependent variable, civil liberties score. Below the line that connects the independent variable and the dependent variable is the Pearson correlation coefficient (r). Write the value of this correlation coefficient.

r = _____

Note that on this screen the program does not indicate the significance level of the correlation coefficient. Thus, the lack of asterisks next to this correlation coefficient does not indicate a lack of statistical significance. On the contrary, you have already seen that this correlation is statistically significant. If you want, you can see the correlation matrix (with significance indicated) by clicking the [Correlation] option under Statistics on the left side of the screen.

Next, note the beta coefficient above the line. When there is only one variable in the regression analysis, the correlation coefficient and the beta coefficient will be the same. Note, however, that the program does indicate the significance level of the beta coefficient. Here there are two asterisks next to the beta coefficient, indicating that this coefficient is statistically significant at the .01 level or better.

The beta coefficient indicates the amount of change (measured in standard deviations) in the dependent variable produced by one standard deviation change in the independent variable while controlling for the effects of other independent variables in the regression analysis. Here, however, there is only one independent variable so far. Thus, we can interpret this beta coefficient as follows: For each standard deviation change in per capita gross domestic product, there is a .608 standard deviation change in civil liberties score.

Next, note the Multiple R-Squared in the upper right corner of the screen. This is not actually a multiple R-squared at this point, because we have just a single independent variable in the analysis at this stage. Thus, with just one independent variable in the analysis, the "multiple" R-squared is the same figure that you would obtain if you squared the Pearson correlation coefficient.

How much variation in the dependent variable (civil liberties score) is explained by the independent variable (per capita gross domestic product)? _____%

Is this "multiple" R-squared statistically significant?   Yes   No

At this point, we would conclude that nations that have higher per capita gross domestic product have a better civil liberties rating for their citizens.

9. What other variables might help to explain variation in civil liberties scores among nations? Let's include newspaper availability and expected education level again. Another possibility would be the degree to which violence is used in cultural conflicts. Let's add these three variables to the analysis along with per capita gross domestic product.

> Data File: **GLOBAL**
> Task: **Regression**
> Dependent Variable: **314) CIV LIBS04**
> ➤ Independent Variables: **138) GDPCAP PPP**
> **213) NEWS/CP**
> **367) EDUC INDEX**
> **344) C.CONFLICT**
> ➤ View: **Graph**

Note that you need to select all four independent variables for this analysis.

First, let's examine the value of the squared multiple correlation coefficient. Write this value below.

Multiple R-squared = _____

Is this squared multiple correlation coefficient statistically significant?   Yes   No

What percentage of the variation in civil liberties scores is explained by the four independent variables (per capita gross domestic product, newspaper availability, expected education level, and the degree to which violence is used in cultural conflict) together?   _____%

worksheet

Write the Pearson correlation coefficients showing the relationship of each independent variable with the dependent variable.

For per capita gross domestic product and civil liberties score, r = _____

For newspaper availability and civil liberties score, r = _____

For expected education and civil liberties score, r = _____

For degree of violence in cultural conflict and civil liberties score, r = _____

We see that each of the independent variables is substantially correlated with the dependent variable. Further, the four together explain a large percentage of variation in the dependent variable.

Now let's look at the beta coefficients to answer this question: What effect does each independent variable have on the dependent variable while controlling for the effects of the other two independent variables?

Write the beta coefficient for each of the independent variables.

Per capita gross domestic product beta = _____

Newspaper availability beta = _____

Expected education beta = _____

Degree of violence in cultural conflict beta = _____

The higher the absolute value (ignoring whether it is positive or negative) of the beta coefficient, the greater the effect of an independent variable on the dependent variable, while controlling for the effects of the other independent variables. Which of these four independent variables has the greatest effect on civil liberties scores? (Circle one.)

Per capita gross domestic product   Newspaper availability

Expected education   Degree of violence in cultural conflict

Note that the beta coefficient is positive for degree of violence in cultural conflict: The higher the degree of violence in cultural conflict, the higher the civil liberties score (1 = most free; 7 = least free).

Let's look again at the relationship between per capita gross domestic product and civil liberties score. The Pearson correlation is strong. However, examine carefully the beta coefficient for per capita gross domestic product. According to this analysis, how much effect does per capita gross domestic product have on civil liberties scores when we control for the effects of the other three independent variables? (Circle one.)

a. None—the beta coefficient is not statistically significant

b. A small effect

c. A large effect

worksheet

We started out with a substantial relationship between per capita gross domestic product and civil liberties scores. However, given the preceding results, we might ask what happens if we eliminate per capita gross domestic product from the analysis. Would this greatly reduce the amount of explained variation? Can we eliminate this variable as well? Let's find out.

Data File:	**GLOBAL**
Task:	**Regression**
Dependent Variable:	**314) CIV LIBS04**
➤ Independent Variables:	**213) NEWS/CP**
	367) EDUC INDEX
	344) C.CONFLICT
➤ View:	**Graph**

Return to the screen that lists the four independent variables for this regression analysis, select 138) GDPCAP PPP and delete it from the list. Then click [OK] to do the analysis with the three remaining independent variables.

How much variation in the dependent variable (civil liberties scores) is explained by the three independent variables (newspaper availability, expected education level, and degree of violence in cultural conflict)?   _____%

Did the elimination from the analysis of the one variable whose beta coefficient was not statistically significant (per capita gross domestic product) make an important difference in the extent to which we can explain variation in the civil liberties scores of nations?   Yes   No

That's all for this lesson.

CHAPTER 14

The Overall Process

INTRODUCTION

In case you feel you have lost sight of the forest because of the trees, this chapter will help you put the overall political research process back together. The chapter consists of three basic parts:

- A brief review of the overall process in political research

- A research example that demonstrates many of the basic steps in the overall process

- The chapter exercise, which sets up a research problem for you to carry through the basic stages of the process

This book was designed to give you information about (and experience with) the basic research process in political science. As you have gone through these materials and worksheets, certain ideas have been emphasized again and again—such as the goal of *explanation*. On the other hand, as you focus on specific topics involved in research, it is possible to lose track of some aspects of the overall research process. Therefore, this final chapter will give you experience with working through the overall research process.

To demonstrate the application of these ideas, an actual example will be presented that incorporates many of the steps of the research process in political science. At the same time, however, it needs to be emphasized that there is no one specific way of performing political research. There are many approaches and variations, so the example is simply an example—not a model that fits all political research.

Last, the worksheet section for this final chapter is arranged to guide you through the overall research process. You learn best by doing the research. Some of the steps are designed in such a way to be easily expanded by your instructor.

REVIEW: THE OVERALL PROCESS IN POLITICAL RESEARCH

Goal

Political science seeks ultimately to explain *all* aspects of political reality. Individual political researchers attempt to explain *certain* aspects of political reality. The goal is to develop tested theory to explain the variation in certain dependent variables that reflect certain aspects of political reality.

As you read the following review, remember that the order of these steps is not necessarily the same for all research projects. Some researchers might go through this series of steps exactly in the listed order; other researchers might, for example, start with the data and work backward to develop the research idea.

The Research Idea

A political researcher develops a research idea based on personal interests, the work of other researchers, suggestions by people with whom the researcher interacts, or some other basis. The researcher might have access to a data file and might examine the possibilities for research based solely on the available data.

Whatever the basis, the initial idea might be very specific or rather vague and general. It might concern new dependent variables, a new explanation for an existing dependent variable, new possibilities for antecedent or intervening variables, and so on. The research idea might simply concern better ways to measure variables that have been used previously, or it might be an update of older research.

The Literature Review

The researcher must know what research has already been done. So, the researcher searches books and professional journals to find any information that is relevant to the research idea. The results of this literature review can effect the research idea. Perhaps the idea was already examined by someone else. Maybe a part of the idea has been researched. The literature review may produce findings that contradict those of different studies that use different research methods.

Based on the literature review, the researcher refines the research idea. What is already known, and what is not yet known in this area? What kinds of new research need to be done? Given the resources and abilities of the researcher, what kind of research can be done? Based on consideration of such questions, the researcher modifies and clarifies the research idea.

Hypothesis Formulation

At some point, the research idea leads to the development of specific, testable hypotheses. At this point, the researcher should have (at a minimum) a loose theoretical framework that provides an explanation of the aspects of political reality with which the researcher is concerned. The researcher derives the hypotheses from this theoretical explanation. The results from the tests of the hypotheses will allow the researcher to draw implications about the theory. A hypothesis is a prediction based on a theory. If the hypothesis is correct, this finding adds support to the theory. If the hypothesis is not correct, this finding does not support the theory.

Our theoretical explanations contain, among other things, beliefs about one variable affecting another variable: Theories deal with *causality*. Because it cannot be proven, strictly speaking, that anything causes anything else, the strategy of political research is based on disproof rather than on proof. Thus, the researcher actually tests the null hypothesis, which states that there is no relationship between the dependent variable and the independent variable.

Conceptual (Nominal) Definitions

The researcher must have a clear idea of what is meant by each major concept used in the research. That does not mean that the researcher will define every concept that is mentioned, but clear meanings must be assigned to the major concepts and to any other concepts about which there is likely to be misunderstanding.

Operational Definitions

Next, the researcher specifies how to measure each concept used in the research. Once the researcher has measured a concept, he or she has a variable. Regardless of what source of data the researcher uses to operationalize concepts, the researcher must be clear and explicit about the way the concept is operationalized so that other people can replicate the procedure.

Measurement

Now the researcher carries out the actual measurement process (unless the researcher is working backward and has already collected the data). The researcher can collect data through various sources (survey data, experimental data, public records, and so on). The measurement process also includes any modifications that the researcher needs to make to the data. Data modification includes such procedures as recoding the data, collapsing the data, and combining several variables into one composite variable.

Statistical Analysis

Next, the researcher carries out the statistical analysis. Such analysis usually begins with descriptive statistics, especially for the dependent variable. Then the researcher selects the appropriate statistical techniques (depending greatly on the levels of measurement of the variables involved) to test the hypotheses.

Drawing Conclusions

On the basis of the statistical analysis, the researcher accepts or rejects the individual null hypotheses. On that basis, the researcher draws conclusions about the hypotheses and the explanatory value of the theory. The researcher might also draw conclusions about the implications for further research.

Writing the Research Report

The type of report to be written on the research depends on the type of audience for which it is written. The manner in which we present the terminology and the specific details will vary depending on the background of those who will read the report. However, no matter who is going to read the report, it should include at least some information on the background of the research question, the literature review, the conceptual and operational definitions, the data-collection procedures, the statistical results, and the conclusions.

EXAMPLE: THE SOURCES OF POLITICAL TOLERANCE

The Research Idea

Suppose you had looked through the GSS 04 data file and became interested in the political tolerance questions (ATHIEST SP, RACIST SP, and so on). You noticed that some people were very politically tolerant, some people were fairly tolerant, some were fairly intolerant, and so on. Thus, there is variation in political tolerance among people in the United States, and you are interested in explaining that variation. What accounts for the variation? Why are some people more tolerant than others? What kinds of people are more tolerant and what kinds are less tolerant?

The Literature Review and Hypothesis Formulation

Given this general concern with the sources of political tolerance or intolerance, you go to the library to do the literature review. What research has already been done in this area? What is known about the sources of political tolerance and what is not known? (To show how the hypotheses are developed out of this process, we will combine the literature review and hypothesis-formulation steps here.)

Actually, in this particular area, you will find that a great deal of research already has been done. There are several books and many articles on political tolerance. Furthermore, there is substantial disagreement among researchers in this area concerning certain relationships. *For the purposes of this example, however, let's pretend that your literature review turned up only theorizing about the topic rather than actual research.* Let's suppose that you turned up the following (untested) ideas concerning the sources of political tolerance in people:

> **Proposition 1:** People with more knowledge are more politically tolerant than people with less knowledge.

One author theorized that people with more knowledge would be more likely to know about basic democratic principles and the rationales that had been presented to justify political tolerance. This author theorized further that sheer knowledge of such topics would lead people to accept such ideas to a greater extent than they would if they had no such knowledge. This line of reasoning could be tested by relating a measure of political tolerance to a measure of education. Therefore, you formulate the following hypothesis:

> *Hypothesis 1:* There is a positive relationship between political tolerance and education.

> **Proposition 2:** People who are exposed to greater social diversity are more likely to accept the legitimacy of social diversity, and that leads to greater political tolerance.

People who live in relatively homogeneous environments are not exposed to as much social diversity as people who live in more heterogeneous environments. When people come into contact with such diversity in their day-to-day lives, it is likely that they learn to accept the legitimacy of differences among people and ideas, and that leads to the development of political tolerance.

That idea sounds good, and you are very interested in it. However, given that you are planning to use a data file that already exists (the GSS 04 file), you are not quite sure how you will operationalize it. One thing you think of is that there are questions that ask people how often they read the newspaper and how much television they watch. Those variables at least roughly suggest exposure to diversity; they might also tie in with the proposition about people's levels of knowledge. On the other hand, it might be necessary to control for one of those variables while examining the effects of the other on political tolerance. For example, how does frequency of newspaper reading relate to political tolerance while controlling for the amount of time watching television? You formulate the following hypotheses:

> *Hypothesis 2:* There is a positive relationship between political tolerance and the frequency of newspaper reading.

> *Hypothesis 3:* There is a positive relationship between political tolerance and the amount of time spent watching television.

> **Proposition 3:** People who are more secure are more politically tolerant.

The idea is that people who feel secure also feel less threatened by other people and therefore are willing to allow greater freedom to other people. People who feel less secure feel more threatened by others and, as a result, are less likely to support freedom for other people—especially for those who are very different in some way.

One thing you think of here is that political tolerance could be related to income. People with more income should feel more secure. Another proposition concerning political tolerance and security is that, in the United States, whites should feel more secure than should African Americans because African Americans would feel less secure because of racial discrimination and prejudice against them. On that basis, you might expect whites to be more politically tolerant. On the other hand, African Americans have been victims of intolerance, and on that basis you might expect African Americans to be more politically tolerant. It also occurs to you that this same kind of pattern might be found in differences between males and females. Therefore, you develop the following hypotheses:

> *Hypothesis 4:* There is a positive relationship between political tolerance and income.

> *Hypothesis 5:* Whites are more politically tolerant than are blacks.

> *Hypothesis 6:* Males are more politically tolerant than are females.

> **Proposition 4:** People become less politically tolerant as they grow older.

It has been argued that people become more "set in their ways" as they age. The argument is that people become more vulnerable, more cautious, and less tolerant. On that basis, you formulate the following hypothesis:

Hypothesis 7: There is a negative relationship between political tolerance and age.

After formulating that hypothesis, however, you come across an argument that people do not become less politically tolerant as they age. That argument suggests that the reason political differences exist among people in different age groups has more to do with the era in which these people were growing up than it has to do with the aging process itself. The argument basically proposes that the kinds of political attitudes people develop are shaped to some degree by the political environment in which they grew up. Once political attitudes are formed, people pretty much retain the same attitudes throughout their lives.

At this point, you see that you cannot really determine from the GSS 04 file whether people become less politically tolerant as they grow older. However, you can determine whether older people are actually less politically tolerant, so you decide that you will test the hypothesis. But keep in mind that if older people are less politically tolerant, we don't know whether they became less politically tolerant as they aged or whether they were also less politically tolerant when they were younger. To test that, we need data from a series of surveys over time rather than just one survey in 2004. (Actual research on that question, using NORC GSS 04 data from a series of surveys over time, indicates that people do not become less politically tolerant as they age.)

Conceptual Definitions

Here, the only basic concept that we need to define is political tolerance. We can do that as follows: *Political tolerance is a willingness to allow freedom of expression to other people regardless of those people's characteristics or views.*

Note that not everyone would agree with that definition. Some might want to make it broader, some might want to make it narrower, some might want it to refer to tolerance of those with whom we disagree, and some might want to change it in other ways.

Operational Definitions

Several of the independent variables (age, education, gender, income, and race) are fairly standard, so it would not be necessary to give operational definitions for them unless they had been measured in an unusual way. However, let's present the operational definitions for frequency of newspaper reading and amount of time spent watching television.

Frequency of newspaper reading is operationally defined in terms of responses to the following GSS 04 data file item:

> **NEWSPAPER?** How often do you read the newspaper—every day, a few times a week, once a week, less than once a week, or never? (The second and third categories have been collapsed into the weekly category, and the last two categories included in the question have been collapsed into less than weekly.)
>
> 1) DAILY   3) <WEEKLY
> 2) WEEKLY

Amount of time spent watching television is operationally defined in terms of responses to the following GSS 04 data file item:

WATCH TV On the average day, about how many hours do you personally watch television? *(The second and third categories have been collapsed into a single category. The same has been done with the fourth and fifth categories.)*

    1) 0–1 HOURS
    2) 2–3 HOURS
    3) 4+ HOURS

Our biggest job, however, is to operationally define political tolerance. There is disagreement among researchers concerning the ways in which political tolerance should be operationally defined. Not everyone would do it as we will here.

The GSS 04 file has five questions concerning whether a speech should be allowed for five hypothetical people: a person who is opposed to all churches and religion, a Communist, a homosexual, a person who believes blacks are genetically inferior, and a person who wants to let the military run the country. Because you have read those questions before, they will not be repeated here.

To develop a measure of political tolerance that is more reliable and more valid than any one of these individual questions, the five questions are combined in the variable FREESPEAK. For each person who answered all the questions, this variable consists of the number of "allow speech" responses given. Thus, each person has a score that varies from 0 (don't allow any of the five persons to give a speech) to 5 (allow all five persons to give a speech). This, then, is our operational definition of political tolerance for present purposes.

Statistical Analysis and Conclusions
Here, we will present the results of the statistical analysis. We will also draw conclusions about the meaning of the results as we go along.

Political Tolerance and Education
Because education in categories is an ordinal variable, we will use Kendall's tau here. Kendall's tau-c is .238** and the significance level is .000 for the relationship between political tolerance and education.

So, there is a statistically significant, positive relationship between political tolerance and education. We reject the null hypothesis that there is no relationship between political tolerance and education. People who have more education are more politically tolerant than people who have less education.

We need to be careful about the meaning we attach to this; our finding actually calls out for more research. Why is it that the variable *years of school* is positively related to political tolerance?

Although we had theoretical reasons for expecting this relationship, we have not delved deeply enough into antecedent or intervening variables to determine the validity of the reasoning behind the hypothesis. We cannot conclude simply that years of school will produce greater political tolerance. Years of school is just a rough indicator to stand for a more meaningful variable, education. Even so, is education itself the factor that produces greater political tolerance? Or does education produce some other variable (e.g., a kind of personality trait or a philosophical outlook) that in turn produces higher political tolerance? Another possibility is that those whose personalities lead to higher political tolerance are also the kinds of people who are more likely to go on for more schooling.

Thus, although the results are in accord with our hypothesis and our reasoning, we need to avoid jumping to conclusions that oversimplify reality. In a sense, our finding simply says, "Okay, you're making progress. Now dig deeper into this relationship." In political research, one piece of research often leads to another. *The scientific process is cumulative: Each research project builds on what is already known.*

Political Tolerance, Newspaper Reading, and Television Watching
Because frequency of newspaper reading and amount of time spent watching television are both set up as ordinal variables, we cross-tabulated each of these variables against political tolerance. The relationship between political tolerance and newspaper reading is not statistically significant (Prob. = .445).

The results concerning television are also discouraging for our initial reasoning. There is a statistically significant (Prob. = .029), weak relationship (Kendall's tau-c = −.090) between political tolerance and amount of time spent watching television. Thus, we were correct to expect a relationship. However, the relationship is negative! We expected that people who spent more time watching television would be more politically tolerant, because they would be exposed to greater social diversity. Table 14.1 presents the results, which have been further collapsed to make the pattern clearer.

This negative relationship between political tolerance and television watching certainly provides an interesting basis for further research. It raises a variety of questions. Does television watching produce lower political tolerance? Are less politically tolerant people simply more likely to spend their time watching television? Does watching television actually reduce exposure to social diversity because it serves as a withdrawal mechanism? Do some shows on television contribute to greater political tolerance whereas others detract from political tolerance? Are there other important variables that affect the ways in which political tolerance and television watching are connected? This even raises some interesting side questions, such as whether the portrayal of violence on television promotes political intolerance. We might also need to control for education while looking at the relationship between television viewing and political tolerance.

Table 14.1 Political Tolerance by Amount of Time Spent Watching Television Each Day

	0 to 1 Hours	2 to 3 Hours	More Than 4 Hours
0 to 2 tolerant responses	19.5% (30)	26.6% (47)	25.0% (27)
3 to 4 tolerant responses	25.3% (39)	28.2% (50)	33.3% (36)
5 tolerant responses	55.2% (85)	45.2% (80)	41.7% (45)
Totals	100.0% (154)	100.0% (177)	100% (108)

Political Tolerance and Income

We reasoned that people with more income would have more political tolerance, because they would feel more secure. Income in categories is an ordinal variable; thus, we will use a cross-tabulation for this part of the analysis. When we cross-tabulate political tolerance by income category, we find that there is a statistically significant (Prob. = .000), moderate (Kendall's tau-c = .151) positive relationship. That supports the reasoning behind the hypothesis.

However, there is a problem: The relationship between income and political tolerance exists primarily because of the relationship between income and education. When we control for education, there is not much relationship between income and political tolerance. That is, when we examine the relationship between political tolerance and family income while using education as a control variable, there is only a statistically significant relationship between political tolerance and income among those with at least one year of college, and the relationships among those with a high school education or less are non-existant.

Political Tolerance and Race

We reasoned that African Americans would be less politically tolerant than whites, because African Americans would feel less secure personally, because of racial discrimination in society. The relationship between race and political tolerance is statistically significant (Prob. = .013). Cramer's V here is .135. Thus, we have a weak relationship: Whites tend to be slightly more politically tolerant than are African Americans.

However, this relationship may simply result from the fact that, because of racial discrimination, the average education level of African Americans is not as high as that of whites. Therefore, we did the analysis again while controlling for categories of education. Only among those with college education was the relationship between political tolerance and race statistically significant. Thus, there is only a partial relationship between political tolerance and race when we control for education.

Political Tolerance and Gender

Males seem to be more politically tolerant than are females, as hypothesized, but the result is not significant (Prob. = .062). Thus, we fail to reject the null hypothesis that there is no relationship between political tolerance and gender.

As with income and race, we were using gender to test the political tolerance–personal security hypothesis. However, this is really "stretching it," and we would actually need variables that clearly measured the concept of personal security. This would require a different set of questions concerning personality attributes.

Political Tolerance and Age

Kendall's tau-c is −.020 for political tolerance and age; but the relationship is not statistically significant (Prob. = .494). As we have seen, this does not answer the question about whether people become less politically tolerant as they age. To answer that question, we would need data from a series of surveys done over time.

Overall, the research has supported some of the hypotheses and some of the reasoning. In some situations, the research raised new questions about the measurement of the concepts or about other variables that might affect the relationships between the dependent variable (political tolerance) and the specific independent variables. In this situation, we certainly managed to raise more new questions than we answered. But we did provide some answers.

worksheet

NAME: _____

COURSE: _____

DATE: _____

In this final exercise, you will go through the overall research process. This project is set up in such a way that your instructor can easily expand it if desired. For example, it might be expanded to include additional hypotheses or an extensive review of the literature. Another possibility is that your instructor might want you to use a different data file (one that you create) rather than one of the five data files included with Student MicroCase.

Important: Before you actually begin the project, read through all of the instructions quickly so that you will see where the project is heading and what you will need to do. Also, as you proceed through a particular part of the exercise (e.g., giving operational definitions for concepts), it would be a good idea to review the relevant chapter in the book.

1. Start MicroCase, select the data file you would like to use, and browse through the variable descriptions. You might want to browse through several data files before deciding which one to select for this project. Then select a variable to be used as a dependent variable. (**Note:** You may want to read Appendix A for ideas.) Then select a variable to be used as an independent variable.

   From which data file did you select the variables? _____

   What is the MicroCase number and name of the variable that you are using as the dependent variable? _____

   What is the basic concept involved in the variable?

   _____

   _____

   _____

   Give a conceptual definition for the concept. (Before doing this part, you may want to review the discussion of conceptual definitions in Chapter 2.)

   _____

   _____

   _____

   _____

Based on the information in MicroCase about the variable, give a complete operational definition for the concept you are using as the dependent variable. (Before doing this part, you may want to review the discussion of operational definitions in Chapter 2.)

_____

_____

_____

_____

What is the MicroCase number and name of the variable that you
are using as the independent variable?   _____

What is the basic concept involved in the variable?

_____

_____

_____

_____

Give a conceptual definition for the concept.

_____

_____

_____

_____

Based on the information in MicroCase about the variable, give a complete operational definition for the concept you are using as the independent variable.

_____

_____

_____

_____

2. State a hypothesis to express the relationship between the dependent variable and the independent variable. **Note:** Before stating the hypothesis, you may want to review the discussion of hypotheses in Chapter 5. Pay particular attention to whether you need a directional format (both variables are ordinal or higher) or a nondirectional format (one or both variables are nominal).

_____

_____

_____

_____

3. State the null hypothesis for the relationship. (You may want to review the discussion of null hypotheses in Chapter 5 before stating the null hypothesis.)

_____

_____

_____

_____

4. Explain why you expect to find the relationship that you have hypothesized. Here you are theorizing. Why would the independent variable have the kind of effect on the dependent variable that you indicated in your hypothesis?

_____

_____

_____

_____

_____

_____

5. At this point, your instructor may want you to do a review of the literature relevant to your hypothesis. If so, then attach your literature review to these pages.

6. What is the level of measurement (nominal, ordinal, interval, or ratio) involved in each of the variables you are using? (Before answering, you may want to review the discussion of levels of measurement in Chapter 3.)

Dependent Variable _____

Independent Variable _____

7. Given the levels of measurement involved in your variables, which measure of association do you need for your analysis? (Before answering, you may want to review the discussion of measures of association in Chapter 10 and perhaps Chapter 13.)

_____

8. Use MicroCase to perform the statistical analysis that you need. What is the significance level for the relationship between the dependent variable and the independent variable? (You may want to review the discussion of tests of statistical significance in Chapter 10.)

_____

Is the relationship statistically significant?   Yes   No

Do you accept or reject the null hypothesis?

Accept   Reject

9. Write below the measure of association that you selected in item 7 above, and write the value of that measure of association (e.g., Kendall's tau-c = .131).

_____ = _____

10. Is that relationship in accord with what you hypothesized? Explain your answer.

11. If you used cross-tabulation, set up a table in the proper format for a report and attach it to these pages. If you are in a computer lab in which you can print results, print the cross-tabulation and attach it as well. It would be a good idea to review the discussion in Chapter 9 about how to set up a table in the proper format for a report.

If you used some other type of analysis (e.g., regression), then print the results and attach them to these pages.

worksheet

12. Controlling for a third variable: Select a variable that you think may affect the relationship between the dependent variable and the independent variable. List this variable below and indicate the basic concept involved.

What is the MicroCase number and name of the variable that you are using as the control variable?

_____

What is the basic concept involved in the variable?

_____

_____

_____

_____

Give a conceptual definition for the concept.

_____

_____

_____

_____

Based on the information in MicroCase about the variable, give a complete operational definition for the concept you are using as the control variable.

_____

_____

_____

_____

13. Explain why you think the control variable may affect the relationship between the dependent variable and the independent variable.

_____

_____

_____

_____

14. Perform the necessary analysis to examine the relationship between the dependent variable and the independent variable while controlling for the control variable. (You may want to review Chapter 12 and/or Chapter 13.) Depending upon the particular statistical analysis that you used, write below the relevant statistical results (significance information and measures of association or beta coefficients) obtained from the controlling process.

_____

_____

_____

_____

15. What do you conclude about whether the control variable affected the relationship between the dependent variable and the independent variable? Explain your answer.

_____

_____

_____

_____

APPENDIX
A

Independent Projects

There are many variables in each of the seven data files that have been little used or not at all used in the chapter exercises. Many of those variables could provide the basis for an independent research project. Such a project need not be limited to your present course or to other courses in political science. You could use your findings to write papers for other social science courses or even for writing courses. We have presented just a sampling of possible research areas below. However, we will begin these suggestions by reiterating the possibilities for the new data file that you can create in MicroCase.

CREATING A DATA FILE

In Chapter 7 you learned how to create a data file in MicroCase. Although you used only a few cases and a few variables to learn that process, the data you entered are real (they are from the U.S. Senate, 109th Congress). Appendix B presents many variables for all 100 U.S. senators. For a research project, you could select several of those variables, set up the data file, and analyze the results. With your Student Version of MicroCase, you can create a data file with an unlimited number of variables and cases. Remember that, after creating such a file, you can create a new file that replaces the old file.

Here are some examples of research questions you might pursue using the U.S. senators data:

*   To what extent does political party affiliation explain the variation in how senators vote on issues in Congress?

*   Does the security of the senator's seat (as indicated by the percentage of the vote received in the most recent election) have an effect on the voting behavior of senators?

*   To what extent are there patterns in the voting behavior of senators? If we know how a senator votes on one issue (e.g., the stem cell research issue), how well does that predict how the senator would vote on another issue (e.g., the tax cuts)?

Remember, however, that you do not need to use just the data provided in Appendix B. You can also gather other data for U.S. senators—for the same session of Congress or from a different session—from sources in your library (e.g., the *Congressional Record*) or from the Internet. Further, you do not need to use data based on senators. You can gather data from other sources. Here are two examples of projects you might engage in:

- Conduct a survey of students in your college or university concerning their political attitudes, background characteristics, social views, and so on.

- Using the types of variables in the STATES file as examples, gather data for a sample of cities in the United States and analyze patterns.

HOUSE DATA FILE

- **Effects of Party Affiliation**

  This file includes variables showing how representatives voted on a number of different issues in the 109th Congress in 2005–2006. To what extent do the political party affiliations of representatives explain how they voted on these issues?

- **Effects of Other Variables**

  To what extent can we explain the voting behavior of U.S. representatives on the basis of their background characteristics (e.g., sex, age, race) or variables concerning their election to the House (e.g., campaign spending, percentage of the vote received, region in which their district exists)?

- **Issue Interrelationships**

  To what extent can we predict how a representative votes on one issue on the basis of how the representative voted on another issue? Are there patterns in the voting behavior of representatives? Are those patterns more likely to appear on some types of issues than on others? You might control for certain variables to see what effect this has on voting patterns. For example, does political party affiliation affect the extent to which those patterns exist? How about region—especially the possible contrast between the South and the rest of the country? Does the Southern Coalition (Republicans and conservative southern Democrats) still exist? (For questions about regional influences, look at 16) REGION and 18) SOUTH DEM.)

GSS AND GSS 04 DATA FILES

- **Abortion**

  There is a series of questions concerning abortion attitudes, and there is a composite measure based on responses to six different abortion-related questions. What accounts for variation in support for, or opposition to, allowing an abortion?

- **Capital Punishment**

  What accounts for difference in attitudes concerning capital punishment?

- **Pornography**

  What kinds of people (in terms of background characteristics, political attitudes, etc.) are more likely to support or oppose laws against pornography?

- **Support for Social Welfare Programs**

  What accounts for differences in people's level of support for government programs to help people economically?

- **Support for Sexual Equality**

  Why are some people more supportive of sexual equality than are others? What kinds of people are most likely to support sexual equality, and what kinds of people are most likely to oppose it?

- **Spending Issues**

  Where do people stand on spending on particular areas (e.g., welfare, health, crime)? What accounts for differences among people in terms of spending attitudes?

- **Euthanasia**

  Where do people stand on the issue of euthanasia? What kinds of characteristics or attitudes of people account for variation in attitudes toward euthanasia?

NES AND NES 04 DATA FILES

- **Presidential Voting Choice**

  What explains why some people preferred one candidate over another candidate in the 2000 and 2004 presidential elections? What kinds of people voted Democratic? Republican? For Perot? How important are political issues, background characteristics, and party identifications in explaining why people vote the way they do? What kinds of people voted for one party in 2000 and for a different party in 2004?

- **Religion and Politics**

  What effects do people's religious orientations (e.g., general religious preference, frequency of praying, interpretation of the Bible) have on their political identifications and views on political issues? Do religious orientations affect political orientations when we control for people's background characteristics such as education?

- **Perception of Party Differences**

  Do people perceive differences between the Democratic Party and the Republican Party in terms of such issues as poverty, crime, and education? What accounts for variation in such perceptions?

- **Political Information**

  What accounts for differences among Americans in terms of political information? What kinds of people are most likely to have greater political knowledge? Are the political-issue views of those who have greater political knowledge different from those who have less?

- **Trust**

  How is personal trust related to political trust? How does trust of the news media relate to personal trust and political trust? What kinds of people have greater political trust?

STATES DATA FILE

- **State Taxes and Spending**

  What accounts for variation in state taxes from one state to another? What accounts for variation in state spending in particular areas (e.g., healthcare, welfare, prisons)? How is state spending in particular areas related to the amount of state taxes? That is, are state taxes more correlated with spending in some areas than in others?

- **Party Competition**

  Several variables show the relative numbers of Democrats and Republicans in the state legislature or in Congress, and there also is information about presidential voting. What accounts for variation from state to state in terms of party competition? Conversely, does party competition affect public policy? For example, does the degree of party competition help to explain variation among states in terms of expenditures for certain programs?

- **Aid for the Poor**

  Several variables in the STATES file concern public aid for the poor, the unemployed, and so on. There is a great deal of variation among the states in the amount of money spent on such programs. What accounts for that variation?

- **Support for Education**

  At least two variables in this file indicate the policy emphasis on education. What accounts for differences among the states in terms of the emphasis they place on education?

- **Percentage of Female Legislators**

  The percentage of female legislators varies from state to state. What accounts for that variation? What kinds of states are more likely to have a higher proportion of female legislators?

- **Social Problems**

  Several variables in this file indicate the extent to which a state has a particular social problem (e.g., crime). What kinds of states are more likely to have higher frequencies of such problems?

GLOBAL DATA FILE

- **Sexual Equality**

  What kinds of nations have greater sexual equality in political and economic roles? To what extent is that related to the attitudes of people about gender roles? To what extent is comparatively high sexual equality related to the education level and economic development of nations?

- **Civil Liberties and Political Rights**

  What explains why some nations are more supportive of the political and civil rights of their citizens than are other nations?

- **External Debt**

  What patterns exist in terms of the amount of external debt of nations, and what kinds of political or demographic variables might account for such patterns?

- **Human Development**

  There is great variation in the human development index scores of these 172 nations. What accounts for that variation? To what extent is human development related to political factors? To economic factors?

- **Inequality**

  Variables 184) INEQUALITY and 183) $ RICH 10% indicate the degree of income inequality within nations. How is that inequality related to other characteristics of nations?

- **Religious Distributions**

  Variables 475–480 concern the percentages of religious groups within each nation. How does the religious makeup of a nation affect its political values and structure?

DATA ARCHIVE

You may also download additional data files from the Web Expeditions site that are not included on your diskette in order to pursue independent research questions. Files include voting records from the 109th Congress (House and Senate), the Canadian National Election Study, selected countries from the World Values Survey, and a time-series archive of the GSS and NES.

B

U.S. Senators Data

This appendix contains data for U.S. senators for the 109th Congress (2005–2006). Your instructor might want you to create a data file based on this data. You can use the following data, or you can gather different information about the senators and use it instead.

DESCRIPTIONS OF VARIABLES

The senator's name, state, party affiliation, and number of years served are obvious. The percentage of the vote received is the percentage of the total votes cast (votes for major party candidates and other candidates as well) received by the senator. Note that when there are more than two candidates in an election, the winning candidate's percentage can be less than 50%.

The remaining variables consist of a series of roll-call votes in the U.S. Senate. Similar to the procedure in the HOUSE data file, each senator's vote on a bill is indicated as Y for *yes* or N for *no,* and a blank is used for missing data (the senator didn't vote on the bill). Each of these roll-call votes is briefly described below.

1. ROBERTS NOMINATION TO SUPREME COURT: Confirmation John G. Roberts, Jr., of Maryland, to be Chief Justice of the United States. [PN 801 confirmed 9/29/2005]

2. DEFICIT REDUCTION ACT: Deficit Reduction Omnibus Reconciliation Act of 2005 [S 1932 passed 11/3/2005]

3. ALITO NOMINATION TO SUPREME COURT: Confirmation Samuel A. Alito, Jr., of New Jersey, to be an Associate Justice [PN 1059 confirmed 1/31/2006]

4. EXTENSION OF TAX CUTS: Tax Increase Prevention and Reconciliation Act of 2005 [HR 4297 passed 2/2/2006]

5. PATRIOT ACT EXTENSION: A bill to amend the USA PATRIOT ACT to extend the sunset of certain provisions of such Act [HR 4659 passed 2/2/2006]

6. IMMIGRATION REFORM ACT: Comprehensive Immigration Reform Act of 2006. Comprehensive Immigration Reform Act of 2006 – Sets forth border security and enforcement provisions, including provisions respecting (1) personnel and asset increases and enhancements; (2) a National Strategy for Border Security; (3) border security initiatives, including biometric data enhancements and a biometric entry-exit system, document integrity, and mandatory detention of aliens apprehended at or between ports of entry; and (4) Central American gangs. [S 2611 passed 5/25/2006]

7. MARRIAGE PROTECTION AMENDMENT: Constitutional Amendment – Marriage Protection Amendment – Declares that: (1) marriage in the United States shall consist only of the union of a man and a woman; and (2) neither the U.S. Constitution nor the

constitution of any state shall be construed to require that marriage or the legal incidents of marriage be conferred upon any other union. Motion to Invoke Cloture on the Motion to Proceed to the Consideration of SJ RES 1; Marriage Protection Amendment [SJ RES 1 rejected 6/7/2006]

8. PERMANENT REPEAL OF ESTATE TAX: Death Tax Repeal Permanency Act of 2005 – Declares that the sunset provisions of the Economic Growth and Tax Relief Reconciliation Act of 2001, which terminate its application to estates of decedents dying, gifts made, or generation-skipping transfers, after December 31, 2010, shall not in fact apply to title V of such Act, which repeals estate and generation-skipping transfer taxes. (Thus makes the repeal of such taxes permanent.) Motion to Invoke Cloture on the Motion to Proceed to Consideration of HR 8; Death Tax Repeal Permanency Act of 2005 [HR 8 rejected 6/8/2006]

9. FETUS FARMING PROHIBITION: Fetus Farming Prohibition Act of 2006 – A bill to amend the Public Health Service Act to prohibit the solicitation or acceptance of tissue from fetuses gestated for research [S 3504 passed 7/18/2006]

10. STEM CELL RESEARCH: Stem Cell Research Enhancement Act of 2005 – To amend the Public Health Service Act to provide for human embryonic stem cell research. [HR 810 passed 7/18/2006; failed to override presidential veto in U.S. House]

11. CLOTURE MOTION ON THE NOMINATION OF JOHN BOLTON: A motion to cease debate and go to a vote on President Bush's nomination of John Bolton as the U.S. Representative to the United Nations. (Cloture motion on PN 326 failed on 6/20/05. Although a majority voted in favor of the motion, 60 votes are required to stop debate.)

12. GREENHOUSE GAS EMISSIONS AMENDMENT: An amendment to provide for a program to accelerate the reduction of greenhouse gas emissions in the United States. [S. Amdt. 826 to HR 6 failed 6/22/05.]

13. HABEAS CORPUS FOR ENEMY COMBATANTS: To provide for judicial review of detention of enemy combatants in U.S. courts, not military tribunals. [S 1042 failed 11/15/05.]

14. IRAN SANCTIONS AMENDMENT: An amendment to authorize, with an offset, assistance for prodemocracy programs and activities inside and outside Iran, to make clear that the United States supports the ability of the people of Iran to exercise self-determination over their form of government, and to make enhancements to the Iran-Libya Sanctions Act of 1996. [S. Amdt. 4234 to S. 2766 failed on 6/15/06.]

15. INCREASE IN MINIMUM WAGE: Kennedy Amdt. No. 4322 – To amend the Fair Labor Standards Act of 1938 to provide for an increase in the Federal minimum wage. [S. Amdt. 4322 to S 2766 failed on 6/21/06.]

16. IRAQ TRROP WITHDRAWL AMENDMENT: A resolution calling for a phased withdrawl from Iraq, with a timeline for future withdrawls provided by the President. [S. Amdt. 4320 to S 2766 failed 6/22/06.]

17. BORDER FENCING AMENDMENT TO DEPT. OF HOMELAND SECURITY APPROPRIATIONS ACT, 2007: An amendment calling for appropriating an additional $1,829,400,000 to construct double-layered fencing and vehicle barriers along the southwest border and to offset such increase by reducing all other discretionary amounts on a prorata basis. [S. Amdt. 4659 to HR 5441 failed 7/13/06.]

Research Methods in Political Science

Name[1]	State[2]	Party	Years	Percentage of Vote Received	Votes on Bills									
					1	2	3	4	5	6	7	8	9	10
Akaka	11	Dem	16	73	N	N	N	N	Y	Y	N	N	Y	Y
Alexander	42	Rep	4	54	Y	Y	Y	Y	Y	N	Y	Y	Y	Y
Allard	6	Rep	10	51	Y	Y	Y	Y	Y	N	Y	Y	Y	N
Allen	46	Rep	6	52	Y	Y	Y	Y	Y	N	Y	Y	Y	N
Baucus	26	Dem	28	50	Y	N	N	Y	Y	Y	N	Y	Y	Y
Bayh	14	Dem	8	62	N	N	N	N	Y	Y	N	N	Y	Y
Bennett	44	Rep	14	69	Y	Y	Y	Y	Y	Y	Y	Y	Y	Y
Biden	8	Dem	34	60	N	N	N	N	Y	Y	N	N	Y	Y
Bingaman	31	Dem	24	63	Y	N	N			Y	N	N	Y	Y
Bond	25	Rep	20	56	Y	Y	Y	Y	Y	N	Y	Y	Y	N
Boxer	5	Dem	14	58	N	N	N	N	Y	Y	N	N	Y	Y
Brownback	16	Rep	10	69	Y	Y	Y	Y	Y	Y	Y	Y	Y	N
Bunning	17	Rep	8	51	Y	Y	Y	Y	Y	N	Y	Y	Y	N
Burns	26	Rep	18	51	Y	Y	Y	Y	Y	N	Y	Y	Y	N
Burr	33	Dem	2	52	Y	Y	Y	N	Y	N	Y	Y	Y	Y
Byrd	48	Dem	48	78	Y	N	Y	N	Y	N	Y	N	Y	Y
Cantwell	47	Dem	6	49	N	N	N	Y	Y	Y	N	N	Y	Y
Carper	8	Dem	6	56	Y	N	N	Y	Y	Y	N	N	Y	Y
Chafee	39	Rep	30	57	Y	N	N	N	Y	Y	N	N	Y	Y
Chambliss	10	Rep	4	53	Y	Y	Y	Y	Y	N	Y	Y	Y	N
Clinton	32	Dem	6	55	N	N	N	Y	Y	Y	N	N	Y	Y
Coburn	36	Rep	2	61	Y	Y	Y	N	Y	N	Y	Y	Y	N
Cochran	24	Rep	28	71	Y	Y	Y	Y	Y	N	Y	Y	Y	Y

[1]When you set up the small data file in Chapter 7, you assigned case identification numbers to each of the 10 senators and then entered each senator's name as the label for each case identification number. However, Student MicroCase allows only as many as 10 labels for a variable. So, just assign each senator a case identification number (1 to 100). Write the case identification numbers next to the senators' names before you enter the data. If you obtain additional data for these senators from another source, make sure that you follow the same sequence of case identification numbers.

[2]Similar to the situation for the names of the senators, just assign numbers for the names of the states (from 1 to 50). Write the state identification numbers next to the names of the states before you enter data.

Name[1]	State[2]	Party	Years	Percentage of Vote Received	Votes on Bills									
					1	2	3	4	5	6	7	8	9	10
Coleman	23	Rep	4	50	Y	N	Y	Y	Y	Y	Y	Y	Y	N
Collins	19	Rep	10	49	Y	N	Y	Y	Y	Y	N	Y	Y	Y
Conrad	34	Dem	20	61	Y	N	Y	N	Y	Y	N	N	Y	Y
Cornyn	43	Rep	4	55	Y	Y	Y	Y	Y	N	Y	Y	Y	N
Corzine	30	Dem	6	50	N									
Craig	12	Rep	16	57	Y	Y	Y	Y	Y	Y	Y	Y	Y	N
Crapo	12	Rep	8	99	Y	Y	Y	Y	Y	N	Y	Y	Y	N
Dayton	23	Dem	6	49	N	N	N	Y	Y	Y	N	N	Y	Y
Demint	41	Dem	2	54	Y	Y	Y	Y	Y	N	Y	Y	Y	N
Dewine	35	Rep	12	60	Y	N	Y	Y	Y	Y	Y	Y	Y	N
Dodd	7	Dem	26	66	Y	N	N	N	Y	Y		N	Y	Y
Dole	33	Rep	4	54	Y	Y	Y	Y	Y	N	Y	Y	Y	Y
Domenici	31	Rep	34	65	Y	Y	Y			Y	Y	Y	Y	Y
Dorgan	34	Dem	14	68	Y	N	N	N	Y	N	N	N	Y	Y
Durbin	13	Dem	10	56	N	N	N	N	Y	Y	N	N	Y	Y
Ensign	28	Rep	6	55	Y	Y	Y	Y	Y	N	Y	Y	Y	N
Enzi	50	Rep	10	54	Y	Y	Y	Y	Y	N	Y	Y	Y	N
Feingold	49	Dem	14	55	Y	N	N	N	N	Y	N	N	Y	Y
Feinstein	5	Dem	14	56	N	N	N	Y	Y	Y	N	N	Y	Y
Frist	42	Rep	12	65	Y	Y	Y	Y	Y	Y	Y	Y	Y	Y
Graham	40	Rep	4	55	Y	Y	Y	Y	Y	Y	Y	Y	Y	N
Grassley	15	Rep	26	70	Y	Y	Y	Y	Y	N	Y	Y	Y	N
Gregg	29	Rep	14	66	Y	Y	Y	Y	Y	Y	N	Y	Y	Y
Hagel	27	Rep	10	57	Y	Y	Y	Y	Y	Y		Y	Y	N
Harkin	15	Dem	22	52	N	N	N	N	Y	Y	N	N	Y	Y
Hatch	44	Rep	30	66	Y	Y	Y	Y	Y	N	Y	Y	Y	Y
Hutchison	43	Rep	13	65	Y	Y	Y	Y	Y	N	Y	Y	Y	Y
Inhofe	36	Rep	12	57	Y	Y	Y	Y	Y	N	Y	Y	Y	N

Name[1]	State[2]	Party	Years	Percentage of Vote Received	Votes on Bills									
					1	2	3	4	5	6	7	8	9	10
Inouye	11	Dem	44	76	N	N	N	N	Y	Y	N	N	Y	Y
Isakson	10	Rep	2	58	Y	Y	Y	Y	Y	N	Y	Y	Y	N
Jeffords	45	Ind	18	66	Y	N	N	N	Y	Y	N	N	Y	Y
Johnson	41	Dem	10	51	Y	N	Y	Y	Y	Y	N	N	Y	Y
Kennedy	21	Dem	44	73	N	N	N	N	Y	Y	N	N	Y	Y
Kerry	21	Dem	22	52	N	N	N	N	Y	Y	N	N	Y	Y
Kohl	49	Dem	18	62	Y	N	N	N	Y	Y	N	N	Y	Y
Kyl	3	Rep	12	79	Y	Y	Y	Y	Y	N	Y	Y	Y	N
Landrieu	18	Dem	10	50	Y	Y	N	Y	Y	Y	N	N	Y	Y
Lautenberg	30	Dem	24	54	N	N	N	N	Y	Y	N	N	Y	Y
Leahy	45	Dem	32	71	Y	N	N	N	Y	Y	N	N	Y	Y
Levin	22	Dem	28	58	Y	N	N	N	Y	Y	N	N	Y	Y
Lieberman	7	Dem	18	63	Y	N	N	N	Y	Y	N	N	Y	Y
Lincoln	4	Dem	8	56	Y	N	N	Y	Y	Y	N	Y	Y	Y
Lott	24	Rep	18	66	Y	Y	Y	Y		N	Y	Y	Y	Y
Lugar	14	Rep	30	68	Y	Y	Y	Y	Y	Y	Y	Y	Y	Y
Martinez	9	Dem	2	49	Y	Y	Y	Y	Y	Y	Y	Y	Y	N
McCain	3	Rep	20	77	Y	Y	Y	Y	Y	Y	N	Y	Y	Y
McConnell	17	Rep	22	56	Y	Y	Y	Y	Y	Y	Y	Y	Y	N
Mikulski	20	Dem	20	65	N	N	N	N	Y	Y	N	N	Y	Y
Murkowski	2	Rep	4	49	Y	Y	Y	Y	Y	Y	Y	Y	Y	Y
Murray	47	Dem	14	55	Y	N	N	N	Y	Y	N	N	Y	Y
Nelson, Ben	27	Dem	6	51	Y	Y	Y	Y	Y	N	Y	Y	Y	N
Nelson, Bill	9	Dem	6	51	Y	N	N	Y	Y	Y	N	N	Y	Y
Obama	13	Dem	2	70	N	N	N	N	Y	Y	N	N	Y	Y
Pryor	4	Dem	4	54	Y	N	N	Y	Y	Y	N	N	Y	Y
Reed	39	Dem	10	63	N	N	N	N	Y	Y	N	N	Y	Y
Reid	28	Dem	20	61	N	N	N	N	Y	Y	N	N	Y	Y

Name[1]	State[2]	Party	Years	Percentage of Vote Received	Votes on Bills									
					1	2	3	4	5	6	7	8	9	10
Roberts	16	Rep	10	62	Y	Y	Y	Y	Y	N	Y	Y	Y	N
Rockefeller	48	Dem	22	77	Y	N	N	Y	Y				Y	Y
Salazar	6	Dem	2	51	Y	N	N	Y	Y		N	N	Y	Y
Santorum	38	Rep	10	53	Y	Y	Y	Y	Y	N	Y	Y	Y	N
Sarbanes	20	Dem	30	63	N	N	N	N	Y	Y	Y	N	Y	Y
Schumer	32	Dem	8	71	N	N	N	Y	Y	Y	N		Y	Y
Sessions	1	Rep	10	53	Y	Y	Y	Y	Y	N	Y	Y	Y	N
Shelby	1	Rep	20	68	Y	Y	Y	Y	Y	N	Y	Y	Y	N
Smith	37	Rep	10	50	Y	Y	Y	Y	Y	Y	Y	Y	Y	Y
Snowe	19	Rep	12	69	Y	N	Y	Y	Y	Y	N	Y	Y	Y
Specter	38	Rep	26	53	Y	Y	Y	Y	Y	Y	N	Y	Y	Y
Stabenow	22	Dem	6	50	N	N	N	Y	Y	N	N	N	Y	Y
Stevens	2	Rep	38	77	Y	Y	Y	Y	Y	Y	Y	Y	Y	Y
Sununu	29	Rep	4	51	Y	Y	Y	Y	Y	N	N	Y	Y	N
Talent	25	Rep	4	50	Y	Y	Y	Y	Y	N	Y	Y	Y	N
Thomas	50	Rep	12	74	Y	Y	Y			N	Y	Y	Y	N
Thune	41	Rep	2	51	Y	Y	Y	Y	Y	N	Y	Y	Y	N
Vitter	18	Rep	2	51	Y	Y	Y	Y	Y	N	Y	Y	Y	N
Voinovich	35	Rep	8	64	Y	Y	Y	N	Y	Y	Y	N	Y	N
Warner	46	Rep	26	53	Y	Y	Y	Y	Y	Y	Y	Y	Y	Y
Wyden	37	Dem	10	63	Y	N	N	N	Y	Y	N	N	Y	Y

APPENDIX C

Variable Names and Sources

DATA FILE: HOUSE

1) NAME
2) SEX
3) RACE
4) YEARBORN
5) AGE (U)
6) AGE
7) RELIGION
8) EDUCATION
9) MARITAL
10) LAWYER?
11) PARTY
12) #TERMS
13) #TERMS2
14) INCUMBENT
15) STATE
16) REGION
17) POSITION
18) SOUTH DEM
19) DIST.AF(U)
20) DIST.AFRAM
21) DIS.HIS(U)
22) DIST.HIS

23) DIST $(U)
24) DISTRICT $
25) $HOUSE(U)
26) $HOUSE
27) %VOTE(U)
28) %OF VOTE
29) TOT RCPTS
30) IND.CONT.
31) PAC.CONT.
32) CAN.CONT
33) TOT EXPEN
34) CSHONHND
35) OPPON$$
36) MED_AGE
37) DIST.WH(U)
38) DIS.ASN(U)
39) MARRIED
40) %SNG.MOM
41) %NON.FAM
42) %UNDER 18
43) %OVER 65
44) HHD.SIZE

45) FAM.SIZE
46) %HOWNERS
47) %RENTERS
48) DIST.HHD$
49) DIST.F$
50) %PEOP.POV
51) $HOUSE2
52) NEW 109?
53) FUEL EFF
54) STEM CELLS
55) TEN COMM
56) FIX UN
57) NET SPEECH
58) TAX CUTS
59) ANWR
60) LEAVE IRAQ
61) GAY MARR
62) BORDER FEN
63) ABORT NOTI
64) TRIBUNALS
65) %VOTE(U)2

DATA FILE: GLOBAL

1) COUNTRY
2) AREA
3) COASTLINE
4) % ARABLE
5) %IRRIGATED
6) %PERM CROP
7) %MEAD-PAST
8) %FOR-WOOD
9) FOREST 90
10) FOREST 00
11) CEREAL
12) POPULATION

13) POP/FEM
14) POP/MALE
15) WOMEN/MEN
16) %POP FEM
17) % UNDER 15
18) %POP 15-64
19) % OVER 64
20) POPDENSITY
21) URBAN %75
22) URBAN %02
23) URBAN %15
24) URBAN GROW

25) RURAL POP
26) RURAL GROW
27) AGE.DEPEND
28) BIRTHRATE
29) MORTL<5 60
30) MORTL<5 90
31) MORT<5 RED
32) MORTAL<5
33) POP GROWTH
34) POPGR15-20
35) POPGR10-15
36) POPGR05-10

37) POPGR95-00	85) HIV:ALL	133) ECON DEVEL
38) POPGR90-95	86) HIV:TEEN	134) THREEWORLD
39) DEATHRATE	87) HIV:PREV	135) WORLDS.7
40) DEATH 70	88) AIDS:DEATH	136) QUAL. LIFE
41) BIRTH 70	89) AIDS:ORPHN	137) CALORIES
42) LIFE EX 70	90) AIDS:LIFE	138) GDPCAP PPP
43) LIFEX FEM	91) NOAID:LIFE	139) GDPCAP PP3
44) LIFEX MALE	92) HIV:BLOOD	140) GDP CAP 5
45) LIFE EXPCT	93) HIV:INFO	141) GDP
46) LIFE FEM	94) HIV:DRUGS	142) GDP CAP GR
47) FERTILE 60	95) HIV:DISCR	143) GDP GROW
48) FERTILE 90	96) HIV:CONDOM	144) GROW 90-99
49) FERTILITY	97) HIV LOW	145) IND GROWTH
50) FERT RED1	98) HIV HIGH	146) DEBT %GDP
51) FERT RED2	99) HIV PREG	147) ACCNT_BAL
52) MORTAL FEM	100) CONDM MALE	148) FDI NET
53) MORTAL MEN	101) CONDM FEM	149) FDI_GROSS
54) NETMIGRT	102) HIV KNOW:M	150) GROSS SAVE
55) REMIT WORK	103) HIV KNOW:F	151) AID/EXPND
56) REMIT RCPT	104) HIV:WOMEN	152) EXP/GDP
57) ASSAULT	105) %HIV/AIDS	153) TRADE %GDP
58) MURDER	106) ANTI RVIR%	154) TRADE GOOD
59) RAPE	107) TUBERCULOS	155) IMP/GDP90
60) ROBBERY	108) TUBE DEATH	156) IMP/GDP02
61) BURGLARY	109) CONTRACEPT	157) EXP/GDP90
62) THEFT	110) SEX MUTIL	158) EXP/GDP02
63) DRUG	111) SEXMUT URB	159) AGRIC EXP
64) POLICE	112) SEXMUT RUR	160) AGRIC IMP
65) PRISONERS	113) IM:DPT	161) FOOD_IMP
66) CAP PUN 95	114) IM:MEASLES	162) FOOD EXP
67) CAP PUN 06	115) IM:MEASL<1	163) FUEL EXP
68) CIRRHOSIS	116) IM:DTP<1	164) TECH_EXP
69) SUICIDE	117) IM:HEPB<1	165) TOUR %IMP
70) AIDS	118) %UNDRWGHT	166) MFG EXP
71) DRUGS	119) ORPHAN ALL	167) MFG IMP
72) ALCOHOL IP	120) DOCTORS	168) TOUR EXPE
73) SPIRITS	121) BIRTH HELP	169) PR_EXP90
74) BEER DRINK	122) ABORTION	170) PR_EXP02
75) WINE DRINK	123) ABORT LEGL	171) MFG_EXP90
76) CIGARETTES	124) MOM HEALTH	172) MFG_EXP02
77) ALCOHOL	125) AB. UNWANT	173) COMMEXP
78) UNDERNOUR	126) HUM DEV75	174) COMMIMP
79) FOOD90-92	127) HUM DEV80	175) POP<1$DAY
80) FOOD:00-02	128) HUM DEV85	176) AID/GNI
81) DIET:79-81	129) HUM DEV90	177) AID/CAP
82) DIET:00-02	130) HUM DEV95	178) FOOD$INDEX
83) FOOD_PROD	131) HUM DEV00	179) FOOD INDEX
84) FOOD_PROD2	132) HUM DEV02	180) KID WORK

181) WOMEN WORK	229) SAN TOT 02	277) BUS.REGS
182) UNEMPL:UNV	230) SAN URB 90	278) INF.MARKET
183) $ RICH 10%	231) SAN URB 02	279) INCOME.TAX
184) INEQUALITY	232) ENERGY.DEP	280) CORP.TAX
185) CARS/1000	233) CARB DIOX	281) CORP:ILL
186) PC/100	234) ELEC/COAL	282) CORP:LEG
187) PHONES/100	235) ELEC/HYDRO	283) CORP:ETHIC
188) TELP/P1 90	236) ELEC/GAS	284) PUB:ETHICS
189) TELP/P1 02	237) ELEC/NUKE	285) LEGAL:EFF
190) CELL PHN90	238) ELEC/OIL	286) CORP:GOV
191) CELL PHN02	239) NRG CONSUM	287) CORRUPT%
192) WEB/1000	240) FUEL_IMP	288) COURT CF%
193) INTRNT:HST	241) ENERGY INV	289) COURT %
194) PRODELECT	242) $DIESEL	290) CRIME %
195) COMPUTER	243) $GAS	291) ELCTRC %
196) RAIL LINES	244) WATER/CHEM	292) FINANCE %
197) RAIL PSNGR	245) WATER/CLAY	293) TAX_CORP
198) RAIL PSG	246) WATER/FOOD	294) TAX_INDIV
199) RAIL TON	247) WATER/MET	295) TAX %
200) RAILT/CP	248) WATER/OTHR	296) VOICE-A:04
201) AUTO	249) WATER/PULP	297) VOICE-A:96
202) AUTO/CP	250) WATER/TEXT	298) POL.STB:04
203) COM VEH	251) WATER/WOOD	299) POL.STB:96
204) COM V/CP	252) MA:CLIMATE	300) EFF.GOV:04
205) HWY VEH	253) MA:BIODIV	301) EFF.GOV:96
206) HWY V/CP	254) MA:RIGHTS	302) REGL.QT:04
207) ROADS/AREA	255) MA:KYOTO	303) REGL.QT:96
208) RADIO	256) MA:POPS	304) RULE LAW04
209) RADIO/CP	257) MA:WTO	305) RULE LAW96
210) RADIOS/CP	258) ENVIR.REG	306) CORRUPT 04
211) TELEVISN	259) ENVIR.EFF	307) CORRUPT 96
212) TV/1000	260) ENVIR.CMPT	308) PRESS.FREE
213) NEWS/CP	261) STABLE.POL	309) INDX:CORPT
214) % AGRIC $	262) RULE.LAW	310) LEVEL:DEM
215) % INDUS $	263) ENVIR.ACC	311) FREEDOM
216) % SERVC $	264) ELECTRIC80	312) FREEDOM2
217) %WORK AG	265) ELECTRIC01	313) LEVEL:CMPT
218) %WORK IN	266) GREENHS80	314) CIV LIBS04
219) F/M EMPLOY	267) GREENHS00	315) CIV LIBS
220) H2O URB 90	268) GLOBAL:EC	316) CIV LIBS95
221) H20 URB 02	269) GLOBAL:PER	317) CIV LIBS90
222) H2O RUR 90	270) GLOBAL:TEC	318) CIV LIBS85
223) H2O RUR 02	271) GLOBAL:POL	319) CIV LIBS80
224) H2O TOT 90	272) GLOBAL	320) CIV LIBS75
225) H2O TOT 02	273) ECON.FREE	321) POL RIGT04
226) SAN RUR 90	274) ECON.FREE2	322) POL RIGHT
227) SAN RUR 02	275) FREE.TRADE	323) POL RIGT95
228) SAN TOT 90	276) PROPERTY	324) POL RIGT90

DATA FILE: GLOBAL cont'd

325) POL RIGT85
326) POL RIGT80
327) POL RIGT75
328) ELECT04
329) ELECT FMLY
330) %TURNOUT
331) GOVERNMENT
332) COMMUNIST
333) COMMTYPE00
334) COMMTYPE06
335) ISLAMPOL
336) ISLAMLEGAL
337) IND DATE
338) IND PERIOD
339) NO CORRUPT
340) WAR
341) WAR2
342) NUKES
343) MULTI-CULT
344) C.CONFLICT
345) REGION
346) REGION2
347) HEALTH EXP
348) HEALTH SP
349) EDUCAT SP
350) DEFENSE SP
351) ARMS EXP
352) ARMS IMP
353) MIL/BUDGET
354) MIL %GDP
355) MIL %LABOR
356) MIL PERSON
357) SEC_EDUCAT
358) P-SEC EDU
359) HEALTH RES
360) PUB EDUCAT
361) HEALTH_CAP
362) HEALTH_PRV
363) PUB_HEALTH
364) HEALTH_TOT
365) HEALTH PAY
366) M/F EDUC.
367) EDUC INDEX
368) PUB HEAL90
369) PUB HEAL01
370) GENDER EQ
371) FEM POWER
372) %FEM.HEADS

373) %FEM/LEG95
374) %FEM/LEG99
375) %FEM.LEGIS
376) LIT:MALE90
377) LIT:FEM 90
378) NET USERS
379) PRIM MALE
380) PRIM FEM
381) KID LABOR
382) BOY LABOR
383) GIRL LABOR
384) KID WED
385) KIDWED URB
386) KIDWED RUR
387) LITYOUTH:F
388) LITYOUTH:M
389) LITYOUTH
390) PRIM FIN:F
391) PRIM FIN:M
392) PRIM FIN
393) PUPILTEACH
394) UNIVRSTY
395) UNIV:FEM
396) UNIV:MALE
397) SEC:FEM
398) SEC:MALE
399) PRIM:FEM
400) PRIM:MALE
401) PRIM.SCH
402) TRAINTEACH
403) EDUCATION
404) ANTI-SEM.
405) ANTI-FORGN
406) ANTI-MUSLM
407) RACISM
408) ANTI-GAY
409) SPOUSE SEX
410) HAPPY SEX?
411) CHORES?
412) FRIENDS?
413) LEISURE?
414) WORK IMPT?
415) UNIONIZED?
416) UNIONS?
417) MERIT $
418) POOR LAZY
419) INJUSTICE
420) WORKER OWN

421) TRUST?
422) TRUST CITZ
423) CHEAT GOVT
424) CHEAT BUS$
425) CHEAT TAX
426) TAKE BRIBE
427) LYING
428) HOT BUY
429) LITTERING
430) COP CONFID
431) EX-MARITAL
432) MINOR SEX
433) GAY SEX
434) PROSTITUTE
435) RELIG HOME
436) VOL@CHURCH
437) LIFESATIS
438) TWOPARENTS
439) SEX FREE
440) HOUSEWIFE
441) TWO INCOME
442) MEN POLLDR
443) WOMEN EARN
444) BOY EDUC
445) CHURCH CON
446) GOV CONF
447) LIFE MEAN
448) GOOD EVIL
449) RELIG KID
450) GOD BELIEF
451) AFTR DEATH
452) SOUL
453) DEVIL
454) HELL
455) HEAVEN
456) SIN
457) RELIG COMF
458) DO SPORTS?
459) VERY HAPPY
460) NATL PRIDE
461) WILL FIGHT
462) FAMILY IMP
463) KID MANNER
464) KID INDEPN
465) KID OBEY
466) KID THRIFT
467) PETITION
468) SIT-IN

Research Methods in Political Science

DATA FILE: GLOBAL cont'd

469) BOYCOTT

470) DEMONSTR

471) STRIKE

472) POL INTRST

473) TALK POL

474) INTERESTED

475) %MUSLIM

476) %CHRISTIAN

477) %CATHOLIC

478) %HINDU

479) %BUDDHIST

480) %JEWISH

481) JEHOV.WITN

482) MORMONS

Given the large number of variables in most data files in the seventh edition, you may need to print your own codebook. Instructions on how to create codebooks like the HOUSE or GLOBAL data files are provided below.

> ➤ Data File: **GSS**
> ➤ Task: **CODEBOOK**
> ➤ Display Summary: **All Variables**
> ➤ Settings: **Number, Name**

Once you have created this codebook you may print it or create a text file. Complete codebooks are also available for download on the book's companion website.

SOURCES

NES and NES 04 – American National Election Studies 2006 and 2004

The NES data files are based on selected variables from the 2004 and 2006 American National Election Study provided by the National Election Studies, Institute for Social Research at the University of Michigan. The National Election Studies (www.electionstudies.org). THE NATIONAL ELECTION STUDY 2000-2002-2004 FULL PANEL FILE [dataset]. Ann Arbor, MI: University of Michigan, Center for Political Studies [producer and distributor].

These materials are based on work supported by, in alphabetical order: the Carnegie Corporation of New York (under grants B7532 and "D B 7532.R01"), the Center for Information and Research on Civic Learning and Engagement (CIRCLE), the National Science Foundation (under grant SES-9707741), the Russell Sage Foundation (under grants 82-00-01 and 83-02-05), and the University of Michigan.

Any opinions, findings and conclusions or recommendations expressed in these materials are those of the author(s) and do not necessarily reflect the views of the funding organizations.

GSS and GSS 04 – General Social Survey 2006 and 2004

The GSS data files are based on selected variables from the National Opinion Research Center (University of Chicago) General Social Survey for 2004 and 2006. James A. Davis is the Principal Investigator and Tom W. Smith is the Director and Co-Principal Investigator. The project has been sponsored by the National Science Foundation. One of the goals of this project is to provide interesting and high-quality data to scholars everywhere, and especially to those who are not affiliated with large research centers.

HOUSE – U.S. House of Representatives, 2005–2006

The data in the HOUSE file are from a variety of readily available sources such as the world almanac, newspapers, magazines, and official government documents. The voting information was obtained from the *Congressional Quarterly* and the United States Congress website (http://thomas.loc.gov).

GLOBAL – 172 Nations with Populations of 200,000 or More

The data in the GLOBAL file are from a variety of sources. The description for each variable uses the following abbreviations to indicate the source.

AQUASTATS: Food and Development Organization of the United Nations Annual Statistics on Food and Water.

CA: Church Almanac, published biannually by the Salt Lake City Deseret News.

FAO: Food and Agriculture Organization of the United Nations, *Food Security Report*, published annually.

FITW: *Freedom in the World*, published annually by Freedom House. www.freedomhouse.org

HDR: *Human Development Report*, published annually by the United Nations Development Program.

HF: *The Index of Economic Freedom*, published annually by The Heritage Foundation and the Wall Street Journal.

IBWR: *Illustrated Book of World Rankings*, 2001.

IDB: International Data Base, 1998, U.S. Bureau of the Census.

IDEA: Institute for Democracy and Electoral Assistance. Turnout data are from the institute's *Global Report on Political Participation* (Stockholm, 2006) Electoral system data and coding from *The International Handbook of Electoral System Design* (Stockholm, 2006).

IP: *International Profile: Alcohol and Other Drugs*, published by the Alcoholism and Drug Addiction Research Foundation (Toronto, 1994).

JWY: *The Yearbook of Jehovah's Witnesses*, published annually.

KEARNEY: Globalization Index, published annually by A.T. Kearney.

KIDRON & SEGAL: *State of the World Atlas*, 5th edition, London: Penguin, 1995.

LE ROY: Coded and calculated by Michael K. Le Roy.

McCORMICK:	Coded by John McCormick, *Comparative Politics in Transition*, (New York: Wadsworth, 1995), p. 9.
NBWR:	*The New Book of World Rankings*, 3rd edition, Facts on File, 1991.
PON:	*The Progress of Nations*, UNICEF, 1996.
RWB:	*Reporters Without Borders*, annual ranking of press freedom published annually.
SAUS:	*Statistical Abstract of the United States*, published annually by the U.S. Department of Commerce.
SOWC:	*State of the World's Children*, published annually by UNICEF.
STARK:	Coded and calculated by Rodney Stark.
SWPA:	Dan Smith, *The State of War and Peace Atlas*, 1st edition (London: Penguin, 1997).
TI:	*Corruption Perceptions Index*, Transparency International, published annually.
TWF:	*The World Factbook*, published annually by the Central Intelligence Agency.
TWW:	*The World's Women*, published annually by the United Nations.
UNCRIME:	United Nations. The Sixth Annual United Nations Survey of Crime Trends and Operations of Criminal Justice Systems, 1997 (Computer files). Vienna, Austria: Crime Prevention and Criminal Justice Branch, United Nations Office at Vienna.
UNMID:	United Nations Millennium Indicators, 2004.
UNPD:	United Nations Population and Development Indicators.
UNSD:	*United Nations Statistical Database*, published annually.
WVS:	World Values Survey, 2002.

STATES—the 50 States of the United States

The data in the STATES file are from a variety of sources. The variable description for each variable uses the following abbreviations to indicate the source.

ABC:	*Audit Bureau of Circulation Blue Book* for the indicated year.
ARIS:	Kosmin, Barry A., and Egon Mayer. 2001. Report: *American Religious Identification Survey*. New York: CUNY Graduate Center.
AMERICAN LEGION:	Data published by the American Legion
BADER:	Coded and calculated by Chris Bader, MicroCase.

BEA: Bureau of Economic Analysis

BJS: Bureau of Justice Statistics

BLS: Bureau of Labor Statistics

CDC: Centers for Disease Control

CENSUS: The summary volumes of the U.S. Census for the indicated year.

CENSUS:
C2SS: Census 2000 Supplementary Survey

CHRON.:   *The Chronicle of Higher Education Almanac* for the indicated year.

CHURCH: *Churches and Church Membership in the United States*, published every 10 years by the Glenmary Research Center, Atlanta, for the year indicated.

DEA: Drug Enforcement Administration

DES: U.S. Dept. of Education, Digest of Education Statistics for the indicated year.

E & E: Bureau of Labor Statistics, Employment and Earnings for the date indicated.

FEC: Federal Election Commission for the indicated year.

HCSR: Health Care State Rankings (Morgan Quitno, Lawrence, KS) for the indicated year.

HEAVEN'S
GATE: Data taken from a publication, "How and When Heaven's Gate May Be Entered," posted by Heaven's Gate on the Internet.

HHS: Health and Human Services

HIGHWAY: Federal Highway Administration, Highway Statistics for the indicated year.

INS: Immigration and Naturalization Service

KINKO'S: Data published by Kinko's, Incorporated

KOSMIN: Kosmin, Barry A. 1991. Research Report: *The National Survey of Religious Identification*, New York: CUNY Graduate Center.

MELTON: Melton, Gordon. 1993. *Encyclopedia of American Religion*.

MMWR: *Morbidity and Mortality Weekly Report* for the date indicated.

NCES: National Center for Education Statistics

NCHS: National Center for Health Statistics

NCSL: National Conference of State Legislatures

NEA: National Endowment for the Arts

RETAIL: *Census of Retail Trade*, published every five years by the Bureau of the Census, for the indicated year.

SA: *Statistical Abstract of the United States* for the indicated year.

SMAD: *State and Metropolitan Area Data Book* for the indicated year.

S.P.R.: State Policy Reference for the indicated year.

S.R.: State Rankings (Morgan Quitno Corp., Lawrence, KS) for the indicated year.

SSA: Data published by the Social Security Administration

UCR: *Uniform Crime Reports* for the indicated year.

UFO NEWS-
CLIPPING
SERVICE: (The UFO Newsclipping Service, AR) 1994–1996

U.S. FISH &
WILDLIFE: Data provided by U.S. Fish and Wildlife Service

WA: *The World Almanac* for the indicated year.

Glossary

Accuracy (or ***margin of error***)—in sampling, the extent to which sample results are representative of the results that would be obtained if the entire population were used rather than a sample. (See Chapter 6.)

Aggregate data—data based on groups of units put together such as census data for states, cities, or counties. (See Chapter 3.)

ANOVA (or ***Analysis of Variance***)—allows the researcher to examine the relationship between variables where the independent variable is nominal or ordinal, and the independent variable is interval or ratio. (See Chapter 11).

Antecedent variable—a variable that occurs before both the independent variable and the dependent variable. (See Chapter 4.)

Beta coefficient—a regression coefficient that shows how many standard deviations of change in the dependent variable are produced by one standard deviation of change in a particular independent variable while controlling for the effects of all other independent variables in the regression equation. (See Chapter 13.)

Case (or ***unit of analysis***)—the item (person, city, nation, or whatever) for which we have data. (See Chapter 3.)

Coding—the assignment of numbers to the categories or values of a variable. (See Chapter 7.)

Collapsing a variable—reducing the number of categories or values of a variable to a smaller number by combining some categories or values. (See Chapter 9.)

Concept—an abstraction based on characteristics of perceived reality. (See Chapter 2.)

Conceptual (or ***nominal***) definition—a statement of the meaning of a particular concept. (See Chapter 2.)

Confidence level—the probability that sample results are outside the specified level of accuracy (margin of error). (See Chapter 6.)

Control variable—a variable whose variation we control in order to determine whether variation in this variable affects the relationship between a dependent variable and an independent variable. (See Chapter 12.)

Correlation—(1) in broad terms, any relationship between two variables; (2) in more specific terms, specific measures of association between interval or ratio variables such as the Pearson correlation coefficient. (See Chapters 4 and 12.)

Cross-tabulation (or ***contingency table***)—a table that cross-tabulates two nominal and/or ordinal variables by one another in order to determine whether there is a relationship between them. (See Chapter 9.)

Data cleaning—the process of checking a data file for errors and correcting the errors. (See Chapter 7.)

Dependent variable—a variable whose variation is to be explained in a study. (See Chapter 4.)

Double-barreled question—a survey question that actually asks more than one question. (See Chapter 6.)

Eta-squared—a P-R-E measure that represents the amount of reduction in the total variance that has occurred as a result of dividing the cases into groups based on the independent variable. (See Chapter 11.)

Exit poll—a survey of people on election day as they leave the polling place. (See Chapter 6.)

Explanation—the practice of relating variation in the dependent variable to variation in the independent variable. (See Chapter 4.)

Frequency distribution—a listing of the values of a variable along with the number (and/or percentage) of cases for each value. (See Chapter 8.)

Haphazard sample—a sample selected in such a way (usually convenience or self-selection) that certain people within a population are more likely to be included than are others. (See Chapter 6.)

Hypothesis—a testable statement of relationship, derived from a theory. (See Chapter 5.)

Independent variable—a variable that is used to explain variation in another variable. (See Chapter 4.)

Indicators—the kinds of observations that are made in order to measure a particular concept. (See Chapter 2.)

Individual data—data that are based on single entities rather than on collections of entities. (See Chapter 3.)

Interval measurement—measurement that assigns real numbers to observations and has equal intervals of measurement but has no absolute zero point. (See Chapter 3.)

Intervening variable—a variable that occurs between the independent variable and the dependent variable and affects the relationship between them. (See Chapter 4.)

Leading question—a survey question worded in such a way that the respondent is led to select a particular response. (See Chapter 6.)

Mean—an arithmetic average computed by adding the values of the variable for all the cases and dividing this sum by the number of cases. (See Chapter 8.)

Measure of association—a measure of the degree of relationship between two variables. (See Chapter 10.)

Median—the value of a variable that has 50% of the cases above it and 50% below it. (See Chapter 8.)

Mode—the value of a variable that occurs most often in the data for that variable. (See Chapter 8.)

Multiple correlation coefficient (R)—a measure of the degree of relationship between a metric dependent variable and a set of independent variables taken collectively. The squared multiple correlation coefficient (R^2) tells us the proportion of variation in the dependent variable explained by the set of independent variables collectively. (See Chapter 13.)

Multiple regression—a statistical technique that expresses a dependent variable as a function of a set of independent variables taken collectively. (See Chapter 13.)

Multistage cluster sampling—a sampling procedure in which smaller units are sampled from larger units through two or more stages until the sample of people is clustered into a fairly small number of areas. (See Chapter 6.)

Negative (or ***inverse***) ***relationship***—a relationship between two variables in which both vary together in opposite directions. (See Chapter 5.)

Nominal measurement—classification of observations into a set of categories that have no direction. (See Chapter 3.)

Normal distribution—a type of symmetrical distribution for a variable in which the mean, median, and mode are all at the highest point in the middle. As you move away from the middle of the distribution in either direction, there are fewer and fewer cases. In a normal distribution, the area encompassed by the mean plus-or-minus one standard deviation includes approximately 68% of all cases. The mean plus-or-minus two standard deviations includes approximately 95% of all cases. (See Chapter 8.)

Null hypothesis—a statement that there is no relationship between the variables in a hypothesis. (See Chapter 5.)

Number-of-cases problem—a problem that occurs when cross-tabulation of variables results in too few cases in some categories for meaningful analysis. (See Chapter 12.)

Operational definition—a specification of the process by which a concept is measured. (See Chapter 2.)

Ordinal measurement—classification of observations into a set of categories that have direction. (See Chapter 3.)

P-R-E interpretation—an interpretation that can be given to certain measures of association that meet Costner's Proportional Reduction in Error criterion: the proportion by which we can reduce the number of errors in predicting the dependent variable by knowing the relationship between the dependent variable and the independent variable. (See Chapter 10.)

Pearson correlation coefficient (r)—a measure of the degree of relationship between two metric (interval or ratio) variables. (See Chapter 13.)

Positive (or ***direct***) ***relationship***—a relationship between two variables in which both vary together in the same direction. (See Chapter 5.)

Probability sample—a sample of a population in which each person has a known chance of being selected. (See Chapter 6.)

Public records data—a very broad category of data that includes any data that can be obtained from any publicly available records. (See Chapter 3.)

Quota sample—a sample in which the goal is to obtain a group representative of the population by setting quotas for selecting various categories of people based on their proportions in the population. (See Chapter 6.)

Random sample—a sample in which each person in the population has an equal chance of being selected throughout the selection process. (See Chapter 6.)

Random-digit dialing (RDD)—a method of selecting a sample for a telephone survey by using random digits for the telephone numbers. (See Chapter 6.)

Range—the difference between the highest value and the lowest value of a variable. (See Chapter 8.)

Ratio measurement—measurement that assigns real numbers to observations, has equal intervals of measurement, and has an absolute zero point. (See Chapter 3.)

Regression—a statistical technique that expresses a dependent variable as a function of an independent variable. (See Chapter 13.)

Reliability—the extent to which a measurement procedure consistently measures whatever it measures. (See Chapter 2.)

Significance level—the probability that a relationship found in a probability sample occurred just by chance (sampling error) and does not really exist in the population. (See Chapter 10.)

Social desirability—a problem for survey results that occurs when there is a socially accepted response for a question and the respondent selects that response in order to avoid looking bad in some way. (See Chapter 6.)

Spurious relationship—an apparent causal relationship between two variables that is actually due to one or more other variables. (See Chapter 4.)

Standard deviation—a measure that expresses the degree of variation within a variable essentially on the basis of the average deviation from the mean. The standard deviation is the square root of the variance. (See Chapter 8.)

Survey data—data, collected through surveys, for which the individual is the unit of analysis. (See Chapter 3.)

Test of statistical significance—a test that determines whether a relationship between variables in a probability sample can be generalized to the population from which the sample was selected. (See Chapter 10.)

Validity—the extent to which a measurement procedure measures what it is intended to measure. (See Chapter 2.)

Variability—the extent of variation within a variable, especially with regard to a particular context such as a population subgroup. (See Chapter 6.)

Variable—a measured concept. (See Chapter 2.)

Variance—a measure that expresses the degree of variation within a variable essentially on the basis of the average deviation from the mean. The standard deviation is the square root of the variance. (See Chapter 8.)

Variation—differences within a set of measurements of a variable. (See Chapter 2 and Chapter 4.)

Z-scores—standardized scores for a variable (usually a variable that is normally distributed or fairly close to being normally distributed) that are computed by dividing the deviations from the mean by the standard deviation for the variable. (See Chapter 8.)